ENRICHING HEALTH

Pathways To Complementary Therapies

M.D. BETZ

Bloomington, IN Milton Keynes, UK

authorHOUSE

AuthorHouse™
1663 Liberty Drive, Suite 200
Bloomington, IN 47403
www.authorhouse.com
Phone: 1-800-839-8640

AuthorHouse™ UK Ltd.
500 Avebury Boulevard
Central Milton Keynes, MK9 2BE
www.authorhouse.co.uk
Phone: 08001974150

First published by AuthorHouse 4/21/2006

ISBN: 1-4259-1394-6 (e)
ISBN: 1-4259-1393-8 (sc)

Library of Congress Control Number: 2006900464

Printed in the United States of America
Bloomington, Indiana

This book is printed on acid-free paper.

FORWARD

As a practicing Gynecologist for 14 years, I have recently come to appreciate many of the health care issues and solutions that Dr. Michael Betz presents with amazing detail in Enriching Health: Complementary Medicine Pathways. Medical Doctoral education stresses the importance of homeostasis, the body's innate ability to make inner changes in order to maintain a constant, balanced, existence. However, the current medical approach to health involves prescribing drugs or surgery for ailments once they are already established. These modalities are often applied near the end-point of disease processes and rarely facilitate the body's inherent ability to heal itself. Medical treatments may improve symptoms of disease temporarily or cause certain laboratory test results to trend toward "normal," but many times this only gives a false sense of security to the patient and doctor. Therefore, the methods of the Western medical system seem at odds with the concept of homeostasis. This discrepancy became apparent to me about two years ago when I took a step back and made a conscious appraisal of the health of my own clients. I realized a trend in which people were losing their vitality, gaining unwanted pounds, carrying a longer list of medications, and generally finding it harder to enjoy life. Some were affected by premature heart disease, premature menopause, cancer, or diabetes. I began to search for better ways to help my clients find true wellness. In the process I have gained knowledge of, and respect for, what is referred to as Complementary and Alternative Medicine (CAM). One of the few incongruous things about CAM is found in its semantics. The use of medicine is actually not a part of many of the individual modalities such as proper nutrition, acupuncture, Yoga, healing touch, or guided imagery. I think Complementary and Alternative Health Methods, or Modalities, or Therapies would be more appropriate. Whatever the exact terminology, the need for a change in our approach to health and wellness is painfully apparent.

In *Enriching Health: Complementary Medicine Pathways* Dr. Betz provides us with a most comprehensive and informative assessment of the current situations in medicine today. He successfully demonstrates why changes to our medical system are desperately needed, both financially and for the sake of our health. He provides plentiful details and informative references. He then shows us how alternative approaches to health are being utilized, outlining some of the results, and provides examples of how those results compare quite favorably with our traditional disease treatment approach. CAM therapies are in general associated with less inadvertent harm (side-effects, medical errors) and lower costs. With an uplifting and inspiring tone, Dr. Betz tells us how CAM therapies are gradually being accepted by individuals, employers, health insurance plans and even governmental agencies. It is exciting to learn how much progress has already been made toward our culture embracing CAM modalities.

This book serves many purposes for people with varying levels of knowledge about Complementary and Alternative Medicine. Dr. Betz convinces the uninitiated or skeptical reader to consider the benefits of taking responsibility for their own health. For readers already familiar with CAM options, *Enriching Health: Complimentary Medicine Pathways* serves as an invaluable resource and a means for spreading the intriguing information to others. Disseminated education and awareness will eventually lead to improvements in our health-related habits. Physicians and clinicians seeking to learn more about the validity of CAM will also appreciate the plentiful supporting studies cited in the references.

From a personal perspective, I have enjoyed a change for the better in the health of my clients by adopting a more natural, holistic approach in my practice. A wellness model, as opposed to a sickness model, provides people with an essential sense of control that automatically promotes emotional and physical wellness. As a result, the use of costly drugs and surgery with their concomitant risks and side-effects can be minimized.

We are now in the early stages of witnessing our reactive medical care system evolves into a proactive health care system. I am fortunate and honored to be a part of the wellness revolution and I commend Dr. Betz for bringing us the timely information presented in Enriching Health: Complementary Medicine Pathways.

Janel L. Meric, MD, FACOG
President
Harmony Health and Wellness
Knoxville, Tennessee

TABLE OF CONTENTS

LIST OF TABLES AND FIGURES

ACKNOWLEDGEMENTS

I am indebted to many. For John Maluso who intuited that I had a mission and supported this journey. For Lenahan O'Connell who enabled this project by "conferring" many times and helping with public policy issues in Chapter 5. Special thanks goes to Ron Felix who helped write and explain mind/body tools found in the Appendix C. For my sister, Beth who gave unwavering support and read several drafts. For librarians such as Linda Sammataro, Sandra Leach and Alan Wallace who helped find materials that mere mortals can not find. Thanks go to the holistic healer, Janel Meric MD for her kind word in the Forward to this book. Gratitude goes to Bill Judge, Sam Wallace, Jim Talley and Nancy Brannon who read and gave me feedback. And last but not least to my editor, Sharon Sharp, who encouraged me to enliven this material. This book has been a personal spiritual journey. My hope is that the reader will feel empowered and experience an expansion in her/his own health consciousness.

PREFACE

The origins of this book stretch back to 1987 when I had a strong inner prompting to drop my university-sponsored, subsidized medical insurance. This spontaneous intrusion arose seemingly out of nowhere while sitting in my office. After examining the wisdom of this inner prompting for one week, I canceled my medical insurance and I've never looked back.[1] I didn't begin writing this book, however, until 2001.

Why did I cancel my medical insurance? Unhealthy illusions were nurtured in my mind by the concept of medical insurance. Part of this awakening arose from having served on two hospital committees for 12 years that helped me understand first-hand the limits of a disease care system funded by 3rd party payers. Doctors are unable to insure my health. I hold the key to promoting and maintaining my own health. Health is not a commodity that can be purchased like an auto or a new suit even though insurance helps pay for the costly consequences of our lifestyle choices. Doctors specialize in disease care and can often help *restore* health but they generally do not *promote* health. I play the central role in maintaining my own health. Medicine is a science of disease and pathology, not a science of health. Physicians use an arsenal of tools to counter disease after it strikes; they focus on biochemistry. Most physicians rely upon drugs as magic bullets and surgery to destroy disease and thereby restore health. Our disease care system helps people *after* they become ill. We need a health enriching system that promotes health and prevents disease.

Can the ill effects from an unhealthy diet be corrected with surgery and pills? Can the ill effects on the heart and biochemical changes caused by stress be corrected with mind mellowing drugs? Can the ill effects on the stomach and the digestive system from overeating be corrected with expensive antacids?

Those who believe there is a pill for every ill occupy one end of a continuum of beliefs about health. At the other extreme are those who believe that health is a natural, normal experience promoted and best maintained by the individual with proper diet, exercise and the mental management of stress. The science of health is about achieving health by strengthening the immune system, cultivating healthy habits and working with others to protect the environment from pollution and toxic exposure. Health promotion relies heavily upon behavioral sciences while disease care relies on biochemical sciences, largely ignoring lifestyle choices and personal responsibility.

A growing number of Americans prefer a health enrichment model as they use more Complementary and Alternative Medical (CAM) therapies. Globalization has brought us different ethno-medical systems that emphasize health promotion more than treatment of disease. For example, in the *Yellow Emperor's Classic of Internal Medicine* (700BC), the chief medical advisor Chi Po states:

> *Health is what the wise person pursues when in good health, not after it is lost... . Who waits until they become thirsty to dig a well?*[2]

Enriching Health examines the rise of CAM therapies and their integration into the medical care system in the new millennium. Integrative medicine combines the strengths of conventional medicine (treating serious acute infectious disease, trauma and emergency medicine) with the strengths of CAM (promoting health by empowering individuals, using a holistic approach, and treating chronic disease with lifestyle changes and more natural therapies). Consumer demand and physician leadership are driving CAM and its integration into medical care. This will result in a softer, gentler and more natural approach with more health promotion by consumers in partnership with their providers.

INTRODUCTION

For over a decade, Maria (not her real name) doctored three chronic conditions with specialists until a dramatic adverse reaction from taking a new drug shocked her into the realization that prescription drugs were not improving her health. This became a turning point, causing Maria to explore more effective pathways than conventional medicine to enrich her health.

Maria, an energetic entrepreneur in good health, had owned and managed a gym where she taught gymnastics with 16 employees to thousands of students for a number of years. She had successfully balanced her business, marriage and parenting three children up to that time. In 1986 during pregnancy with her fourth child, her business was audited over a three-month period that caused great stress. Her health remained good through her pregnancy but three months after giving birth, Maria experienced an erosion of her health. The first symptom of allergies came during ragweed season. She could not breathe. She used Seldane and other over-the-counter medications. Maria declared:

> *This initial attack started a three-year process of trying to discover on my own what was causing the allergic reactions. After finding no relief, I finally went to an allergist and had the scratch test to identify the culprits. I was allergic*

to everything so I started allergy shots weekly at first and then monthly. The allergist assured me that I could become immunized to these things within three years but I ended up taking allergy shots for seven years.

Soon after the onset of allergic reactions, Maria started suffering from migraine headaches once or twice every month without connection to the menstrual cycle. At first, the headaches were not severe, but subsequently they ranged from bad to devastating. She explained:

Sometimes during a migraine, I would throw-up and lose my eyesight. I consulted a specialist who prescribed many different kinds of drugs. Nothing helped very much so he kept experimenting with all the latest drug updates.

The third chronic problem to erode her quality of life was a skin rash. Maria had never had skin problems before. She consulted a skin specialist who initially prescribed Acutane but Maria refused any more after one month because it had so many nasty side effects (drying her skin, mouth, eyes and joints). Tetracycline was prescribed along with many other types of antibiotics over a prolonged time period but they did nothing to clear her skin problems.

In 1998, her migraine specialist prescribed a new drug that caused an asthma attack, severely restricting Maria's capacity to breathe. This adverse drug reaction triggered an avalanche of events that propelled Maria toward exploring alternative therapies. Maria was already getting allergy shots and taking an allergy medicine and Tetracycline for her skin rash. Not being able to breathe got her attention and prompted a return trip to her allergist. The allergist was upset with her for taking another medication that reacted with his treatment regimen. None of the three specialists ever communicated with one another nor asked about other medications she might be taking. While Maria was reasonably knowledgeable, she had relied upon her medical experts for the literature she had read about these maladies and how to treat them.

> The adverse drug reaction triggered an avalanche of events that propelled Maria toward exploring alternative therapies.

The allergist retested Maria's response to a second scratch test after seven years of treatment. She was as allergic to those same things as she had been before! This event exposed the limits of doctoring symptoms and propelled her to explore a wider set of choices and to become an active steward of her own health. Maria recalled:

I left the doctor's office dazed and disappointed with my misplaced trust in these treatments. As I was returning to the gym, I passed a chiropractic office adjoining my business. I pondered whether my many problems might be due to damaging my neck/spinal column from gymnastic stunts. I walked in, had an x-ray and filled out the most thorough 4-page intake I had ever seen! After examining the intake material and X-ray, he said, "You do not need my chiropractic skills because your spine is fine but you have Dysbiosis, a digestive tract disorder that is causing your symptoms.[3] Your prolonged use of antibiotics has caused an imbalance of bacteria in your digestive tract, causing allergies, skin rash and other problems. This can be fixed but you must get off all your prescriptions and change your diet." I was asked to adopt a new diet with no wheat, no soda pop, and limited dairy and to take several herbs. Within four months, all my allergies and migraine headaches were gone. This caused me to totally commit to natural health. However, three more years would pass before my skin would clear up with a more alkaline diet I adopted a year later.

> "Your spine is fine but you have leaky-gut syndrome or Dysbiosis, a digestive tract disorder that is causing your symptoms. Your prolonged use of antibiotics has caused an imbalance of bacteria in your digestive tract, causing allergies, skin rash and other problems."

When Maria's family moved to an adjoining state, she decided to manage a health food store where she could learn more about natural health. Maria recalled:

> *I met a man who was totally into diet. He helped me learn that my body was very acidic and that foods should be selected and balanced in terms of alkalinity/acidity. I wanted to learn more about the chemistry of foods to improve my skin and enrich my health. He requested that I commit to the discipline and only eat within strict guidelines. I agreed to the regimen. He taught me to select foods by these criteria and to start out the day with a glass of water with squeezed lemon juice, pure honey and organic natural vinegar (with the mother in it). I learned how to lower my acidic levels with different types of foods. This new set of guidelines cleared up my skin, helped me grow great fingernails and significantly enriched my level of health.*

Food continues to be Maria's primary strategy for maintaining health now that her health has returned fully. As she expressed it: *Good health does not primarily depend on a pharmaceutical pill or even natural supplements but on food itself.* She regards food as the most important key to health. Maria lives out the ancient wisdom as taught by the Greek physician, Hipprocrates who asserted, "Let food be your medicine."

Maria's exploration of pathways for enriching health with complementary and alternative therapies is not unusual. An adverse drug reaction was her turning point but for others, the turning point may be to avoid the intrusive and toxic therapies of conventional medicine or the failure of the conventional medical therapies to treat chronic illness effectively. For others, it is the positive appeal of promoting health, becoming more engaged in one's own health and/or the gentler methods of alternative therapies.

Modern conventional medicine has been in crisis for some 30 years with the inability to stem the growing avalanche of chronic diseases. According to an editorial in a prestigious medical journal in 1968[4] and later quoted by President Richard Nixon, *the 'germ theory' of disease and its use of drugs is ineffective in treating chronic diseases.*[5]

Conventional medicine's failure to adapt to changing disease patterns reflects a frozen mind-set. Unable to change its mission or tactics after winning the war against diseases of poverty (infectious communicable diseases caused by nutritional deficiencies, germs and parasites), conventional medicine uses the same tactics with chronic lifestyle diseases that include heart, cancer, diabetes and kidney disease. Chronic diseases are caused by a lifestyle of affluence as we over eat, under exercise and pollute our environment. We overly consume calories (portion distortion) without burning off the extra caloric intake and managing stress. We also fail to protect the water and food supply against contamination.

> Chronic diseases are caused by affluence as we over eat, under exercise and pollute the environment.

Medical educators and most physicians utilize the old model that was used to fight infectious disease; each disease was believed to have one cause (a pathogen) that could be destroyed with one drug— the magic bullet. Medicine remains locked into the old strategy that won the last war against acute diseases rather than dealing with the present challenge posed by chronic disease that has multiple causes. Chronic diseases are largely preventable. Most physicians wage war with magic bullets. The solutions reside in behavioral and institutional change more than with high-tech tools of drugs or surgery.

> Our medical care system focuses on treating people after they become ill instead of promoting health.

Our medical care system focuses on treating people after they become ill instead of promoting health.[6] Waste and inefficiency abound from doctoring preventable chronic diseases with expensive drugs that primarily mask symptoms. Our medical care system swallows one out of every seven dollars in our economy. Medical insurance policies are helpless to control escalating costs. Consumers are temporarily insulated from the costly consequences of their lifestyle choices as they clamor for unlimited services. None of the major parties shoulder responsibility for the waste and inefficiency they each create according to the Center for Practical Health Reform.

Simply using the medical care system now causes more deaths than heart disease[7] (see Chapter 2). In its aggressive efforts to fight disease, modern medicine kills patients by prescribing drugs with lethal adverse reactions, performing unnecessary surgery, spreading infections and making a wide-range of other mistakes.

Explosive growth in complementary and alternative medical (CAM) therapies is bringing the most dramatic, far-reaching changes in medical care in nearly a century. More Americans are embracing health enrichment over doctoring disease. Some pioneering physicians are championing 'integrative clinics' offering both CAM and modern therapies. More consumers are seeking to enrich their health. Not only are most chronic diseases preventable, the skills involved in building health differ greatly from those used in fighting disease. As the US military learned in Bosnia, Haiti, Somalia and now Iraq, the skills required in destroying an enemy differ from those in building peace and harmony! Medical schools still largely prepare physicians to wage war against disease rather than promoting healthy lifestyles and behavioral change.[8] The curriculum focuses on the biochemistry of disease, rather than promoting health. America needs more health promoters, empowering patients in the collaborative work of enriching health and preventing disease. Waiting to treat chronic disease after the damage occurs is costly, often ineffective and too often fatal.

This book is about a cultural shift in America from doctoring disease to enriching health. The popularity of complementary and alternative medicine (CAM) expresses this shift from a disease centric to a health centric model.

Plan of the Book

Chapter 1 describes four major markers that signal a shift from doctoring disease to enriching health. This big shift moves from a fear-based focus on disease toward a positive goal of health, from reliance on quick fixes to adopting healthier life styles, from reactive to more proactive roles for consumers, and from an emphasis only on the physical to a holistic view of health. CAM therapies are used disproportionately by more educated individuals with higher incomes, insuring it will persist and be adopted by others.

Chapter 2 discusses the public's many grievances with our modern conventional medical care system such as cost, side effects, mistakes, inability to treat chronic illnesses effectively and the failure to promote health. Chronic diseases increase as physicians over-medicate and under-educate patients for conditions that are mostly preventable. Disaffections are causing many to explore alternative therapies for their chronic conditions.

Chapter 3 examines the attraction of complementary and alternative therapies. CAM therapies attract many users because they promote health, are holistic, less intrusive and cultivate personal stewardship; CAM therapies supply much of what patients with chronic conditions want and their CAM practitioners help affirm a worldview that more people are embracing. Changing values are facilitating a shift toward CAM usage.

Chapter 4 examines the central role of social support systems in behavioral change. Self-help groups are a special type of support system that requires its members have the same illness, addiction or problem. Self-help groups serve as transition-assisters to lifestyles that enhance physical, emotional, and spiritual health while empowering participants to become more active stewards of their own health. These self-help groups also become lay referral systems for other CAM therapies. Online or off, self-help groups represent a new form of "community" consisting of social support circles which enhance the adaptive skills of some 20 million Americans. Such groups have healing power.

Chapter 5 examines conditions and lifestyle choices that undermine health, including the fast food industry, stressful workplaces that provide few opportunities to grow, transportation systems that discourage walking and biking exercise, and the use of a "pill for every ill." We must reform some institutional practices to reduce their unhealthy consequences. Both public policy and active personal stewardship must reduce the seductive lure of advertising to over-consume, for "instant gratification" and stressful conditions that undermine health.

Chapter 6 examines the role of business leaders of large corporations in championing a new approach to medical care and health promotion. Employers are dealing with costly consequences of chronic illness by forging new institutions and incentives to promote health. By applying what they've learned from implementing quality improvement in their core businesses, private employers are promoting health as a cost-effective way to prevent illness and reduce disease-care expenses, thereby increasing their productivity.

Chapter 7 examines how CAM therapies are being integrated into the medical mainstream. CAM therapies promote health and lower medical care cost. CAM therapies/therapists are joining new 'integrative clinics' within major medical school centers, hospitals and pain clinics. Obstacles to bringing CAM therapies into the system include: closed mindedness, limited research on CAM, the training of CAM practitioners, limited insurance coverage of CAM therapies, and limited incentives to change behavior.

The *Afterward Chapter* predicts that Energy Medicine will expand dramatically and become the medicine of the new millennium. Energy therapies are based on the principles of physics and range from acupuncture and applied kinesiology to qigong and therapeutic touch. A wide range of soft and hard tissue healing occurs from magnetic pulses, whether from human hands or high tech machines. Health is enhanced by the infusion of energy.

CHAPTER 1.
SHIFTING FROM DISEASE TO HEALTH

Health is the soul that animates all the enjoyments of life, which fade and are tasteless without it.

William Temple

In June 1997, disability and depression enveloped Margo[9] like a dense fog. Ten months earlier the 38-year-old had qualified for a highly selective eleven-week training program for marketing telephone services to small business customers. She knew this position would be stressful but had no idea what would follow. After six months of dealing with daily sales quotas, Margo's health began to falter. First, she contracted a virus that would not subside, even after repeated visits to her medical group for treatment. Then fatigue descended upon her like a lead blanket. With each visit to her medical group, a different doctor treated the lingering viral infection and a growing list of maladies. With fatigue and depression mounting, a disability leave-of-absence seemed to be her only option.

Barely managing to eat, swallow pills, and care for herself, Margo dropped into a depressive slump that lasted nearly six months. The doctors eventually diagnosed the aches, pains, and fatigue she experienced as fibromyalgia and chronic fatigue syndrome. By January

1999, Margo also had stomach problems. A colonoscopy showed that she had Crohn's disease.

Nearly three years after dropping into a personal hell-hole, Margo was at her lowest point. When she saw no possibility of returning to her former job or of working anywhere else, she lost all hope of improving. Previously, a very active, healthy, independent person, Margo was near despair. She had no energy and experienced pain in many parts of her body. Doctors prescribed numerous medications and trigger point injections. Neither conventional medicine nor psychotherapy seemed to help.

At this low point Margo saw a sign advertising Reiki, a gentle hands-on energy therapy. Desperate for hope and healing, Margo was ready to try alternative healing methods. She checked out Reiki on the Internet and learned that it is a way to direct energy from what is called the universal light into different parts of the body. Margo explained,

> I called the number on that sign and the Reiki therapist said it might help energy flow into blocked parts of my body. I was so intrigued that I immediately made an appointment. I was pleasantly surprised at feeling both relaxed and energized from my first 45-minute treatment. When the therapist told me I could learn to do this hands-on healing treatment for myself, I enrolled immediately and started taking classes. I used Reiki to energize myself each morning.

Still Margo had pain in her legs and by March 2000 the pain became unbearable. When Margo felt she had tried everything conventional medicine had to offer, she made an appointment to see a local acupuncturist hoping to reduce her level of pain.

> I had learned about acupuncture for pain from friends and the Internet when I first got sick. But I had no money and I was afraid of needles. I remember believing that acupuncture would help. And it did the very first time! Then I adopted the macrobiotic diet the acupuncturist suggested. With each visit, the pain lessened, and within eight months it was gone!

My health turned a corner and started improving. That man changed my life!

Reflecting on her experience with alternative therapies, Margo concluded

I learned the importance of attitude. Attitude is everything. Physically, I am 60 percent better and steadily improving. I am much stronger physically, emotionally, and spiritually. I know I am getting better and I am certain I will work again!

Soon after my interview, Margo enrolled in college to pursue a new direction in her life. She no longer followed the macrobiotic diet but she was actively cultivating health with her diet, food combinations, exercise, relaxation and the use of affirmation to direct her life.

The Rise of Alternative Approaches to Health and Illness

Margo's experience is not unusual. Millions of Americans are seeking different treatments for their chronic illnesses. In their quest, they are transforming the American medical care system. These people, along with some of their physicians and the alternative therapists they visit, are forging a more holistic approach to health and illness.

In this emerging approach, the whole person is treated, not just the physical ailment. They look for root causes of chronic illness. Treatment expands beyond relief of symptoms to encompass the patient's lifestyle and, at times, the patient's ultimate values and spiritual practices. This transformation involves a shift from doctoring disease to promoting health.

Margo experienced dramatic improvement in her condition when she moved from passive reliance upon her doctors to more holistic approaches that required her active involvement. The transition from the largely physical approach of doctoring to the holistic perspective of promoting health involves changes in an individual's perspective, a shift from

- Fear of disease to the hope of health and improved quality of life,
- Reliance on quick-fix symptom suppressers to health enriching lifestyle changes,
- Dependence on experts to a more active stewardship of one's own health, and
- Emphasis on physical health to a holistic view of health.

A new health care system is being sculpted by consumers in response to widespread dissatisfaction with conventional medicine and its increasing costs. The emerging system focuses on the prevention of illness through the use of a variety of complementary and alternative medical (CAM) therapies, including the ones Margo used to regain and enhance her health. CAM therapies might well transform our system from one that rewards physicians and pharmaceutical firms for providing disease care services to one that offers rewards for promoting health and healthy lifestyle habits. At this time, there are no incentives that reward providers or patients for health promotion. (In Chapter 6, I discuss companies that reward employees who commit to exercise and other healthy habits. Companies such as Quaker Oats and Northeast Utilities offer incentives.)

Because our current system fails to invest in health promotion, we spend billions of dollars each year on unnecessary hospitalization, treatment, and disability. Waiting to treat diseases that are preventable costs much more than targeting risk factors and promoting healthy lifestyle choices. Most doctors certainly do everything in their power to help cure their patients after they succumb to disease. However, our system must move upstream to patient education to promote health and healthy lifestyle habits rather than waiting downstream to perform surgery or prescribe drugs for desperate patients. Cardiologists Robert Elliot, M.D., describes our current situation as: *A medical system waiting at the bottom of a cliff for people to fall off. When we suggest building a fence at the top of the cliff to prevent people from falling, the answer from the bottom is, 'We can't afford it. We're spending all our money down here.'*[10]

What Is Alternative Medicine?

Alternative medicine or alternative therapy is a broadly inclusive label applied to different ethno-medical systems and therapeutic practices. Although different in many respects, these therapies share one major attribute; they fall outside the legal monopoly of modern Western biomedicine. The medical establishment has maintained exclusive control of the licensing of physicians for nearly 90 years. The American Medical Association asserted monopoly control when they "reformed" medical education and licensure early in the 20th century. All 50 states have medical practice laws that confer monopoly power on physicians who pass state licensing examinations after graduating from an accredited medical school.[11] All options for medical treatment other than those prescribed by licensed physicians were excluded until recently.[12]

Modern Western medicine uses the metaphor of war and fights disease after it develops. For this reason, it is also called allopathic, from the Greek word "allo" meaning to counter or resist and the Greek word pathos meaning disease. In line with its mission to fight disease, Western medicine is more invasive than alternative approaches. Modern medicine's primary therapies include surgery and drugs. Of course, invasiveness varies by degrees relative to other therapies. Figure 1.1 illustrates a continuum of invasiveness comparing alternative and modern Western therapies.

Fig. 1.1 Continuum of Invasiveness of Therapies Used by Different Ethno-medical Systems

Most Invasive	→	→	→	→	→	*Least Invasive*
Modern Western Medicine	Ayurveda	Chinese	Chiropractic	Naturopathy	Energy Therapy	**Mind-body Therapies**
Injections Drugs Radiation Surgery	Diet	Acupuncture	Manipulation	Herbs	Healing Touch	Biofeedback
	Herbs	Food	Nutrition	Homeopathy	Light	Hypnotherapy Imagery
	Massage	Herbs	Lifestyle	Massage	Reiki	Psychotherapy
	Yoga	Massage		Nutrition	Therapeutic Touch	

Adapted from Claire Cassidy "Cultural context of CAM systems" in *Fundamentals of Complementary and Alternative Medicine*, by Marc Micozzi (Ed), NY: Livingston, 1996: page 19.

The use of alternative therapies does not imply rejection of conventional therapies. Most Americans who use alternative medicine also utilize Western therapies for other ailments. Over the last decade, the original term "alternative" has given way to "complementary" to describe the increasingly common practice of using alternative medical practices as a complement to conventional treatment. Studies show that approximately 80 percent of those using one or more alternative therapies had used conventional medicine for the same problem and most continue seeing their physician.[13]

Combining the best of conventional and alternative therapies is gaining widespread support and is being codified into "best practice" protocols. In 1992 the National Institute of Health established the Office of Alternative Medicine (OAM) with a budget of $2 million. OAM was upgraded to a center in 1998 and renamed the Center for Complementary and Alternative Medicine with a budget of $80 million.

There are six major categories of complementary and alternative medicine (CAM) as shown in Table 1.1 below. Some of these therapies are complete systems, e.g., Indian Ayurvedic Medicine, Traditional Chinese Medicine, naturopathy, and homeopathy. These therapies are used to treat a wide range of ailments with a number of specific preparations and practices. Other therapies, however, are more focused tools designed for specific conditions or are suitable for use with a number of conditions such as hypnosis, guided imagery, herbs and energy therapies such as acupuncture, Healing Touch and Reiki.

Complementary medicine is compatible with Western medicine because it is non-invasive. Acupuncture is the one exception of being invasive but it remains gentle in comparison to major surgery. Thus, unlike drugs that can clash with each other and produce serious side-effects, many alternative therapies can be used with conventional medicine because they gently complement the modern Western treatments by enhancing the health and well-being of the individual.

Table 1.1 Complementary and Alternative Medical (CAM) Therapies/Products—Major Domains of CAM

Alternative Medical Care Models
Ayurvedic medicine
Chiropractic
Homeopathic medicine
Native American medicine (e.g., herbs, sweat lodge, drumming
      and chanting)
Naturopathic medicine
Traditional Chinese Medicine (e.g., acupuncture, herbal)
Mind-Body Therapies
Art therapy
Dance therapy
Guided imagery
Hypnosis
Prayer and mental healing
Biological Based Therapies
Herbal therapies
Individual therapies (e.g., bee pollen)
Orthomolecular medicine (e.g., megavitamin)
Special diets (e.g. macrobiotics, low-fat diets)
Therapeutic Massage and Somatic Movement Therapies
Alexander Method
Feldenkrais
Massage
Energy Therapies
Healing Touch
Qigong
Reiki
Tai Chi
Therapeutic Touch
Bio-eletromagnetics
Magnet therapy

Modified from *the Final report of the White House Commission on CAM Policy*, March 2002, chapter 2, page 1, US printing office.

Who Uses Complementary and Alternative Medicine?

Alternative therapies are gaining acceptance and legitimacy across the country from the coastal villages of Maine to the sprawling cities of California. The number of adult Americans using CAM therapies grew steadily from the 1960s through the 1980s, and then surged dramatically in the 1990s. The percent of adults using CAM within a one-year time-period increased from 34 percent in 1990 to 42 percent in 1997.[14] This surge in the number of people using CAM treatments is reported in over 20 studies. Studies that ask about use over the person's lifetime find over 60 percent have used CAM-therapies.

Why People Use CAM Therapies?

Many factors are causing a shift toward health promotion and the use of CAM therapies. The growing trend toward CAM can be explained as a combination of negative experiences with conventional medical treatments along with positive attractions to gentler therapies. Some people are attracted by the prospects of enriching health and vigor while others are pushed away from conventional medicine by negative experiences. A government survey in 2001 found that over half (55%) of the adult CAM users use CAM because of its therapeutic benefit; over one in four (26%) used CAM because a conventional medical provider suggested they try it; one in eight (13%) used CAM because they felt Western medicine was too costly; and others wished to enrich their health.[15]

Clearly, many people with chronic conditions, like Margo, turn away from Western medicine because it fails to help significantly with their chronic condition or because the interventions have toxic side effects that result in decreased quality of life. Most people using CAM are very satisfied with their treatments.[16] People who use CAM cite its holistic orientation; its gentle, more natural therapies; and its focus on enhancing health and quality of life as the reasons for their satisfaction levels.

Many patients also seek an active role in maintaining their health. CAM users typically are more educated with higher income levels than nonusers. CAM users are attracted to CAM by the prospect of greater control over their health. Thus, the use of CAM is a personal choice made by people who want to improve the quality of their life; users choose the type of therapy they believe best addresses their particular health challenges.[17] No doubt, a variety of predisposing, enabling, and medical factors also operate in each case. The people who utilize CAM do not all hold the same beliefs, motivations, and needs.[18]

Satisfaction levels among those receiving alternative treatments are very high. In one study, 84 percent were very satisfied with the results of their experience with alternative therapies and over 87 percent would recommend them to others. Satisfied patients return, so use of alternative therapies is rarely a one-time experience. Not only do a majority of satisfied patients continue using alternative treatments after initial usage, they frequently explore additional lifestyle changes and therapies.[19]

How is this Shift from Doctoring to Enriching Health Possible?

A wise man realizes that health is his most valuable possession.
Greek physician Hippocrates

To enhance one's health like Margo demonstrated is now increasingly common among Americans. These qualities are cultivated by higher education. The number of college graduates continues to grow dramatically. More people work with ideas and abstract concepts in creative tasks such as computer programmers, lawyers, teachers, managers, professionals, and the like. Creative work requires flexibility of thought and opinion. Increasingly, Americans are less trusting of traditional authority—be it religious, political, or medical—but we are very pragmatic and goal oriented. We focus on what we want rather than focusing on fear and what we don't want.

People are more receptive to new ideas and approaches to health and personal lifestyle than ever before. Moreover, popular magazines and television programs are aware of these changes and devote more coverage to CAM therapies, often with lead stories in *Time, Newsweek,* and *US News* and *World Reports*. Broad cultural changes are reflected in four behavioral and value shifts toward health. Today more Americans are likely to

- Seek treatments that enhance quality of life,
- Exercise more self-care and personal stewardship in health,
- Change toward healthier lifestyles, and

- Use a more holistic and spiritual view of health.

This overall shift from doctoring to promoting health is summarized in Table 1.2.

Table 1.2 Differences in Doctoring and Promoting Health

From Doctoring → → → → → → → → → *To Promoting Health*		
Fighting disease	→	Promoting health and positive affirmations
Depending on expert help	→	Using more self-help and personal stewardship
Relying on quick-fixes	→	Willingness to change lifestyle
Focusing only on the physical body	→	Taking a more holistic view of health and illness

Promoting Health and Hope

An increasing number of Americans place health at the top, or very near the top, of personal values. In one study, 39 percent described themselves as those who work at staying healthy.[20] Americans are more interested in their health than ever before. Increasing numbers read the health sections, surf health web sites and phone the ever-growing number of help-lines offering advice on all types of health problems.

More individuals are seeking ways to enhance health as suggested by the rise in popularity of such magazines as *American Health, Prevention, Body & Soul (formerly New Age),* and *Spirituality and Health* as well as by the many exercise magazines, nutrition newsletters, and the increased numbers of health food stores. The White House Commission on CAM Policy declared: *our national focus must shift to promoting health rather than only fighting disease.*[21]

Resources devoted to health promotion initiatives have increased over the last twenty years at both the state and national levels. Agencies such as the Office of Disease Prevention and Health Promotion, the Center for Disease Control and Prevention (CDC), and the Department of Health and Human Services (HHS) play an important role in stimulating and coordinating health promotion efforts. The National Center for Chronic Disease Prevention and Health Promotion now publishes a peer-reviewed electronic journal with the mission of addressing applied prevention research and public health practices.[22]

Health promotion utilizes the language of a positive goal and rewarding experiences while disease care focuses on pathology and what to avoid with scare tactics and grim pictures. Health promotion is positive and something to enjoy. Tommy Thompson, the former Secretary of Health and Human Services, reflected this new, more positive view of health promotion when he commented on negative messages used in weight control: *We've made the waist a terrible thing to mind...making people believe they need to go to extremes to achieve good health.* He called for a fresh approach to promoting health. *We need to make it fun and achievable. We need to stop the guilt-ridden lectures and start showing people the enjoyable and doable steps to better health.* In other words, we need to cut out the negative "scare-care" and become "health builders."

Employers are among the most active supporters of health promotion. They are learning that a healthier workforce is a win-win situation; health promotion enriches the employer's bottom line while enriching the quality of life for their employees. Promoting health not only reduces expenditures on medical care and insurance premiums, it also lowers absenteeism and employee turnover, while raising morale and productivity. Over 90 percent of qualified studies indicate that health promotion is cost-effective with an average saving of $4.90 in medical care costs for every dollar invested.[23] CitiBank, General Electric, General Motors and many more companies are promoting health among their employees as detailed in Chapter 6.

Using More Self-Help and Personal Stewardship

Americans love the idea that they can fix what's broken. Three out of four adult Americans say they prefer treating health problems themselves. The limits of doctoring and the limitless amount of information on the Internet enhance the appeal of self-help even more. Americans surfed more than 12,000 websites devoted to mental health alone and spent $563 million on self-help books at the start of the new millennium.[24] More than 2,000 self-help books are published each year. The entire August 2002 issue of *Monitor on Psychology* focused on self-help and health related issues, such as exercise, the treatment of phobias, etc. Increasingly health is being seen as more of a personal responsibility.

Nearly three out of four (74%) adult Americans believe their health is affected by how they take care of themselves according to a recent Harris-Interactive survey. Over 50 percent of adults in the US now use dietary supplements. Herbal product use jumped 50 percent from 1997 to 2002. Nearly one in five adults uses herbs for symptoms as diverse as menopausal hot flashes and memory problems.[25]

People who take more personal responsibility for their health are referred to as optimists. Optimists are more proactive, look on the sunny side of events and expect favorable outcomes in contrast with pessimists. Optimism can be learned by changing the internal dialogue (mind-talk) from feelings of helplessness and holding negative, destructive thoughts to regulating emotions, and affirming a more resilient long-term and proactive stance.[26]

Some physicians unwittingly motivate their patients into taking more personal responsibility for their health. One woman with lupus described her reaction after one particularly frustrating day in which she felt patronized and put-off by her physician:

> *I knew that day with absolute certainty that things were going to be different...I knew for sure that if doctors couldn't help me, then I was going to have to do it myself. The biggest change was taking control, believing that I knew more about myself and my body than anyone else did. Now I'm feeling the best that I have in at least ten years.*[27]

Reynolds Price, author and teacher had a ten-inch long eel-like tumor inside his spinal cord that took away his ability to walk. Five years after his bout with cancer, Price wrote about the value of taking personal responsibility for your own health: *You're in your calamity alone...If you want a way out, then [you must] dig it yourself.*[28]

Chronic illness and health crises often serve as a reset button, a turning point, a transforming experience, changing one's worldview and lifestyle. Life-threatening illnesses often serve as catalysts of spiritual transformation, sculpting a new life, both inside and out.[29]

Self-help takes many forms. The more popular forms of self-help include exercise programs, stress management tools, positive affirmations, diet, food supplements and self-help support groups. Millions of Americans have joined self-help support groups. Each year, more and more Americans use self-care manuals written to help them cope with specific illnesses (e.g., manuals for arthritis, diabetes and hypertension). Studies show self-help manuals increase satisfaction and confidence in decision-making among those who use them.[30] The sale of medical home-testing tools has become a billion dollar a year industry. There are take-at-home tests for blood sugar, pregnancy, cholesterol, the AIDS virus, colon cancer, blood pressure, blood type and many more.

Among the factors behind the trend toward self-care are:

- Rising costs of medical care and prescriptions,
- Increasing dissatisfaction with experts and their complexities and
- The accessibility of health information on the Internet.

Willingness to Change Lifestyle [31]

Change does not come easily for most people. Changing ones' lifestyle requires motivation, commitment, and a support system to sustain that change. In 1997, the Center for Advancing Health launched *the Decade of Behavior Initiative* program because:

- 58 million Americans were obese,
- 47 million were smokers,
- 18 million had a depressive disorder,
- 16 million had diabetes,
- 14 million abused alcohol,
- 13 million used addictive drugs and

- 50 percent of all patients with chronic illness quit using their prescription drugs altogether.[32]

Behavioral and psychosocial factors influence the onset and management of all chronic diseases. In fact, nine out of the ten leading causes of death in the United States are primarily due to behavioral and social factors such as the use of tobacco products, excessive alcohol consumption, poor diet, and lack of exercise.[33]

Time Magazine reports that 80 percent of Americans wish to improve their health by changing some aspect of their lifestyle, but don't know how to do so successfully. Changing a habit is not easy as anyone who has tried to lose weight or quit smoking will admit. Since behavior is nurtured and sustained in social environments where beliefs, values, and actions are cultivated and reinforced, we need support to change. Three aspects of the social environment help motivate change:

- Appropriate information (manuals and easy to follow routines),
- Rewarding/enjoyable/successful experiences and
- Support and reinforcement in a social network.[34]

Over 25 years ago the call for a shift toward disease prevention and the promotion of healthy habits first sounded.[35] But little has changed within medicine since then in the techniques used to motivate behavioral change in patients. The current approach to prevention relies on fear and other scare tactics even though studies consistently show that fear and other negative emotions fail to motivate change. People avoid painful feelings and mental discomfort. Conventional medicine uses *scare-care* messages as a tactic even though fear suppresses the immune system. Ancient wisdom asserts, *"What you resist will persist."* Fear fails to motivate sustainable change especially when delivered in short, impersonal scripts by a physician. Focusing on what you want to happen enhances physical, emotional and mental health far more than fretting over what you fear might happen!

Tools for motivating change are available. Behavioral tools help mobilize the individual's inner mental and emotional resources for change in conjunction with the person's social support system. Self-help groups are part of the 'culture of lifestyle change' deploying effective tactics of peer support and experience enrichment (examined in Chapter 5). The broader environment, or climate of support, has received more attention recently with public and private policy changes resulting in tax incentives for investing in health promotion, cafeterias that offer healthy meals and laws that restrict smoking.[36] Healthier lifestyles become easier when friends support healthy choices and medical providers model healthy habits for their patients. Health promotion programs are more effective when social support systems nurture, support, and reinforce healthy choices. Such programs promote health while reducing the public and personal burden of illness and medical care costs.[37]

A Holistic View of Health

Prior to 1970, most Americans viewed health as simply the absence of physical disease. Today an increasing number of Americans view health as a positive state of physical, emotional, mental, and spiritual well being that they can consciously nurture through appropriate lifestyles, habits and practices. Health and healing are multi-dimensional as suggested in Figure 1.2 below. Although the physical dimension of health has dominated Western thinking and practice for several hundred years, the integration of the mind-body connection is once again being recognized. Spiritual and medical practices are reconnecting as they existed earlier in Western thought and even now persist in most non-Western societies. Nearly all religious traditions proscribe balance for the emotions, development of the mind, physical practices for the body (e.g., diet, internal cleansing) and spiritual rituals that unite and bridge the visible with the invisible.[38]

Figure 1.2 Holistic Model of Health

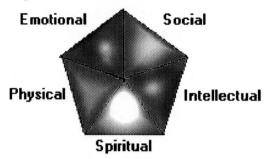

Nearly all religious traditions proscribe balance for the emotions, development of the mind, physical practices for the body (e.g., diet, internal cleansing) and spiritual rituals that unite and bridge the visible with the invisible.

Most adult Americans surveyed (86%) believe personal prayer, meditation, or other spiritual and religious practices can accelerate the healing effects of medical treatment. Nearly half claim that personal prayer or meditation either cured an illness or significantly improved their condition.[39] Herbert Benson, M.D., author of *Timeless Healing,* claims spiritual practices reduce distress and kindle hope.

The spiritual dimension satisfies our need for meaning and fulfillment as it activates hope and faith in healing. Spiritual meaning serves as a compass, providing direction and comfort through sickness and health, bringing coherence to life. Faith buffers stress, calms and encourages a more optimistic worldview. Robert Schuler's classic *The Power of Positive Thinking* inspired others to know that when you change the way you see things, the things you see change. Individuals with faith cope more effectively with problems and life disruptions. Spiritual beliefs woven into the larger tapestry of life bring more flexibility and resilience.

Summary

The increasing use of alternative therapies expresses a major shift from a disease centric to a health centric model. The big shift is from a fear-based focus on avoiding disease toward health and hope, from reliance on quick fixes to adapting healthier life styles, from reactive to more proactive roles for consumers and from an emphasis on the physical to a more holistic view of health. Alternative therapies arose from outside the medical monopoly but they are largely used to complement modern Western medicine. Complementary and alternative therapies are disproportionately used by individuals who are more educated and with higher income. Females use these complementary and alternative therapies more frequently than males.

Complementary therapies are often used for chronic illnesses and to enrich the quality and level of health. These therapies are more natural, help build health and are more holistic in orientation. The big shift from doctoring disease to promoting health became possible with changes in American values and behaviors. In the next chapter, we examine the grievances against modern Western medicine that cause many to turn toward alternative therapies.

CHAPTER 2.
MODERN CONVENTIONAL MEDICINE: AGGRESSIVE AND DEADLY

> *The physician celebrates computer tomography while the patient celebrates the outstretched hand.*
>
> Norman Cousins

More Americans die from their encounters with our modern system of medical care than from any other cause declares a panel of medical researchers.[40] Simply passing through the system exposes patients to risks that end up killing more of them than does heart disease or cancer (711,000 and 553,000 deaths in 2001, while "medical care system" deaths numbered 784,000).[41]

In its assault on disease and pathology, modern medical care kills patients by prescribing the wrong drugs, doing unnecessary surgery, spreading infection, mis-communicating orders, using invasive high-tech tools, and making a wide range of mistakes. Public awareness of this grim reality skyrocketed in the 1990s,[42] eroding confidence in modern medicine.[43]

A national poll conducted by the National Patient Safety Foundation in 1997 found:

- 42% experienced a medical error, either personally or through a friend and
- 32% claimed the error had a permanent negative effect on their health.[44]

Although doctors swear "to do no harm," they unintentionally do a great deal of it. Correcting this situation requires that we learn to "see" healing and health differently. These problems cannot be solved by the same mindset that created them.

Our medical care system is disease centric, focusing on disease and disease-care services instead of promoting or maintaining health. Most chronic diseases (89%) are preventable and those remaining can be delayed according to the Center for Disease Control and Prevention (CDC).[45] When chronic diseases are allowed to envelop the person, they cascade into costly and elaborate treatments.

In this chapter, I focus on the medical care system's ineffective treatments for chronic illness, high cost, over reliance on drugs, medical errors and general failure to promote health. These grievances cause patients to turn away from modern medicine and motivate them to search for alternative ways of healing.

Chronic Disease: The term chronic disease has its etymological root in the Greek word 'chronos' which means time. Chronic diseases:

- Persist for three or more months,
- Are caused mostly by life style behaviors,
- Are not self-limiting, and
- Involved few early symptoms during their latency periods.

Chronic diseases are prolonged illnesses that are either caused by (or greatly aggravated by) lifestyle choices, such as poor diet and lack of exercise or by exposure to environmental toxins. Some of the most common and deadly of these conditions include heart disease, cancer, asthma, and Type II diabetes. Chronic diseases often impair people from performing their routine life tasks such as walking and disable many over time.

The percentage of Americans afflicted with one or more chronic disease grew nearly 110 percent over the last sixty years. In 1935, the country's first National Health Survey, found 22 percent of the population suffered from a chronic condition. In 1995, a similar survey sixty years later found nearly half the population (46 percent) suffered with one or more chronic condition. Chronic disease leads to long-term costly care with more physician visits, drug dependence, repeated and lengthy hospitalizations, nursing home stays and a lower quality of life.

> The percentage of Americans afflicted with one or more chronic disease grew nearly 110 percent over the last sixty years.

While the likelihood of chronic illness increases with age, it is not confined to old age. One in four children age 17 or less also have a chronic illness, as shown in Table 2.1, column one. The percentage of children with chronic conditions surged over the past 30 years with an explosion of numbers suffering from chronic asthma and Type II diabetes.

Over four out of ten (44 percent) of those with chronic conditions are in the two youngest age categories as shown in Table 2.1, second column. The elderly represent only 26 percent of all Americans who are afflicted with chronic conditions. Working age adults, 18 to 64 years of age, account for 60 percent of the total while children under the age of 18 account for 14 percent.

Table 2.1 Prevalence of Chronic Disease in Four Age Groups

Age Range	Percent of Persons With a Chronic Condition	Percent of Total Chronic Conditions
65 and over	88	26
45-64	68	29
18-44	35	31
0-17	25	14

Adapted from Hoffman et al, JAMA vol. 276 (18): 1476.

Many Americans in all age categories suffer from chronic conditions and these conditions are often quite serious, some life threatening. Table 2.2 presents the percent of the population suffering from the most common chronic ailments with many individuals having more than one chronic condition.

Table 2.2 Percent of Population with Specific Chronic Conditions

Condition	Percent of Population	Millions of People
Allergy (pollen)	10.0	26.0
Alzheimer's		4.0
Arthritis	12.5	33.0
Asthma	6.0	17.0
Cancer	3.6	8.0
Clinical depression		17.0
Coronary heart	10.5	21.2
Depression		17.0
Diabetes	3.3	18.0
Emphysema		14.6
Hypertension	11.4	29.9
Heart disease	8.1	
Migraine headache		11.5
Osteo-arthritis	5.0	16.0
Sinusitis (chronic)	14.1	35.0
Stroke		2.6

Adapted from CDC Fact Sheet series 10 Jan 2000 and Hoffman et al, JAMA vol. 276 (18): 1476.

Ineffective Treatment for Chronic Illnesses

Every year, chronic diseases claim the lives of more than 1.7 million Americans. These diseases are responsible for 7 of every 10 deaths in the US and cause major limitations in daily living for more than 1 of every 10 Americans, or 25 million people.[46]

All the celebrated arsenal of tools of modern medicine is not helpful to millions of patients suffering from chronic illnesses. How is it possible that physicians who know so much about disease processes are so often ineffective with chronic illness?

Too often physicians leave the underlying problem of chronic conditions intact by merely suppressing symptoms. There is also limited research on the effectiveness of their treatments. A good example is the customary treatment for heartburn and acid reflux. Some 44 million Americans at some point in their life will experience heartburn from acid reflux, with nearly half being diagnosed with Gastro Esophageal Reflux Disease or GERD. GERD arises most often after the age of 40 and is heavily influenced by lifestyle choices, such as smoking, being overweight, eating quickly without chewing, eating just before bedtime, and not eating enough raw fruits and vegetables with enzymes that aid digestion.[47]

Reflux is nothing more than acid slipping past the junction of the stomach and esophagus. The stomach is designed for acid but the esophagus is not, so a sphincter muscle or gate separates the two areas. Acid in the stomach helps digest food. If antacids or acid blockers are used continually to destroy the acid, the sphincter muscle weakens with disuse because the body saves the energy required to protect the esophagus. When the sphincter muscle weakens, acid can rise up to irritate the esophagus. Taking an antacid soothes the sensitive esophagus because less acid remains, but digestion is weakened along with this sphincter muscle.

Most physicians treat the symptoms of heartburn by placing patients on acid-inhibiting medicine. In many cases, physicians are acquiescing to the requests of their patients who read about medications or watch drug advertisements on television. The Boston Globe Magazine described the marketing of Prilosec, one prescription heartburn drug, as follows:

> *Prilosec...became the world's best-selling prescription drug, and the number one medication prescribed for seniors, taking in $6 billion a year. Prilosec is so good...that doctors jokingly call it 'purple crack.' It's an expensive habit, about $4 for each daily pill, or $1,500 a year.[48]*

The success of Prilosec and other prescription antacids may seem like a great advance until you count the cost and the lifetime dependency on this symptom-suppressing therapy. Neutralizing stomach acid, if pursued over time, is a serious mistake with long-term consequences. Taking antacid reinforces the need for more antacid, since it only deals with the symptom. The short term 'fix' insures that the problem persists.

Is it possible to escape from this vicious cycle? Allan Spreen, M.D. devised a simple, cheap and effective treatment for chronic heartburn that liberates one from dependence on such a medication. He writes:

> *Using readily available acidophilus and digestive enzymes stop over 2/3 of all cases. The more difficult cases that may include overt ulcers require a more aggressive approach, but omitting really serious GI illness, the results are nearly always very positive....A powder form of acidophilus supplements protects the esophagus without killing acid while killing the pain almost immediately. You must keep it handy and take it often if you don't solve the whole problem, which involves tightening the sphincter. This GE muscle can be tightened by using the English herb, Potter's Acidosis or by improving the environment of the stomach, which then tightens the junction on its own.*[49]

The solution, along with acidophilus protection, is to add both acid and digestive enzymes at the same time. Proper digestion allows for a higher concentration of acid while tightening the GE junction and protecting the esophagus. Spreen suggests using digestive enzymes at mid-meal when food is in the stomach.[50]

One man described his going off a prescription heartburn medication in the following way. *I began getting a sharp pain on my left side near the stomach area when not taking Prevacid. So I asked my gastro doctor who said that going off Prevacid often causes some hardening of matter in the upper colon and thus the pain. I am back to being a slave to the Prevacid.*[51] [So when his colon ruptures from the blockage and he develops peritonitis, no one will suspect antacids were the initial problem.]

Side effects of Prilosec include abdominal pain, headache, diarrhea, dizziness, rash, and constipation. For Pepcid, the effects are the same as Prilosec plus seizures, palpitations and depression.[52] Suppressing acid in the stomach causes a four-fold increase in the risk of pneumonia by weakening the sphincter muscle, allowing acid to irritate the membranes leading into the lungs and possible infection.[53]

Many medical practices are simply grounded in past medical practices rather than on scientific evidence or even patient outcome studies. Professor David Eddy, M.D., a leading expert on medical information and decision-making, contends that only 15 percent of medical interventions were supported by scientific evidence in 1990.[54] Many treatments were never scientifically assessed at all! Eddy found a strong tendency for the most rigorous studies (randomized controlled trials) to report less clear-cut significant results compared to less methodically rigorous studies which often did attain significant results. Since clear results are much easier to publish than statistically insignificant results, confidence in the effectiveness of treatment becomes falsely inflated.

A 1990 report of the US Congress's Office of Technology Assessment also concluded that approximately 85 percent of all therapies and procedures commonly used by physicians and hospitals had never received any rigorous evaluation. Surgical procedures are evaluated less often. In 1991, the editor of the British Medical Journal concluded that solid research evidence existed for only two of 21 medical practices he examined; the evidence ranged from poor to none for the other 19. More recently, Ezzo and Berman found only one in five (21%) of 159 medical practices were supported by scientific evidence. Research showed that one in twelve (7 %) medical practices were harmful. Clearly, the belief that all of medicine is based on science and that all medical interventions produce positive results is unfounded. Prior to the 1990s, much of the "science" was lab or bench-research, not "evidence-based" or patient outcome research as noted below.

Until the 1990s, few surgical procedures were examined in clinical trials. Surgical procedures that have no benefit to patients can persist a long time. Mastectomies were used for over a century before anyone studied its effectiveness. Heart bypass operations kill 28,000 Americans every year even though two studies found bypass surgery fails to prolong the patient's life. In 2002, research on arthroscopic knee surgery for osteo-arthritis, a popular surgery that costs insurance carriers more than $1 billion a year, found it no more effective than placebo (mock surgery with marks but no actual intervention).[55]

The earliest attempt to standardize care was proposed in the early 1900s by a Boston surgeon and professor at Harvard Medical School. Ernest Codman M.D. proposed a system for tracking the outcomes of surgical interventions to determine the best treatments. His goal was to carefully measure the impact of a given treatment on the patient's functional status at specific intervals after surgery. Codman's reward for proposing this systematically sophisticated method was ostracism. In 1910, the Massachusetts General Hospital ousted him and he was forced to leave teaching at Harvard. Only now, after nearly a century later are these types of studies being done.

Modern medicine's approach to chronic disease wastes billions of dollars for many treatments that fail to bring benefits beyond the placebo effect that averages 30 percent. Despite the best efforts of physicians, many patients suffer immensely—especially the 40 million Americans who are functionally restricted by at least one chronic illness.[56]

Why are we stuck in this quagmire? Why don't we abandon practices that are so costly with little or no benefit to patients? The inability to see or think outside the "conventional box" has created a "paradigm paralysis." Most patients suffer from conditions that are either preventable or subject to great improvement by simply promoting good health, eliminating toxins and/or changing lifestyle choices.

Chronic Disease is Conventional Medicine's Vietnam.

The long and painful US military involvement in South Vietnam is not only a common metaphor for policy failure, but for failure of an especially ironic kind. In Vietnam, the United States had overwhelming material, technological, and military superiority. The US won most significant battles, and yet lost the war. After devoting billions of dollars over a decade, and sacrificing more than 50,000 American lives, the US gave up. In retrospect, the war was not so much a military defeat as a self-defeating strategy with an enemy we didn't understand. We used inappropriate high-tech weapons without success against an enemy we didn't understand. We also wasted piles of money.

Conventional medicine finds itself in a position even worse than that of the U.S military in Vietnam—medicine is losing many of the battles as well as the war against chronic diseases. Over the past 30 years, countless billions of dollars were spent. The latest scientific and technological missiles in conventional medicine's arsenal of weapons were used on chronic disease; and yet we gained very little, and for some conditions, nothing. As in Vietnam, victory is elusive. We are no more stemming the rising tide of chronic disease than the US military stemmed the flow of men and materials from North Vietnam into South Vietnam along the Ho Chi Min Trail. Just as the military brass ordered the use of "agent orange" to defoliate, medicine uses radiation and chemotherapy to destroy cancer cells. Both result in great suffering and damage with little overall long-term results!

Our greatest failure in Vietnam was one of vision. Many of the politicians and generals who planned the war were veterans of WWII and viewed Vietnam through a lens shaped by World War II. Based on their experience, the army with the greatest firepower that inflicted the most casualties won. Thus, they unleashed an awesome amount of weaponry and created such bogus measures of success as "body counts."

Something analogous is occurring with conventional medicine. We are using the tools for fighting acute disease—the last medical war, as it were—to confront a different enemy, chronic disease, on a different battlefield. Our ill-fated "war on cancer" illustrates the creation of entrenched vested interests and wastefulness of this approach to chronic disease. Despite the expenditure of more than $20 billion on research since President Nixon launched "the War on Cancer" in 1971, little significant improvement came in treatment or survival rates for most common cancers. In reality, the overall incidence of cancer increased by 18 percent between 1971 and 1990 and the mortality rate grew by 7 percent. Over 25 percent more people under the age of 65 died of cancer in 1990 than in 1975 (National Cancer

Advisory Board). The age-adjusted death rates for total cancers show a slow and steady increase since the 1950's! The effectiveness in treating and curing most common cancers has remained virtually unchanged.[57]

The world cancer expert Dr. Samuel Epstein alleges the National Cancer Institute and the American Cancer Society have misled and confused the public and Congress by false claims that we are winning against cancer. Such claims help create public and Congressional support for massive increases in budgetary appropriations. Samuel Broder, former National Cancer Institute director, charged that the NCI has become *"what amounts to a governmental pharmaceutical company."* The cancer establishment has either ignored or criticized the proponents of non-toxic alternative cancer drugs.[58] Nevertheless, over 80 percent of cancer patients today use complementary and alternative therapies, a 30 percent increase since the 1970s and the 1980s.

Since most chronic diseases are preventable, the incentives are misplaced for disease-care services (medical doctors and pharmaceuticals) that don't reward prevention and health promotion. Waiting for illness to occur when it's preventable becomes much more expensive than prevention with environmental and lifestyle change. Since "disease-centric" providers are rewarded for providing services, they do. The ideal conditions for the pharmaceutical and the medical industry comes when patients have a disease that never gets better but the patient never dies. Patients return again and again to find temporary relief from disease-care services.

High Cost

Americans spend more money on medical care than any other country. Still, in terms of the health and life expectancy of its population, the US ranks next to the bottom of the 13 most industrialized nations based on 16 indicators of health. In another study by the World Health Organization, the US ranked 15th of 25 industrial nations. How can so much money be spent on achieving so little?

Seventy-five percent of all medical care spending in the US goes toward treating chronic conditions.[59] By failing to promote health and preventing chronic disease, our medical care system becomes costly, cumbersome and ineffective. In delivering disease care, one-third of the total expenditure is spent on administrative overhead.[60]

Chronic conditions consume more services, drugs and hospital beds. They account for 80 percent of all hospital days and 69 percent of hospital admissions. Their average length of hospital stay is 7.8 days compared to 4.3 days for persons without a chronic condition. Persons with chronic conditions consume over four out of every five prescription drugs, two out of every three physician visits and over half of all emergency department visits.[61]

Chronic diseases cause three-quarters of all deaths in the US. People with chronic conditions die 14.8 years prematurely, on average. In response to these grim statistics, the defenders of conventional medicine point to extensions in life expectancy since 1964. But, the Center for Disease Care and Prevention contends that access to medical care contributes only 10 percent to increases in longevity. Extended years of life came from improvements in public health, sanitation and immunizations rather than medical treatment. Public health factors are the cause for nearly all the increased longevity.

Chronic diseases cause three-quarters of all deaths in the US. People with chronic conditions die 14.8 years prematurely.

Prolonging life has not increased life quality because chronic illnesses impair and cause despair for many. Longevity gains are being lost to more years of impairment from chronic illnesses. Women on average suffer nearly 15 years with some disability while men on average suffer 12 years with disability. Thus, although women on average live longer than men (78.8 compared to 72.6 years), they also spend more of those years "doctoring" a chronic condition.[62] *Most of us want to add life to years, not just years to life.*

In 2001, American physicians wrote nearly 3 billion prescriptions at a total cost of $180 billion dollars. The average person filled 12 prescriptions each year with the elderly filling even more.

Between 4–18 % of all medical patients experience adverse drug effects that require spending even more money. They often require further visits to physicians, additional prescriptions, emergency room visits, hospital admissions and even long-term care as shown in Table 2.3. In 1992, the cost of repairing the damage from adverse drug reactions was $76.5 billion beyond the $74 billion initially spent purchasing the drugs.[63] The cost more than doubled in 2000, rising to $177 billion.[64]

Table 2.3 Drug Reactions Bring Added Cost and Use of More Services[65]

Additional Services	Number in millions	Cost in Billions 2000
Physician visits	116	13.8
Additional prescriptions	77	3.5
Emergency room visits	17	5.8
Admission to the hospital	8	121.5
Admission to long-term care	3	32.8
TOTAL	**221**	**177.4**

See Frank Ernst and Amy Grizzle, "Drug-Related Morbidity and Mortality," in *J Am Pharm Assoc* vol. 41(2):192-97, 2001.

The Cost of the Legal Drug Trade

The ties between the drug industry and the medical establishment are many. These ties increase the cost of medical care and influence the practice of medicine. The arrangement smacks of economic and career contamination. Virtually no accountability exists to counter the conflicts of interest that inevitably arise.

Physicians, medical schools, and hospitals are handsomely funded by drug companies to study, publish ghost-written articles, and use their drugs. Drug companies devote billions to advertise, market, and distribute free samples of medications approved by the FDA. Individuals write proposals for grant money, publish articles and build careers based on their biomedical research. Medical school leadership leaves the development of drugs, their testing and even continuing medical education of practitioners up to drug companies. Some refer to these tactics as bringing a Trojan horse into the medical compound as they infiltrate, subvert and subjugate the practice of medicine into a for-profit industry.

An exhaustive review of studies on the influence of the pharmaceutical industry on medicine concluded that pharmaceutical companies affect physicians' prescribing behavior.[66] This influence stems from three types of interactions:

- Most physicians see sales representatives often and attend drug-sponsored educational courses.
- Drug-company funding of clinical trials affect the quality and the type of research that physicians undertake.
- Drug company-sponsored educational courses often have a commercial bias.

The pharmaceutical industry markets its products aggressively and spends a large percentage of its budget on advertising directly to the public. Consumer-directed drug advertising increased dramatically in the 1990s and helped change the practice of medicine by persuading consumers to request brand name drugs from their physicians. Ads for drugs used for skin, HIV/AIDS and ob/gyn conditions were most common. Women were targeted more often than men and the most common appeals were drug effectiveness, symptom control and convenience.[67]

Lavish amounts are also spent on "educating" physicians of their products as the pharmaceutical companies fly physicians to the Bahamas and other resort locations. The drug industry spent $2 billion in 2001 on events for doctors, double what it spent five years earlier. Like other businesses, they defend their market share with bulldog tenacity. Marketing dollars rose sharply in response to the efforts of managed care companies to switch patients to less expensive generic drugs. In 2001, pharmaceutical companies spent more than 11 billion in promotion and marketing, rising from the $5.5 billion spent in 1995.[68]

The pharmaceutical industry spends $13,000 annually on each physician according to Wazana Ashley M.D. This investment serves the interests of the drug companies much more than it serves patients.

This money largely becomes a seductive sales tactic with a personal touch, as company representatives begin contacting physicians before graduation from medical school. Upon entering practice, a weekly visit ensues. This cultivation of relationships pays handsomely, as it affects the prescribing behavior of doctors on multiple levels. Physicians prescribe more drugs sold by companies that pay for their continuing medical education credits; hospitals prescribe more of the drugs from the companies who sponsor administrators' travel to conferences; and physicians' prescribe more of the company's drugs after a pharmaceutical representative "teach-in."[69]

Physicians who rely on company representatives for knowledge are less able to spot false claims about a medication. They prescribe more new drugs, and they make more formulary requests for medications that rarely hold important advantages over existing ones. They prescribe fewer generic drugs and more of the expensive, newer medications, even when the new drugs demonstrate *no advantage* and do not adhere to "best practice guidelines" developed by MDs![70]

Pharmaceutical sponsorship of drug research influences the framing of the results and skews what gets reported.[71] Drug industry support of research often taints the results. When scientists evaluating a medication's efficacy have financial relationships with pharmaceutical or product manufacturers, they less often analyze the safety or efficacy of the drug under study as documented in a number of medical journal articles. Drug company-funded studies were seven times less likely to report unfavorable qualitative conclusions than non-profit-sponsored studies (5% vs. 38%). Conversely, quantitative results were overstated in studies sponsored by pharmaceutical company 30 percent of the time versus 13 percent for non-profit sponsored studies.[72]

Many physicians view free drug samples, being flown to resorts for a drug education, and gifts as simply perks and part of the medical culture. A majority of medical students in one study approved of drug reps bringing gifts to doctors; 85 percent felt it improper for politicians to accept a comparable gift but only 46 percent believed it improper for themselves to accept such gifts from a pharmaceutical company. The culture of medicine accepts as proper what the wider public views as improper. *Self-interest drives the practice of medicine, the marketing of drugs, and the medical-pharmaceutical industry.* Changing these practices in the short-term may be more difficult than changing the direction of a glacier.

Eight of the nine doctors advising the government in 2004 on new cholesterol guidelines were making money from the very companies whose cholesterol-lowering drugs they were urging upon millions of Americans. Two own stock in these companies. Two others went to work for these drug companies shortly after working on the guidelines. Another was a senior government scientist who moonlights for 10 companies and who also serves on one of their boards![73]

In his book, *On the Take*,[74] Dr. Jerome Kassirer, former editor-in-chief of the prestigious *New England Journal of Medicine*, examines the pervasive payoffs that physicians receive from big drug companies and other medical suppliers. Kassirer contends that America's medical-care system is being converted into a commercial cash-cow.[75] Twenty years ago, only one-third of medical research funding at universities came from private industry but today two-thirds comes from private industry.

Kassirer documents the range of conflicts of interest between profit-centered business and a service-centered medicine: the drug industry's huge expenditures for courting doctors to use their products; recruiting physicians to sell their drugs; or to present 'seemingly objective drug education' that favor their products over others.[76]

In America, we permit the principle of *caveat emptor*—let the buyer beware—generally guide the relationship between the industry and the public. This may work well with most consumer goods; but not with medications, for the simple reason that neither the patient nor the attending physician is able to evaluate the products until the damage has already been done. In the case of pharmaceuticals, if the product does not work, there may not be a next time. Because the stakes are high and there is little room for error, we seek assurance that the product is safe and works as promised but to whom can we turn for such assurances?

The pharmaceutical industry is not a competitive market. They receive patent protection for new medications that lasts for 20 years from the date of patent application to expiration.[77]

Additional Costs

Kickbacks and rebates help inflate the cost of drugs even more. In 2003, New York and six other states filed lawsuits against two major pharmaceutical companies—GlaxoSmithKline and Pharmacia Corporation—accusing them of paying doctors and pharmacists to choose their companies' drugs over other medicines. The suit focused on the practice of kickbacks to MDs at the expense of patients and third party payers. Drug companies establish a price for their drugs that the government and insurance companies pay in reimbursement, but pharmaceutical companies allow the doctors and pharmacies to buy their drugs at a much lower price than what is reported to the government. For example, a doctor may pay as little as $7.40 for 10 milligrams of Adriamycin, a chemotherapy drug produced by Pharmacia, after the discounts from the drug maker. Medicare would reimburse the doctor $34.42, based on Pharmacia's average wholesale price, and a Medicare patient in New York would make a co-payment of $8.60. The doctor would pocket $35.62, the difference between the amount paid for the drug and the payments received from the patient and from Medicare.[78]

Medco Managed Care, a unit of the pharmaceutical company Merck, received more than $3.5 billion in rebates in the late 1990s from drug companies promoting sales of certain drugs. According to documents filed in a class-action lawsuit in 2003, Medco received rebates as incentives to promote some of the most costly drugs. Merck's own drugs were promoted especially vigorously. Medco retained most of the $3.56 billion in rebates from the drug companies from the 1997 to 1999 time period, not informing their customers of the rebates.[79]

A growing number of questionable marketing practices prompted the FDA to issue guidelines for PHARMA which were instituted on July 1, 2002. Health and Human Services also issued a 39-page compliance guidance booklet for the pharmaceutical industry in May

2003, identifying three major areas where they 'cross the line' most often. The guidelines identified:

- Inaccurate or inadequate payment data submitted to state and federal agencies,
- Marketing tactics that amount to kickbacks, or other improper remuneration, and
- Violations of drug sample laws.

The HHS' inspector general's office asked the pharmaceutical companies to make formal, explicit commitments to ethical behavior.

Drug Side Effects

Every drug is like a triangle with three faces: —one face represents the healing it can bring, the second face represents the hazards it can inflict, and the third face represents the cost of each. The triangle suggests the tradeoffs between risk, effectiveness and cost.

Prescribed drugs often produce side effects and, sometimes even death.[80] Many physicians exhibit an "addiction to writing prescriptions." Quick fixes come with a price that often is delayed and hidden. In 1994, the overall incidence of adverse drug reactions (ADRs) among hospitalized patients was 6.7 percent.[81] An estimated 2.2 billion hospitalized patients had serious ADRs and 106,000 died, making drug reactions the fourth leading cause of death in the US. Excluded were patients whose problems arose from errors in administration, noncompliance with doctor's orders, overdose, drug abuse, therapeutic failures and suspected but unproven drug reactions.[82] Not surprisingly, the frequency of adverse drug reactions in hospitalized patients increases with the length of hospitalization and the number of drugs prescribed.[83]

The situation may actually be worse in teaching hospitals where patients are more ill and stay longer in the hospital. Most hospitals rely on spontaneous and voluntary reporting of ADRs. Only about 1 in 20 ADR is reported. Unfortunately, the FDA does not generally identify drugs that cause death. Drug research rarely determines if the benefit of a drug outweighs the risk.[84]

Before the FDA approves a drug, the company must submit two trials that show clearly positive effects. Often no one knows the number of trails conducted before two trials show positive effects. The manufacturers of Prozac needed five different trials to collect two; the makers of Paxil and Zoloft took even more trials.[85] In summer 2004, the AMA considered a proposal to require that all drug study results be made public, even unpublished research funded by pharmaceutical companies that might reflect poorly on their drugs.[86] Still such research continues to be shrouded in secrecy.

Non-compliance

Side effects from prescribed drugs cause nearly half the patients to quit taking their medication for chronic conditions. Eight out of ten people taking antidepressants report side effects such as nausea, headache, anxiety, dry mouth, insomnia, sexual dysfunction, diarrhea, gastrointestinal bleeding and tremors. Prescribed drugs bring side-effects that send 17 million people to the emergency department, 8 million to the hospital and 3 million to long-term admissions. As many as 106,000 die from adverse reactions in the hospital to drugs properly prescribed and taken as directed as shown in Table 2.4.[87] A study in 2002 studied deaths from adverse drug reactions. When adding patient deaths from drugs both inside and outside the hospital, the number rose to over 200,000 per year.[88]

> Side effects from prescribed drugs cause nearly half the patients to quit taking their medication for chronic conditions.

The use of prescription drugs often leads to the use of additional drugs to counter unwanted side effects of the first drug. The first drug becomes a "gateway drug," leading to the use of more drugs to suppress its negative side effects. This progresses until the average person over age 65 is taking 12 prescriptions.

Since drugs are often prescribed to patients presenting symptoms that are of an unknown origin, a new prescription may be used to treat a side effect of a medication being used at the time. Molly recalled an incident that happened in her family several years ago:

When my grandmother moved closer to us, we studied the medicines she was taking at the time. We discovered only two of the ten prescriptions were for original problems. All the others were treating the side effects arising from the two original drugs.

Male sexual dysfunction is a common side effect of antidepressants. As a result, a patient will often stop using medication in order to resurrect his sex life, hoping it might lift a depressed mood. So Pfizer, the maker of Viagra, funded a study, hoping to demonstrate how a depressed man taking Prozac can protect his sex life by using Viagra. Pfizer sponsored a continuing medical education event in New York in the fall of 2002, at which Professor Irwin Goldstein called Viagra a "miracle drug" that should be taken on a daily basis *to prevent impotence.*[89] Viagra sells at $10 or more per tablet that certainly elevates the profits of the drug company.

Only one in three patients with depression is adhering to their drug regimen. Depressed patients are among the lowest to adhere to taking pills. Adverse side effects are the primary reason for not taking their medications.[90]

Non adherence with a drug regimen is common because of side effects. Half the patients with chronic disease fail to adhere to doctors' recommendations, irrespective of disease, treatment, or age.[91] A simple search on Medline yielded nearly 60,000 citations since 1980 related to adherence/compliance.

Adverse side effects are the primary reason for not taking their medications.

Half the people with hypertension receive drug treatment and in half of these cases blood pressure is controlled with drugs; half stop taking their drugs during their initial year of treatment, largely because of adverse side effects. Ninety days is the median time before hypertensive patients discontinue their drug regimen.[92]

Clinical trials recently revealed the harmful effects of combined estrogen and progestin therapy for postmenopausal women over shadowed its benefit. The risks of using these hormones included: more heart attacks (29 percent), more cases of breast cancer (26 percent), more strokes (41 percent) and more blood clots to the lungs (112 percent). An estimated 14 million American women take hormone therapy to help relieve hot flashes and other menopausal symptoms as well as to prevent heart disease.[93] Drug treatments can increase the risk of heart attacks, strokes and cancer.

Traditional Chinese medicine (TCM) has treated menopausal symptoms for millennia without hormones. Ancient herbal formulas, adapted for contemporary needs are effective in treating these conditions.[94]

The FDA is responsible for protecting us from harmful drugs, but many approved drugs are unsafe. The FDA is not doing nearly enough to protect the public against adverse reactions to drugs. The FDA maintains that a drug is safe unless reviewers establish with 95 percent certainty that it is not claims David Graham, associate director of the Office of Drug Safety for the FDA. This rule protects drug producers more than it protects consumers.

Over half of all drugs introduced between 1976 and 1985 required either withdrawal or re-labeling because of serious adverse reactions found after the marketing of these drugs. These side effects included heart, liver and kidney failure, birth defects, severe blood disorders, respiratory arrest, seizures and blindness. Changes to the labeling either restricted a drug's use or added major warnings. *One in seven hospital beds are filled by patients suffering from adverse drug reactions* according to Marcia Angell M.D, former editor of the *New England Journal of Medicine.*[95]

The problem is systemic and requires changing because the FDA has an inherent conflict of interest when safety questions emerge about drugs it has approved.[96] The approval process focuses on effectiveness more than safety of drugs during clinical trials. Few safety problems are detected prior to FDA approval because: few people (1000-3000) are involved in a clinical trial; only one drug is used by clinical subjects at a time; the drug is used over a short time period with relatively young healthy test subjects; and the content of the placebo pill is not disclosed. Some contend placebo pills are being used to *rig results* that portray a drug as both significantly better than the placebo and not producing more unwanted side effects of nausea, depression, headaches, tremors, anxiety or diarrhea than the placebo.[97]

This method for evaluating drugs is overly artificial. Many people take more than one medication at a time and drugs often interact with each other and some foods to produce side effects. In addition, many side effects are not detectable in the short time-period of the study.[98]

A more realistic safety picture emerges only after a drug becomes widely used for several years and the trickle of reports on adverse reactions arrive at the FDA. Reports are submitted by physicians, pharmacists and now patients. By FDA's own admission, 10 adverse reactions go unreported for every one reported. Professionals are not required to report drug reactions. Cautious doctors wait for two or three years to prescribe new drugs until the risk becomes "road tested" more realistically. Sorting out the risk is a messy process.

Before conducting human trials for drugs, pharmaceutical companies are often fully aware of the side effects of the products they're testing. So if a drug is known to cause dizziness and nausea, the drug company may create a placebo to mimic the same side effects. Drug companies make their own placebo pills for research purposes, sometimes including ingredients in the drugs being tested.[99] The advertising campaign for a popular allergy medication has TV ads that list the side effects. The voice-over says, "The most common side effects - including headache, drowsiness, fatigue and dry mouth - occurred about as often as they did with a sugar pill."[100]

Dr. Beatrice Golomb, MD, PhD, a professor of medicine at the University of California, San Diego, is fighting the claim that placebos are inactive substances. Professor Golomb wants scientists to provide a list of placebo ingredients so trial results can be properly evaluated by comparing the placebo ingredients with the ingredients in the new drug. Standardized placebos would help eliminate the cynical manipulation of test data against a moving standard rather than a fixed reference point.[101]

Since the FDA has an inherent conflict of interest between approving drugs and monitoring the drug's safety afterward, Congress is considering the creation of an independent board of drug safety to ensure the safety of drugs *after FDA approval.* The case of Vioxx highlighted the safety issue after learning that its use for arthritis increased the risk of heart attack and stroke by two-fold. This followed the more controversial use of Prozac for depressed adolescents that increased their risk of suicide by three-fold compared to depressed adolescents not taking any medications. Five other worrisome drugs deserve further safety scrutiny:

- Meridia, a weight-loss drug linked to risks of higher blood pressure and stroke,
- Crestor, an anti-cholesterol drug linked to renal failure and other serious side effects
- Accutane, an acne drug liked to birth defects,
- Bextra, a painkiller linked to cardiovascular risks and
- Serevent, an asthma treatment linked to deaths.[102]

Over Reliance on Drugs Undermines Health

Prescription drugs constitute conventional medicine's primary therapeutic tool for any given malady. Over three billion prescriptions were filled in the US in 2002, averaging 12 prescriptions per person. Drugs are a tradeoff between risk, benefit and cost.

Drugs are the third leading cause of death in the US.

With so many prescriptions being filled, millions of patients suffer side effects each year. Gentler, less expensive life-style changes are rarely explored. One out of every four people taking prescription drugs experience adverse side effects, and the use of four prescription drugs increases the chance of a drug interaction according to a recent article.103 While some side-affects of drugs may be only a minor inconvenience, others are lethal. Drugs are the third leading cause of death in the US.

Many doctors prescribe "a pill for every ill" and substitute drugs for balanced diets, exercise and stress management. Drugs introduce dangerous chemicals into the body's internal eco-system. Elmer Green of the Menninger Clinic contends that changes in lifestyle are superior to drugs for approximately 75 percent of all medical problems.[104] Dr. Allen Roses, Glaxo, Smith and Kline's vice president of genetics contends that less than half of patients prescribed drugs get any benefit because people respond to the same medicine differently because of their biochemical differences.[105]

Drugs Deplete Nutrients from the Body.

Virtually all prescription drugs deplete nutrients from the body as they are being metabolized so drug therapy is like "robbing Peter to pay Paul." This depletion of nutrients stresses biochemical processes in the body, potentially impairing health in new ways.[106] The Kellogg Report documented the role of prescription drug-use in undermining the absorption of nutrients from food.[107] The friendly flora of our stomach is under attack from overuse of antibiotics and many other drugs. Like weapons of mass destruction, antibiotics destroy both the *good* and *bad* bacteria alike. Compounding this problem is our exposure to antibiotics that are fed to poultry, dairy and beef animals. Eating non-organic meat, milk or other animal products greatly elevates the intake of antibiotics into our bodies. Each year roughly half of the 32 million pounds of antibiotics produced are fed to animals for our meat, milk and egg supply.

Many other drugs also deplete the body of nutrients, including laxatives and birth control pills. Blood tests reveal significantly lower serum levels of critical nutrients like alpha-tocopherol, beta-carotene, and co-enzyme Q-10 among those taking cholesterol lowering statin drugs (like Zocor).[108]

Depression is a serious and common problem afflicting some 17 million Americans. Depression can be treated successfully with various treatments that range from supplements to psychotherapy and/or medication. Sometimes one or the other, or a combination is best. Now, however, millions are using only quick-fix medication, which often brings deleterious effects.

Over the last 20 years, alternative approaches to treating depression (psychotherapy, diet, herbs) have been shouldered aside by drugs. Two out of three patients diagnosed with depression received an antidepressant with most being prescribed a new generation of medications, known as selective serotonin reuptake inhibiters or SSRIs.[109] The most frequently prescribed are: Zoloft, Prozac, Celexa and Paxil. Together, these four medications brought in over $8.3 billion in the year 2001 for treating depression.

SSRIs work by manipulating the brain's use of serotonin, the chemical largely responsible for mood. Under ideal conditions, the brain cells secrete serotonin in response to signals from other parts of the brain. The serotonin then travels across synapses and bonds with serotonin receptors on other cells. When all the receptors are full, the original cell reabsorbs any unused serotonin, a process known as "reuptake." Antidepressants work by interfering with the reuptake process, allowing more serotonin to circulate freely in the brain. More circulating serotonin makes people feel calm, peaceful, and content.[110]

Serotonin levels can be boosted by other means. But very few patients are treated with natural supplements and/or foods to relieve depression. Dietary changes are very helpful in combating depression in a majority of cases. Depressed people are often deficient in magnesium, a mineral found in whole grains, nuts, bananas, and leafy green vegetables. Herbal supplements like valerian root, chamomile, black cohosh, and rosemary may also help manage depression. Equally effective as a drug for mild and moderate depression is St. John's Wort, the "natural Prozac" herb. Lastly, those who experience mild to moderate depression sometimes find relief with an increased intake of omega-3 fatty acids found in fish or fish oil supplements.

Medical Errors

In 1994, Lucien Leape M.D. of Harvard Medical School declared that one million hospital patients nationwide each year were injured by errors during treatment. Leape and his associates estimated that one in every 500 patients admitted to a hospital died as a result of a medical error, making it the third most common cause of death.[111] At a 1997 press conference, Dr. Leape updated his 1994 statistics, noting that medical errors in inpatient hospital settings nationwide could be as high as three million and could cost as much as $200 billion.

Infections alone strike one in ten hospital patients killing over 80,000 Americans every year.[112]

Medical errors include any unintended act (by omission or commission) that produces an adverse outcome or injury. Some adverse events are unpreventable and reflect the risk associated with treatment, such as a life-threatening allergic reaction to a drug when there was no way of knowing the patient's reaction to it. However, the patient who receives an antibiotic to which he or she is known to be allergic, and subsequently goes into anaphylactic shock and dies, represents a case of medical error, which is preventable.[113]

Errors can occur in all medical settings from hospitals, outpatient surgery centers, nursing homes to doctors' offices and patients' homes. Since most fatal errors occur in the hospital, the hospital is where most of the relevant research occurs. Medical errors include:

- Medication error, e.g., being given the wrong medication or the wrong dosage.
- Mishandled surgery, e.g., amputating the wrong leg or nicking an artery.
- Diagnostic errors, e.g., a misdiagnosis leading to an incorrect choice of therapy, a failure to use an indicated diagnostic test, a misinterpretation of test results, or failing to act on abnormal results.
- Equipment failure, e.g. a defibrillator with dead batteries or intravenous pumps whose valves are easily dislodged or bumped, causing over-dosage of medication.
- Lab-report error and misinterpretation of medical orders, e.g. failing to give a salt-free meal.
- System failures, e.g., an infection entering a post-surgical wound or a blood transfusion-related injury, or giving a patient an incorrect blood type. Each year 2 million patients acquire hospital infections after admittance.

Simply using the medical care system causes more deaths than from any other single cause according to a panel of medical researchers in 2003.[114] They combined adverse drug reactions and medical mistakes together. Medical errors, adverse drug reactions, malnutrition from drug treatments and hospital-acquired infections cause the largest number of deaths as shown in Table 2.4 below. These data are from the report Death by Medicine.[115]

Table 2.4 Causes of Annual Deaths From Using the Medical Care System

Causes of Death	Deaths per Year
Adverse drug reactions	106,000
Medical error	98,000
Bedsores and ulcer prevention	115,000
Hospital infections (Nosonomial)	88,000
Malnutrition in nursing homes	108,800
Outpatient & nursing home drug reactions	199,000
Unnecessary procedure	37,136
Surgery-related	32,000
TOTAL	**783,936**

Adapted from *Death by Medicine*, 2003, Gary Null et al.

Chronically ill patients suffer disturbing rates of medical errors, lack of care coordination and poor communication with their doctors according to a 2002 survey of five English-speaking countries funded by the Commonwealth Fund.[116] Among comparably ill patients in all five countries, the US reported the highest percentages:

- Seeing four or more providers (43%),
- Using four or more prescriptions on a regular basis (36%),
- Repeating their health story to multiple providers (57%),
- Having duplicate tests/procedures by different providers (22%),
- Receiving conflicting information about their care from different providers (26%), and
- Reporting either a medication or medical mistake in the past two years (28%), with 63% of these causing serious health problems.[117]

Nearly half (47%) the US respondents reported that their personal physician did not ask for their ideas or opinions about treatment, 31 percent leave without getting important questions answered, over one in four reported a medication or medical mistake in the past two years and 39 percent do not comply with their doctor's medical treatment plan.[118] These statistics highlight the problems of relying on specialists and high tech solutions. Tracking systems, electronic medical records and computerized systems for prescribing drugs offer some hope for improving the quality of medical care. An individual can also become proactive in matters of their own health and this is sure to reduce medical errors.

Failure to Promote Health

The root problem is relegating health to the doctor's domain of expertise and depending on doctors for *health*. Yet medical practice is disease-centric, waiting for patient self-care efforts to fail. They encourage patients to depend on experts and pills to counter ills rather than teaching response-abilities and self-empowerment. Rather than promoting health, doctors tend to provide brief, high-tech units of service. They use high-tech tools on disease rather than promoting health.

Conventional medicine's world-view conflicts with the quality movement that promotes improvement rather than waiting to correct problems after they develop. Conventional medicine focuses on disease and fixing problems after they arise rather than promoting health before disease descends.

Advocates of quality improvement warn against short-term thinking and focusing on *downstream problems* after they emerge. The quality improvement approach shifts attention upstream so as to build-in quality and monitoring the process to safeguard health. Promoting health requires creating a healthy lifestyle and an environment that protects health and enhances healing. Quality improvement involves connecting cause and effect over a longer time horizon—a view far more expansive than that of specialists who focus on repairing diseased organs as separate parts of an ailing physical body.

Conventional medicine's world-view conflicts with the quality movement that promotes improvement rather than waiting to correct problems after they develop.

Conventional medicine largely fixes downstream problems after they emerge along with trauma and medical emergencies. The medical model focuses on fixing the effects of unhealthy choices and toxic environments after individuals have fallen over the cliff as cited in Chapter 1. Most physicians are not promoting health and building a fence to prevent people from falling over the cliff. Conventional medicine relies on using complex, invasive, high tech tools to "fix" problems.

Health promotion is both cheaper and more effective, but requires a 180-degree turnabout in thinking. Doctoring involves more biochemical and pharmacological skills whereas promoting health requires more interpersonal and behavioral change skills.

The medical care system indulges human weakness and passivity by waiting to treat disease rather than cultivating human strengths by teaching self-care skills. By focusing on disease after it descends, medical people unwittingly cultivate dependency; they fail to counter unhealthy behaviors by individuals and corporate actors who are causing disease. By simply reacting to disease and biochemistry, medical providers become biochemical mechanics treating physical disorders as you would repair a car.

Summary

Growing numbers of Americans are losing faith in conventional medical treatments. The failure to promote health, the ineffectiveness of many treatments for chronic diseases and their high cost erodes confidence in modern medicine. In addition, the high-tech intrusive treatments too often bring toxic side effects and medical errors that cause death, further undermining trust. Medicine is part of a high tech medical/pharmaceutical industry that seeks to "kill the enemy" but too often results in "friendly fire" killing many patients.

A growing number of Americans live out their days under the cloud of chronic ailments. They turn to their physicians for relief, but all too often lose quality of life and hope. In many respects, chronic disease has become an important part of how we define ourselves, of our middle-age identity. Many wish to change this identity and enrich their health. The failure of modern medicine to effectively treat chronic conditions prompts the search for alternatives. Not everyone with chronic problems turns to alternative treatments, but the inability of conventional medicine to alleviate suffering from chronic diseases fans the flames of discontent and the search for alternatives. In the next chapter we turn to the positive reasons that attract people to complementary and alternatives therapies.

CHAPTER 3.
THE RISING POPULARITY OF
COMPLEMENTARY THERAPIES

Atoms are ageless. Atoms in your body existed since the beginning of time, cycling and recycling among innumerable forms, both non-living and living. You don't "own" the atoms that make up your body; you borrow them...we are made of the same atoms—atoms that cycle from person to person as we breathe, sweat and vaporize.... Within six years, every person in the world breathes an average of one of your exhaled atoms in a single breath and with each breath....We literally breathe each other.
From Paul Gittewitt Conceptual Physics, 1985.

In January 2004, I received an e-mail from a 51-year-old friend, Heith, about a dream that he said provided guidance for treating the arthritic pain in his knees. The e-mail subject caption read "A really wild dream!" His e-mail read as follows:

I have a great dream to share with you. Here is some background: I have arthritis, especially in my knees. Lately, my knees have been hurting to the point that my prescription medication wasn't even helping. The other night after meditating, I had a spiritual dream, full of light that seemed to "strobe" or have its own energy. The minister of my church was in the dream, as was Edgar Cayce, the "psychic." I was being served spinach to eat that looked and tasted like brown nuts. I thought this odd in the dream. The next day,

I couldn't stop thinking about this dream. I became curious what the Cayce readings had to say about spinach, so I did some research.[119] To my surprise, spinach was mentioned as a preventive for arthritis in several of his readings. I had never eaten spinach, certain that I would not like it but I had nothing to lose so I tried it. The first thing that struck me upon eating spinach was its taste. It seemed to have a nutty taste, as in my dream. I knew then I was onto something.

Nearly all my knee pain vanished the next morning and within 48 hours my knee pain was 90 percent better. I haven't needed any medication for several days now. This is unheard of for me. It is a miracle! That dream contained great guidance.

I e-mailed Heith a positive comment and he responded three days later with this:

I decided to try another Cayce treatment I read about while researching the spinach—hot castor oil packs. I applied the oil packs to both knees for two evenings and now I am completely pain free. You wouldn't believe the pain and discomfort I had before. Usually the first thing I would reach for in the morning would be the bottle of arthritis medicine but this morning I laughed because I didn't need them anymore. I don't need those drugs anymore! [What his body needed was food, real food to combat the inflammation in his joints.]

Some time later I received a third e-mail from my friend proclaiming:

I have not taken any medication since the dream over two months ago. The important thing about this experience was recognizing and acting on the spiritual guidance that arose from within. I knew this dream had an important message, and I had the good sense to heed its guidance. I am grateful!

Most complementary and alternative medical (CAM) therapists believe that dreams and intuition can greatly enhance our quest for health and healing. CAM belief captures a spiritual legacy in our language with words such as "inspiration" or "insight" which is also often referred to as "wisdom of the body" and "built-in intelligence."

In this chapter, five core tenets/beliefs common to CAM therapies are identified and later in the chapter they are linked to cultural values that arose out of the social movements of the 1960s and 1970s.[120] CAM therapies supply what many Americans find absent in conventional medicine, namely a holistic approach to health that softens conventional medicine's over-emphasis on the physical body and high tech tools.

CAM's Five Core Tenets

Derived from many different traditions, the wide variety of CAM therapies seems to share little in common, except for being outside mainstream medicine. Yet, their variety notwithstanding, they share five prominent themes and assumptions that distinguish them from conventional medicine:

- The body has self-healing mechanisms and a built-in intelligence.
- It is better to promote health than fight disease.
- Patient participation is central to health and healing.
- A holistic focus that recognizes the confluence of body, mind, and spirit on health and
- It is best to use natural processes and products.

These unifying beliefs foster a mutually enhancing set of practices and teachings, common to CAM therapies. Woven together, they constitute a natural wellness paradigm that stands in contrast to the conventional biomedical model.[121]

The body has self-healing mechanisms and a built-in intelligence.

A central defining quality of CAM is the belief in the healing power of the body with its built-in intelligence for repair of wounds, bone fractures and emotional hurts. CAM asserts it is better to rely on the healing power of nature first, and technology second. The human body heals itself with proper support, rest and nutrition. Activating natural processes becomes an important task for the practitioner. Strengthening the body's healing forces is emphasized over fighting disease because high tech medicine often uses a crutch or synthetic substance that interferes with the body's responsiveness.[122]

Living organisms all exhibit an adaptive intelligence. Intelligence directs plants toward sunshine and guides amoebas away from noxious agents. Humans possess built-in healing and defense mechanisms when the immune system is supported and functioning. Andrew Weil in his book *Spontaneous Healing* identifies DNA repair, wound healing, bone mending, cellular repair and emotional healing.

Intelligence also operates as intuition in dreams or insights and those "a-ha" moments during waking states. Judith Orloff, a medical doctor and Intuitive, asserts *We all possess an intuitive healing code that contains the blueprints for our health and happiness... listening to intuition is sacred to me.*[123] Intuition is about empowerment. It may come as a flash of insight, a gut feeling, a hunch, or a dream. If you follow your intuitive voice, you can't go wrong, she asserts. This "inner physician" can help maintain health and bring remedies in times of illness. Our dreams can guide us toward health and healing as it did for Heith's arthritic pain. By attuning to our body as it sends us signals, we learn to maintain health and enhance healing if it slides into dis-ease. To inhabit our body means listening and trusting the intelligence of the messages sent. Unfortunately, neither the educational system nor medical care providers encourage us to trust this innate bodily intelligence and its signaling systems.[124]

Symptoms are helpful signals from the body. These signals are warnings and messages to be examined, decoded and interpreted before being suppressed or eliminated with medications. Once interpreted, the patient frequently can eliminate the symptoms through a change of lifestyle rather than defaulting to medication or surgical intervention. Thus, one task of the CAM practitioner is to teach patients how to interpret and decode symptoms.

Considering our physical body as a teacher may seem novel, but the champions of CAM believe that patients must learn to respond and understand their "inner physician" to cultivate health. Attuning to the body requires living in the present moment and monitoring the messages from within. Lynn Robinson's book presents 52 ways intuition can guide you toward health, happiness and wholeness.[125]

It is Better to Promote Health than Fight Disease

CAM therapies focus more on promoting health than on fighting disease. By strengthening internal systems like immune functioning and detoxification, one becomes less vulnerable to the agents of disease and fewer disease episodes occur. The *Yellow Emperor's Classic of Internal Medicine* (700BC) from China expresses a message that is common to many other ethno-medical systems as it asserts: *Health is what the wise person pursues when in good health, not after it is lost. Who waits until they become thirsty to dig a well?*

A number of tools are used in promoting health, such as relaxation techniques, dietary supplements, massage, diet and exercise. More than half the interest in CAM is motivated by the desire to enhance health and wellbeing and to stay healthy. Between 60 and 80 percent of all CAM usage is for promoting or maintaining health.[126]

Patient Participation is Central to Health and Healing

CAM calls for *active participation* from the consumer. Giving away personal power to "experts" leads to dependency. Any system that cultivates dependence brings a lower quality of life, less health and lower self-esteem. This applies to our welfare system, school system and also the medical care system. Individuals who take responsibility for managing or directing their own lives stay healthier, live longer, and heal faster than those who do not. Individuals use CAM therapies because they want more control over their lives. CAM users become more active stewards of their own health and well being.

In a classic study, elderly residents in a nursing home were given plants to care for and were encouraged to be a more active caretaker for themselves rather than letting the staff care for all their needs. Another group of patients of similar age and disability received no encouragement for self-care responsibility. Within three weeks, significant improvements in the health and vitality arose in the more active stewardship group. Eighteen months later, the death rate in the "self-care" group was half that of the other group.[127]

This study illustrates the benefits of self-care and personal responsibility in maintaining or improving one's health. *"The next major advance in the health of the American people will come from their assuming more responsibility for their own health and changing their lifestyle"* proclaimed John H. Knowles, former president of the Rockefeller Foundation.

A Holistic Focus

CAM practitioners assert that physical, mental, social, and spiritual conditions all influence health and illness. Thoughts and emotions can directly influence biological functioning as research demonstrates. The new field of mind/body medicine shows unequivocally that individuals can learn to use their thoughts to control internal processes (neurons and muscles cells). The mind can relieve a broad spectrum of ailments from tension headaches and hypertension to incontinence, temporal mandibular joint (TMJ) syndrome, involuntary muscle spasms and more. Patients can learn ways to lower their blood pressure, to reduce certain malfunctions of the heart, and to modify gastrointestinal secretions and irritable bowel syndrome.

Repressed or angry emotions over time produce physical symptoms. Emotions become stored in specific bodily parts where they express inner conflict. CAM can be used to release pent-up emotions with such tools as massage, applied kinesiology, self-exploration and talk therapy.[128] One writer expressed this wisdom: *Hate does more damage to the vessel in which it is stored than the object on which it is poured.*[129] Fear and hate are very destructive to our health and vitality. These destructive mental-emotional states are rooted in our sense of separation from one another and from our Source. CAM practitioners believe that emotional and physical healing is greatly enhanced when we release emotional toxins and become reunited with others and our Source, the infinite creative intelligence that the New Physics defines as the 'Unified Field.'

> Hate does more damage to the vessel in which it is stored than the object on which it is poured.

Some CAM systems arose out of different religious traditions that shed their parochial view as they migrated in the global marketplace. Many CAM therapies posit a broader view of health and illness beyond the physical/mechanical level with concepts such as spirit, life force, chi and prana. CAM practices such as yoga, chi kung, prayer, healing touch, and Reiki are broadly spiritual healing practices. All these practices reject the exclusive emphasis on the physical body as an overly simplistic and mechanical view of health and healing.

Best to Use Natural Processes and Products

Nature's benevolence is a defining metaphor in CAM. Virtually all CAM therapies use more natural and whole substances. CAM writers posit moral polarities between natural versus artificial, whole versus processed, organic versus synthetic, and pure versus toxic. Natural therapies such as massage, herbs, organic foods, acupuncture and chiropractic are preferred, as well as other energy therapies, such as Reiki and healing touch. Changing one's lifestyle to conform to "nature's norms" is seen as wholesome and less artificial. The term "natural" also is associated with environmentalism, organic foods, sustainability and self-healing mechanisms.[130]

The most common CAM therapies used are food supplements—herbs, minerals and vitamins. While half the adult population takes supplements regularly, over seven out of ten CAM users take supplements regularly.[131] A national survey in 2000 found that 40 percent of adults in America had used one or more herbal remedy to treat symptoms as diverse as menopausal hot flashes and memory problems. [132] Three out of four Americans want a more natural approach to health care. Herbal product use jumped 50 percent from 1997 to 2002.

Popularity of CAM

CAM's "American debut" came in the 1990s, as a few conventionally trained medical doctors in the 1980s became active advocates,
popularizing CAM therapies.[133] The CAM message struck a responsive chord in the public at large, and the popular media picked up the
story line with a feature of "the 20 super-heroes of alternative medicine."[134] Two of the more recognized names in alternative therapies
were Deepak Chopra and Andrew Weil. Each sold millions of copies
of their books.[135] A third person, Jonathan V. Wright was awarded the
very first Linus Pauling Award for Lifetime Achievement in Natural
Medicine by his medical peers. They also gave special praise to his
cutting-edge health advisory newsletter, *Nutrition & Healing.*

Each year an increasing number of Americans are using some form
of complementary and alternative therapy from the list in Appendix
A. In 1991, a groundbreaking national survey showed that more than
one-third of American adults used one or more non-conventional
therapies in the previous year of 1990. By 1997, that number had
increased to 42 percent.[136] Table 3.1 shows the increasing use of virtually all categories of CAM therapies used in these two surveys.

CAM usage continues to rise among younger age cohorts, suggesting that it is growing in popularity. Approximately 30 percent
of the respondents in the pre baby-boom category, 50 percent of the
baby-boom category, and 70 percent of the post baby-boom category
used one or more of the 16 CAM therapies found in Table 3.1 by age
33. CAM use became more common in each younger category, more
than doubling from the oldest to youngest age category. Overall, 67
percent of the respondents used a CAM therapy in their lifetime
with approximately half continuing to use CAM after their initial
use. [137]

This surge in CAM usage is especially surprising since most CAM
therapies are not covered by medical insurance. Approximately 60
percent of all users paid out-of-pocket for their "alternative choice"
(64% in 1990 and 58% in 1997). Clearly, the willingness to pay for
alternative therapies expresses a commitment to these therapies.

Table 3.1. Percent Using Each Alternative Therapy in 1990 and 1997

Alternative Therapy Type	Use in 1990 (%)	Use in 1997 (%)
Acupuncture	.4	1.0
Biofeedback	1.0	1.0
Chiropractic	10.1	11.0
Dietary: Commercial	3.9	4.4
Lifestyle	3.6	4.0
Megavitamins	2.4	5.5
Energy healing	1.3	3.8
Folk remedies	.2	4.2
Herbal or plant therapy	2.5	12.1
Homeopathy	.7	3.4
Hypnosis	.9	1.2
Imagery	4.2	4.5
Massage	6.9	11.1
Relaxation techniques	13.1	16.3
Self help groups	2.3	4.8
Spiritual healing	4.2	7.0
Sum total using one or more therapies listed above:	**34.0**	**42.0**
Percent of persons using CAM for health promotion:	**33.0**	**58.0**

Adapted from Eisenberg et al, "Trends in Alternative Medicine Use in the US" *JAMA,* vol. 280 (18): 1572.

The number of Americans visiting a CAM practitioner also rose markedly from 22 million to 39 million between 1990 and 1997. The most frequently consulted practitioners were for chiropractic, acupuncture, massage, hypnosis and biofeedback therapies. Most people do not consult a practitioner before using dietary supplements and herbal therapies. The total visits to CAM practitioners each year rose from 427 million in 1990 to 629 million in 1997; this represents an increase of almost 50 percent. In 1997, nearly 63 percent more visits were made to CAM practitioners than to primary care physicians.[138]

The dramatic growth in CAM use should not be construed as a rejection of conventional medicine. Eight out of ten CAM users simultaneously use conventional medicine, clearly pointing to a complementary reliance on a mix of conventional and CAM therapies. CAM usage occurs in a series of incremental steps away from exclusive reliance upon conventional medicine. Most still consult their medical doctors for serious acute diseases, trauma, and emergencies. CAM therapies are used for reasons ranging from improvement of health to relief from illness, mostly chronic in nature. Many use CAM to improve health—one in three in 1990 growing to nearly two in three by 1997.[139] Over one in four (28%) turn to CAM because conventional treatments were not working.[140] People use CAM therapies for chronic conditions such as back and neck pain, cancer, HIV, anxiety, depression, headaches, arthritis and fatigue.[141]

> More visits were made to CAM practitioners than to primary care physicians in 1997.

CAM use is higher among women (11% more than men), higher among individuals with post-secondary education (14% more than with no post-secondary education) and higher among those with incomes greater than $50,000 (6% more than among those with lower incomes). CAM use is also higher among residents of the East and West coast and greater among those having some type of transformational experience that changed their "view on life" due to a crisis or a chronic illness.[142]

Transformational experiences propel not only patients, but physicians too, as described in the recent book *From Doctor to Healer*. This book describes the catalysts inducing a transformational change in the lives of MDs who practice a more holistic and eclectic medicine. [143] The common thread running through the lives of these "healers" was a life transforming experience, mostly derived from having their own chronic illness and finding conventional therapies ineffective. They became healers because of their own wounds. Healers are likely to agree with the assertion: It is more important to know what kind of a person has a disease than what kind of disease a patient has.[144] Diagnosis and healing become a task of collaboration involving both the practitioner and patient working together collaboratively. As the expression goes, "the best healers are wounded healers."

> It is more important to know what kind of a person has a disease than what kind of disease a patient has.

A physician in charge of patient education at an HMO in Kentucky illustrates this transformation. Trained in the conventional model, he wrote:

In 1977, I was exposed to applied kinesiology [a technique for testing the electrical flow through muscle to identify physical problems such as food allergies] by a dentist in Lexington. He told me that sugar and caffeine were killing me. I changed my diet mainly to prove him wrong. Immediately, my health dramatically improved. Encouraged, I learned to practice relaxation. Within six months, the combination of relaxation, a whole-foods diet, and aerobics totally eliminated all my chronic conditions. Now ten years later, there has been no recurrence. An added bonus has been complete freedom from colds and influenza during all that time.[145]

Personal treatment experiences often convert a person to an alternative view of health—a type of conversion experience. Typically, conversion changes how a person sees the world through the lens of a new set of experiences and beliefs. Conversion involves a dramatic turning away from one viewpoint to embracing another. Radical change in world-view or paradigm is at the core of all conceptions of conversion or transformation, whether theological, political, or scientific. Rarely does this occur suddenly. Rather, it evolves over time, bringing a new set of beliefs and a different lifestyle. With a change in worldview, a paradigm shift brings a new vocabulary. Ideas and beliefs that were central become irrelevant, and some that were peripheral become central.[146]

What causes a conversion to a new *view on life*? Two reasons help explain this: crisis such as chronic illness, loss of family, or job loss; and participating in new social networks, where people *see the world* differently.

As more people experience crises and new social networks are established, more individuals discover a more holistic approach to health and illness. The holistic approach is an individual journey as well as a shared, social one. As people with similar problems join together, they forge a common identity with a common history. They interact with each other, sharing symbols and attitudes towards events. Such networks of support enable lifestyle changes that involve transforming their "interior space." They discover new powers and a spiritual core that enables healing.

Factors Fueling CAM's Growth

Three trends are fueling the growing popularity of CAM in American society. These factors include the dramatic growth in the incidence of chronic disease, the increasing exposure to CAM therapies and the rise of postmodern values that enhance CAM usage.

Growth in the Incidence of Chronic Ailments

Chronic disease and disability plague approximately half our adult population and continues to increase as discussed in Chapter Two. As the population ages, more Americans experience the discomfort and restrictions associated with the effects of life-style induced diseases. Practitioners of CAM promote their therapies as effective for preventing as well as treating chronic illnesses. Ample research supports their claims. In addition, satisfied patients pass their positive experiences on to friends and family through the lay-referral system known as the 'grape vine,' which is the BEST advertisement in the world—a satisfied customer.

CAM users were asked why they use these therapies in a large US government survey in 2003. They uncovered the following reasons for using CAM: over half (55%) used it for its therapeutic benefit or effective relief from chronic symptoms, 26 percent used it because a conventional physician suggested it, and 13 percent used it because conventional medicine was too expensive.[147] Other surveys also show many turn to CAM for a sense of hope, control, more involvement in decisions and CAM's focus on the whole person.

Increasing Exposure to CAM Therapies

The explosion of health information also helps sculpt a new health model. Americans are voraciously consuming information about health, wellness and CAM therapies in bookstores, newsstands and the Internet. The media age is like a room with a thousand windows—wherever you look there is information on health and CAM therapies. Over the past 25 years, a wave of books and tapes has surged, filling bookstores with information on CAM therapies as noted in the box below. At the end of 2004, more than 90,000 titles in complementary medicine were in print, with dozens more coming on-line every month.

In October 2004, a computer search of books carried by Barnes and Noble yielded
- 6,765 titles with the terms "alternative health,"
- 3,213 titles with the terms "complementary health,"

while Amazon.com yielded
- 135,166 titles with "alternative health," and
- 90,319 titles with "complementary medicine."

While online booksellers listed 327,756 "health" titles, Natural Business Communications estimates that Americans spent $563 million on self-help books in 2000.

Such books and tapes are promoting the new health paradigm by informing the public about choices for treatment and prevention, choices that were largely unknown by many people only ten years ago. An entire infrastructure is forming, including CAM seminars, conventions, newsletters, clinics, web sites, scientific journals, popular magazines and professional organizations devoted to complementary and alternative medicine. Over 20 new scientific journals, over 20 magazines, and over 100 professional organizations focus on complementary and alternative therapies.[148]

The Internet provides a vast digital library on CAM with websites devoted to helping locate a practitioner near one's home. By the end of the 1990s, half the adults in the US had gained access to the Internet at work and/or at home. The Internet propels the public's growing awareness of therapeutic options. As it unlocks a vast storehouse of health information, the demand for it seems virtually limitless. Over three million websites on health and medicine existed in September 2005.

Americans increasingly use the Internet to obtain information about health, disease, therapies, medications and support groups. Access to health information became the number one reason for new online subscriptions, according to a recent Louis Harris poll. Internet subscribers report that obtaining health information was the most common reason for going online, after email. Today, the web provides more health information to more people for more purposes than any other single source.

The Internet is fueling a quiet revolution. It provides the first opinion for some, while for others it provides a second opinion after getting a diagnosis and treatment regimen from their doctor. Nearly half of those diagnosed with a chronic disease sought additional information to that given by their physicians.[149] As Molly who joined an on-line breast cancer support group said, *I never would have had the guts to ask for a second opinion without hundreds of people online telling me I was crazy not to ask for another opinion. They helped me with information and gave me the confidence I needed to obtain a second opinion and use alternative therapies.*

Many general web sites sponsor message boards and chat rooms that help people suffering from a range of ailments to discuss it with others. Examples include: www.allhealth.com, www.healingwell.com, www.medhelp.org, www.webmd.com, www.drkoop.com, and www.drweil.com.

Dr Weil's web site receives over a half million hits per week. He also had 450,000 subscribers to his *Self Healing Newsletter* in 2002. Web sites such as weightwatchers.com and the American Cancer

Society's website, http://www.cancer.org, average 200,000 to 300,000 visitors a month according to NetRatings, an Internet media and market research firm. Spurred on by the Internet, phone inquiries to the Public Health Service's health information clearinghouses more than doubled in the early 1990s.[150]

Reliance on the Internet expands as the baby boomers age and increasingly use this information highway. The percentage of online users seeking health information grew from 38 percent in 1996 to 43 percent in 1997 and then to 56 percent by March 2000. As previously mentioned, the single most important reason for new Internet subscriptions is to access health information.

Postmodern Values Call For A New Model of Medicine

Journalists, authors and TV pundits observe that American cultural values are changing. A growing number of Americans hold beliefs and values that call for a new model of medicine. The results are reflected in CAM's growing popularity. In this sense, consumers are finding in the global marketplace a set of ethno-medical therapies for health promotion and healing.

The social movements of the 1960s spawned a significant shift in values according to sociologist Paul Ray. Based on surveys of over 100,000 US adults conducted over a 13-year period, Paul Ray identifies three distinctive value clusters that characterize different Americans: Traditionalists, Modernists, and Cultural Creatives which I will hereafter call Post Modernists. These three categories constitute differing percentages of the population in 2001 as shown in Figure 3.1 as they embrace different values and different visions for America.

Figure 3.1 Value Clusters in America in 2001

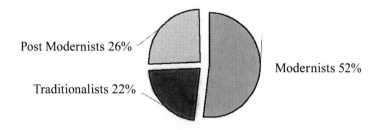

Post Modernists 26%

Traditionalists 22%

Modernists 52%

Traditionalists emphasize a stable life organized around the idealized standards of small town America that prevailed in the early 20th century. Traditionalists are critical of modern standards and all large institutions in society, including corporations and government. Religious authority, family life and political independence constitute their core values. The Moral Majority and most home school families and groups are representative of traditionalists. Individuals holding traditional values constitute some 22 percent of the population in the year 2001.[151]

Modernists presently dominate our institutions in business, government, science, entertainment and the arts in the US. They number slightly more than half our population. Modernists value occupational achievement, economic growth and making money. They subscribe to secular authority and rational/legal standards. In essence, modernism is a philosophy of worldly achievement:

> *If you follow the yellow brick road to success, you will end up with the good life—the diploma, the job, the house and cars, the promotion, or the stock options or both, the children and their education. But this road is really not so much a life path as a career path. The guideposts to success are really signs to the marketplace.*[152]

Post Modernists reject the Modernist emphasis on materialism and challenge the assumption that knowledge is certain, objective and good. Post Modernists are less concerned about financial success and more concerned with authenticity in life, at work and even in business and politics. They value personal growth, spirituality and a more natural environment as shown in Table 3.2 below. Post Modernists form the core supporters and users of CAM therapies, although people in the other two categories also use CAM but in lower percentages. While often as well educated as Modernists, they support environmental reforms to improve global ecology and the well being of people on the planet. They support issues concerning equality of the sexes, cultural diversity, and tolerance. The number of Post Modernists in the population rose dramatically by 2001 to more than 50 million people in the US or 26 percent of our adult population.[153]

Table 3.2 Different Values in America

Traditional Values	Modern Values	Post Modern Values
• Religious authority	• Rational/legal	• Personal authenticity
• Stable life in a small	authority	• Meaningful work
community	• Career achievement	• Quality of life
• Traditional standards	• Material success	• Eco-environmental-
• Critical of large insti-	• Technical progress	ism
tutions		

Post Modern values arose out of the social movements of the 1960s and 1970s among the younger and more educated people who moved into the information-based occupations within the new economy. These people work with words and abstract concepts and value creative work. The people of these movements, especially the environmental and counter culture movements, were rebelling against the emphasis on materialism and artificial environments created by Modernists. Post Modernist values champion health promotion, a more holistic orientation to life, greater self responsibility and more "natural therapies."

These are the values that spawned the holistic health movement of the 1970s and 1980s according to June Lowenberg.[154] She noted there are shared themes across three or more of movements of the 1960s and 1970s which included: holism, distrust of established authority, naturalism and the quest for personal empowerment.[155] These values propelled many individuals to join a variety of self-care movements that grew in the 1970s and 1980s including organic and whole foods, personal fitness,[156] and the use of yoga, tai chi, meditation and massage. Holistic health spawned both "home grown" therapies and imported therapies from India, China and Tibet. Figure 3.3 visually summarizes Lowenberg's thesis.

Figure 3.2. Social Movements and the Values They Championed

Movement	Common Themes Across Groups	Results
Civil rights →	Taking more individual responsibility	Support for holistic and "naturalistic" values in healthcare— medicine, nursing and psychology
Counter culture →	The desire to live closer to nature	
Environmental →	Distrust of basic institutions, science anti high-tech	
Human potential →	Holistic—mind, body and spirit	
Peace →	Tolerance of lifestyle diversity	
Self-help group →	Intuition valued above knowledge and science	
Women's →	Community-building	

The Role of Spirituality in CAM

The holistic approach incorporates the mind/spirit dimensions with the body, reconnecting what was severed in the 16th Century in Western tradition.[157] Historically, health/medical practices arose out of different religious/philosophical traditions that connected the visible to the invisible dimensions of human experience. Most religious traditions prescribe physical practices for the body (e.g., diet and cleansing), knowledge for the mind, and rituals for bridging the physical and spiritual. As these ethno-medical practices migrated to new lands and to peoples with different cultures, they morphed into less sectarian and less parochial practices. Concepts such as spirit, chi, life force and prana are specific terms for a similar idea. Many in the US accept ideas in the Traditional Chinese Medical model that contends human beings are given three treasures at birth: a body essence, the life force or chi, and a mind/spirit. Mind/spirit is believed to be best for directing a long and healthy life. The Native American tradition teaches that health is similar to a wheel that has four spokes: spirit, mind, heart, and body. Health arises from balancing all four elements.

Another example is Herbert Benson's work with Transcendental Meditation where he converted their sectarian mantra into a less sectarian tool for his generic "relaxation response." He suggested that the sacred Sanskrit words be substituted with verses or affirmations from one's own sacred scripture or tradition. Tools/rituals from one religious/spiritual tradition are being harnessed for benefit into another cultural tradition.

Western medical education, especially in the 20th century, declared that its materialist and biochemical approach to medical care was the only scientifically acceptable way to treat the physical ailments of humankind.[158] The physical-spiritual rift is being reconnected over the three eras of conventional medicine, as shown in the box below.

Until recently, the public deferred to medical experts on all issues of disease and treatments. That deference is now being qualified by new insights into the complex and subtle interplay between the mind and spirit on the one hand and the physical body on the other. Growing numbers of Americans are embracing a multi-layered view of health and moving away from the one-dimensional, materialist emphasis of fighting disease.

Figure 3.3 Three Eras of Conventional Medicine[159]

ERA	Description
1	Medicine focused almost exclusively on the physical body. This is mechanical medicine where the body is viewed as a mindless machine. If the body is not functioning properly, the "doctor mechanic" uses the tools of drugs, surgery, and radiation to fix the problem. The doctor-patient relationship is brief and impersonal. Little or no concern is given to the emotional, interpersonal, or spiritual aspects of the patient.
2	Medicine arose in the 1940s, upon the discovery that beliefs and expectations influence health and illness. Medicine initially focused only on the role that negative thoughts had on the body, psychosomatic disease but later expanded to their positive role as well, placebos. Era 2 medicine confines the impact of the individual's thoughts, feelings, and beliefs to their own health to become Mind/Body medicine.

3   "Transpersonal" or "Non-Local" medicine arose in the 1990s. Focusing on the ability of the mind to function non-locally by affecting the physical health of a distant living organism such as plants and people. Increasingly we hear of distant healing via Reiki, prayer work, etc. The mind has some quality that allows it to effect change across space and time. Prayer and transpersonal imagery are examples of the mind's ability to function at a distance that Dossey presents in his book, *Healing Words*. "Conscious intentionality" affects things beyond what brains can do.

Spirit and Health: Some Empirical Evidence

Adherence to a religious/spiritual pathway enhances physical health. Professor Harold Koenig, an expert in this area, offers three reasons why religious activity enhances health. Religious/spiritual adherents have: healthier lifestyles, stronger social support networks, and healthy coping mechanisms—prayer, meditation and faith in "who is ultimately in control."[160] Belief in a higher power promotes health and protects against illness, whether they follow the Buddhist, Christian, Islamic, Jewish, Native American or Hindu path. Religiosity strengthens three relationships: a vertical one with their God, a horizontal one with other people, and, an internal relationship with one's self. Believers, on average, exhibit more positive emotions and hold beliefs that calm and bring coherence, connecting all the separate parts into a healthier whole.[161]

Frequent religious attendees report higher levels of well-being and experience less disability, fewer days in bed and fewer physical symptoms than less frequent attendees. According to Jeffrey Levin in his book *God, Faith, and Health* monthly religious attendance reduces the risk of death in half from heart disease, emphysema, suicide, and some cancers[162]

Most Americans (86%) believe that personal prayer, meditation, or other spiritual and religious practices accelerate the benefits of medical treatment, and nearly half claim a personal experience where prayer or meditation either cured an illness or significantly improved their conditions. Experts agree. Ninety-nine percent of family physicians and ninety-four percent of health maintenance organization executives believe that prayer enhances healthy outcomes.[163]

Religious commitment and participation are also related to faster recovery from surgery, lower blood pressure, reduced depression and enhanced immune system functioning to name a few. Those with faith diminish their risk of early death by 25 percent and prolong their life by seven to fourteen years.[164] And fear factors have less of an affect on those who are faith-filled.

The spiritual needs of patients are important to address—something many doctors have done informally for years and many medical schools are now teaching. Today more than half of the 125 American medical schools offer courses on spirituality and healing.[165]

Summary

Health promoting therapies are being used by more Americans which is fueling the growth of CAM therapies and their holistic approach. Surveys in the 1990s and into the new millennium reveal a dramatic increase in the usage of CAM therapies. CAM constitutes a new vision or model of healing and health. CAM practitioners promote self-care and self-healing and recognize the spiritual/mental component as well as the physical basis of health.

This chapter identified five core beliefs/values of CAM therapies that distinguish them from conventional medicine. In contrast to conventional medicine, CAM works with the body's own self-healing mechanisms, promotes the forces of health, engages the patient as an active participant, is holistic and utilizes more natural processes and materials. These unifying beliefs form a common credo of the new health model of CAM therapies.

A growing number of Americans identify with the beliefs and values of this new health promotion model. Changed lifestyles produce new identities. As CAM therapies are being adopted by more educated Americans, CAM carries a positive connotation.

Three trends are fueling the growth of CAM: The growing number of Americans with chronic illness, the dissemination of CAM information and therapeutic choices via the Internet and the rise of Post Modern values (rejecting one-dimensional thinking, the tyranny of experts and the toxic side-effects of high-tech solutions). These changes do not mean that Americans are abandoning conventional medicine, but they are moving increasingly away from a total reliance upon it. Correlatively, more Americans are becoming more active stewards of their health and even using self-help groups in support of lifestyle changes as I show in Chapter 4.

CHAPTER 4.
LIFESTYLE CHANGE AND SOCIAL SUPPORT: GROUPS AS TRANSITION-ASSISTERS AND HEALTH ENHANCERS

Love heals—both the ones who give it and the ones who receive it.
Karl Menninger

Some 80 percent of Americans want to change their habits so as to improve their health.[166] At any given time, 35 percent of Americans are attempting to lose weight but only 5 percent have any long-term success. Some 47 million Americans smoke cigarettes with over half wishing to quit. Approximately 14 million adults abuse alcohol and 13 million individuals experiment with addictive drugs. Many desire to quit their harmful habits.[167] But all too often, dieters fail, smokers continue smoking, and substance abusers can't break the grip of addiction. Change is challenging. People need support and ongoing encouragement to change. Most individuals mobilize their inner resources for change within supportive relationships.

This chapter discusses a specific type of social support system, the self-help group and its role in health enrichment. These groups, growing in popularity and success, require that each individual suffer from the same illness, addiction or other crisis for membership. Self-help groups are spotlighted, because these groups dramatically illustrate the key role of social support in creating and sustaining life-style change. When resolve is bolstered in supportive group settings, individuals can mobilize their inner resources for behavioral change. Destructive habits can be whittled down to a manageable size with "a little help from our friends."[168]

Currently, self-help groups are the most prevalent formal social support system after Sunday school and Bible study groups.[169] Americans make more visits to self-help groups than to all other forms of professionally designed programs.[170] Frank Riessman of the National Self-Help Clearinghouse contends that 60 million people will participate in a self-help group at some point in their lives.[171] The numbers are large, and as Table 4.1 shows, these groups fulfill a diverse range of needs.

Table 4.1 Types of Self-Help Groups[172]

The self-help movement is easy to overlook because most groups are small, local, and private rather than public and political. Self-help groups are organized and run by people who get together on the basis of a common experience or goal to mutually help one another. Five main types of groups arise to help individuals cope. They include the following:

1. Addiction groups (often based on twelve-step principles) are one of the most popular types of self-help organizations, e.g., substance abuse such as alcohol or narcotics; process abuse such as gamblers, debtors, or over eaters. These programs are based on the spiritual premise that turning one's life and will over to "a higher power" (i.e., God, Allah, or a spiritual entity) for guidance and self-evaluation is the key to recovery.

2. Mental or physical illness groups exist for every medical condition listed by the World Health Organization, e.g., AIDS, multiple sclerosis, muscular dystrophy, cancer, prostate, Tourette's Syndrome, organ transplant patients, Emotions Anonymous, Recovery, Inc., GROW.

3. Family caretakers of ill, disabled or troubled family members or those affected by the behavior of troubled family members are numerous, e.g., caretakers of Alzheimer's patients, Families of the Mentally Ill, Mothers of Twins Clubs, Tough Love, Al-Anon (for friends and family of alcoholics), Alateen (a program for teenagers who have been affected by alcoholics.)

4. Lifestyle oriented or rehabilitation groups share interests or circumstances such as breast-feeding (LaLeche League), vegetarians (vegan societies), exercise groups, singles, older adults, new parents, Single Mothers by Choice, stroke recovery, transplanted organs.

5. Groups for transitions, loss or bereavement (due to divorce, disability or death) such as Compassionate Friends, Survivors of Suicide, Widow to Widow.

Social Support and Health

Social support from friends and relatives decreases the incidence of illness and premature death from all causes.[173] Lack of social support is equal to if not more important than smoking as a risk factor for the onset of chronic illness and early death. People who feel lonely, depressed and isolated are three to five times more likely to become ill and die prematurely writes Dean Ornish, a medical heart specialist. In his book *Love and Survival*, he notes that alienation from supportive friends and family leads to more heart attacks, more open-heart surgeries, and more deaths from cardiovascular disease. From his earlier work with reversing coronary heart disease, Ornish notes:

> *At first I viewed our support groups simply as a way to motivate patients to stay on the other aspects of the program I considered more important such as diet, exercise and stress management. Over time, I realized that group support was itself one of the most powerful interventions.*[174]

Connectedness is as protective a factor as lowering your blood pressure, losing weight, quitting smoking or wearing a seat belt claims psychiatrist Edward Hollowell, MD, of the Harvard Medical School.[175] Participating in self-help groups improves the physical and emotional health of patients.[176] People who attend self-help group meetings become empowered and feel less depressed.[177] Self-help support groups become a healthy antidote for chronic conditions and other life shocks.[178] Exchanging stories and tools for coping improves the quality of life and longevity. Self-help groups offer a unique venue for social support, hope and improving one's immune system functions for health enrichment.

Disruptive life situations can undermine health as they jeopardize sleep, emotional stability and self-esteem. Some turn to alcohol, mood food or other abusive actions to cope with stress. Sometimes sanity and life itself are at risk. Substance abuse or chronic disease can turn life upside down both physically and emotionally.

In response to a crisis, many seek the company of others with the same problem for understanding, comfort and possible help. People in misery not only love company, they can benefit from it. Participating in self-help groups enhances physical, emotional and social health because it decreases anxiety, isolation and depression, thereby enhancing immune functioning; it increases self esteem by enhancing adaptive skills; and it raises the quality of life through creating a circle of supportive friends.

Recent History of the Self-Help Group as a Health Enhancing Tool

The modern era of self-help groups began in 1935 with the formation of Alcoholics Anonymous. In the late 1960s and 1970s, the women's movement played a pivotal role in promoting self-help. By the 1970s, recognition of self-help group effectiveness was growing. In 1978 President Carter's Mental Health Commission recommended investing in self-help groups as a useful therapeutic intervention and called for the creation of self-help clearinghouses as a way to inform and direct participants into local groups. In 1978, the New Jersey Self-Help Clearinghouse formed, followed by more than 60 regional clearinghouses in the 1980s. Surgeon General C. Everett Koop endorsed the self-help concept by convening a conference on self-help groups in 1987. Developing self-help clearinghouses became a national health goal in the report "*Healthy People 2000.*" Self-help clearinghouses went online in the 1990s with almost 300 headings of problems fueling a 20-50 percent increase in participants for the following decade according to Kathryn Davison.[179] *Newsweek*'s cover story in 1998 profiled Dean Ornish's program to reverse heart disease; *join a self-help group for your health,* he prescribed.[180]

Self-Help Groups as Complementary Therapy

Approximately one million small local self-help groups meet across the US. They are organized and run mostly by peers facing the same problem or crisis—be it obesity, fibromyalgia, an eating disorder or over 350 other problems. Their purpose is mutual help through sharing experiences, providing support, and learning how others cope with their problem. Not only are self-help groups highly useful and effective, they generally are cost free because they are self-run even though professionals may serve as consultants or advisors. Participation in self-help groups prolongs life, lessens pain, calms anxiety, and enhances immune function while improving quality of life.[181]

Self-help groups are modern *'transition assisters'* that facilitate the discovery and adoption of new coping behaviors. In previous generations, parents and local communities could prepare their children more completely for the challenges of adulthood by living in closer proximity as extended households with less mobility and less fragmented families. Now, with the accelerating pace of change, people often find they must navigate demanding transitions to new occupations, new friends, new mates and new ways-of-life without the proximity of family support. And with more chronic illness, more individuals must cope with these challenges alone. Self-help groups are now helping more people surmount the disruptions of modern life. Self-help groups are the most frequently used treatment for addictions and nearly half of all visits for treatment for mental health problems (some 40%) involve self-help group meetings.[182]

Self-help groups are an important adjunct for many physical conditions as well, including chronic ailments such as heart disease, cancer, fibromyalgia, chronic fatigue, breast cancer, headaches, rheumatoid arthritis, epilepsy and Multiple Sclerosis. As *transition assisters*, their record of success is outstanding. For instance, research shows one of the more successful therapies for fibromyalgia involves no drugs, but simply a combination of exercise and participation in a self-help group in which members share their stories of what worked for them. One patient exclaimed: *The most gratifying part was the ability to do something for ourselves to feel better, while not depending on doctors.*[183]

At first blush, self-help groups may not appear to be a form of complementary and alternative medicine. Yet they share with CAM most of the same assumptions and beliefs about the nature of health and illness. Like other CAM therapies, the self-help group movement embraces a holistic approach, the self-healing capabilities, the importance of self-help and the value of using more natural and whole products. They also share the belief that chronic disease is best treated through the adoption of a more balanced and healthy lifestyle.

Social support is central to health promotion, because health requires balancing aspects of the whole person: physical, emotional, mental and spiritual. Health deteriorates in the absence of love, social support and meaning. People do not thrive without support from significant others. Just as the physical body requires good nutrition, the emotional body needs nurturing relationships in which love and compassion are given and received. Having a social support system becomes central in most lifestyle change projects. Finding others who share the same challenges increases the likelihood of success by strengthening the individual's motivation and resolve. The mind does best with a positive self-image and self-supportive attitudes. Having a spiritual practice brings inner calm that protects one against feeling lost and without direction.

Figure 4.1. A Holistic Model of Health

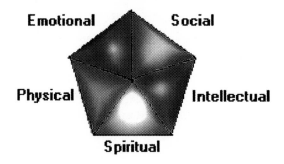

Self-help groups are part of the CAM movement in another respect as well. Participating in a self-help group increases the use of other CAM therapies. The self-help group serves as a gateway or a stepping stone toward other CAM and conventional therapies. In one study, over half of CAM users learned about other alternative therapies from their circle of social support, "they heard it through the grapevine." More than 90 percent of alternative users with breast cancer recommended their therapies to their friends.[184] Additionally, participants in self-help groups hold values and beliefs that are similar to others supporting CAM therapies. These beliefs and values are: distrust of professionals, pure rationality, and the medical care system; rejection of large bureaucratic, and impersonal systems in favor of smaller groups where they find a sense of belonging;[185] and they value experience over expertise, being cooperative and democratic.[186]

A Record of Success

Self-help groups are popular because they create help, support and hope. There are few patients with chronic conditions that are not helped by participating in a supportive group. Brief summaries of research findings are arrayed in Table 4.2. Participation in groups helps patients with physical as well as psychological conditions. For example, people attending self-help groups for diabetics experienced a significantly greater drop in glycated hemoglobin levels compared to diabetics not participating in a self-help group.[187] Self-help group participants in another study for diabetics reported less stress and greater family involvement in controlling glycemic levels.[188] Breast cancer patients participating in a weekly support group increased longevity and quality of life as well.[189]

Participation in self-help groups is beneficial even when there is no face-to-face contact. One stroke victim wrote of his online support system: *The forum was a lifeline for me as I became isolated socially after leaving my job. They helped me adjust to the physical and mental aspects of being disabled.*

Table 4.2 Benefits From Self-Help Group Therapy

Support for—	Benefits
Melanoma	Half of the patients with malignant melanoma at UCLA were enrolled in a support group and compared to those not in a support group; those in the support group showed more natural killer cells (more immune system functioning) and higher survival rates than those in the control group.[190]
Breast Cancer	Breast cancer patients who participated in a support group showed significantly greater declines in traumatic stress symptoms and in total mood disturbance compared with the individuals not in a support group. Self-help groups reduce distress in patients with metastatic breast cancer.[191]
Scoliosis	Adults with scoliosis and undergoing surgery or bracing treatment who participated in a support group experienced fewer psychosomatic symptoms, higher self-esteem, and a better patient-physician relationship than those not participating in a support group.[192]
Rheumatoid Arthritis	Adults suffering from rheumatoid arthritis and participating in a support group experienced reduced joint tenderness compared to patients not participating in a support group (Shearn and Fireman, 1985).
Arthritis	Arthritis patients who take the Arthritis Self-Help Course of six 2-hour weekly sessions reported pain reductions of 15-20% and 17% higher levels of self-efficacy which persisted even four years after taking the course.
New Mothers	Among new mothers, those participating in a support group experienced less emotional distress in the six months after childbirth and had healthier infants than those not involved in a support group. Follow up studies four years later showed that new mothers in the experimental self-help groups compared to the controls had fewer physical illnesses, marital conflicts, sexual problems and divorces. A self-help network empowered mothers for adjusting to a broad range of life adjustment problems.[193]
Widows	Persons widowed and joining a social network for helping others consistently exhibited better outcomes on depression, anxiety, somatic symptoms, use of psychotropic drugs, self-esteem, coping and mastery as compared to those not joining a social network.[194]

Mental Patients	Eighty mental patients being discharged from a nine-week intensive treatment unit were randomly assigned to a control group or a self-help group network for mutual aid. After ten months, only one-half as many project members as control subjects required re-hospitalization (17.5% vs. 35%), and their average length of stay was less than one-third as long as that of the controls (7 vs. 24.6 days). Twice as many network members were able to function without any contact with a mental health system (52.5 vs. 26%).[195]
Weight Loss	Average weight loss over 8 weeks in a sample of 10,000 participants in a self-help group for weight loss was 15 pounds; most maintained their weight loss one year later.
Smokers	Smokers viewed a quit smoking program and read a manual with half additionally being randomly assigned to a peer led self-help group; those assigned to the self-help group experienced nearly double the initial quit rates as non self-help participants.[196]
Alcoholics	A meta analysis of more than 50 studies of Alcoholics Anonymous (AA) found AA involvement reduced alcohol problems and improved psychological adjustment.[197]
Cognitive Behaviors	Patients treated in 12-step programs compared to those treated in cognitive-behavioral programs averaged only half the outpatient visits after discharge (13.1vs 22.5), received significantly fewer days of inpatient care (10.5 vs. 17.0 days), which resulted in 64% lower annual costs (45.7% vs. 36.2%) after one year.[198]

Why Self-Help Groups are Effective

Students of self-help groups have identified three principles that explain the transformative power of self-help group participation: the peer principle, the experience enrichment principle and the helper-therapy principle. The *peer principle* asserts that because peers understand a problem as an insider, they can help in ways that an outside expert or family member cannot. Peers bring more empathic understanding from their own personal experience. This common experience (the *like-me* factor) forges an empathic bond of understanding between group members. As the co-founder of AA wrote, *Drunks don't need a drink; they need a drunk to support their mutual commitment to abstain from drinking.* Similarly, patients with cancer seek peers to talk about things not possible with their family or doctor. And family caretakers of mental patients often prefer other caretakers as confidantes. Those with firsthand experience bring more self-disclosure and greater empathy which increases effectiveness of helpers. *Just as the most effective healers are wounded healers, the most effective helpers are "wounded helpers."*

Self-help groups counter the isolating tendencies created by a crisis or illness. Many people feel embarrassed with a crisis or chronic illness.[199] Opening up to others enduring the same kind of pain, suffering, stigma or loss becomes easier because their wound puts them in the same boat. As one person in a self-help group explained, *this is one place where I can share this stuff because I know they understand.* Individuals from diverse backgrounds can forge a tight circle of support. Where else in America can a person from a park-bench interact as an equal with a person from Park Avenue? Often this interaction extends beyond the meeting room, because self-help groups utilize the peer principle with telephone support (75%), peer counseling (42%), as well as buddy systems (36%).[200]

The experience enrichment principle asserts that each member's experience is a valuable asset that can enhance the adaptive skills of all when shared with others. When experiences are shared, skills are enhanced, options become multiplied, hopes born and motivation strengthened. Self-help groups serve as "cultural incubators" for increasing the pool of adaptive resources and survival skills. They provide an adaptive training program that empowers members with chronic conditions, addictions, or loss. Self-help groups become living laboratories that are less stigmatizing and more supportive than expert systems.

Self-help groups place high value on sharing of their members' experiences by telling their story. A Gallup poll showed that 85 percent of self-help group members claim "hearing others share their story" was important to them and 78 percent reported "hearing what worked and what didn't" was very helpful.[201] Self-help groups give substance to the expression "two heads are better than one," as veteran survivors mentor newer members.

Self-help groups use patient stories for a wide range of purposes. A recent survey of 309 organizations found that 22 distinct uses were made of patient stories and 65 percent of the groups used them extensively. All the organizations devoted some time in meetings for members to tell their stories. Thirty-seven percent used the stories for interviews or articles in the group newsletter; 15 percent used the stories for inclusion in a newspaper article or media broadcast; and 12 percent kept a database of patients' stories.[202]

The helper-therapy principle asserts that the act of helping another heals the helper more than the person being helped. As giving and receiving are exchanged, helping another unfreezes one's fear and self-absorption, replacing it with positive emotions, often called the "helper's high."[203] The "helper's high" is a pleasurable physical and emotional sensation of energy, warmth, and euphoria that results from helping others.[204] When suffering from the same illness or challenge, helpers develop an even greater empathic bond, further enhancing the "high."

Helping another dissolves the boundary between individuals as they forge a heart-to-heart connection, claims Allan Luks. In his national survey of volunteers, 95 percent of these volunteers claimed that helping others gave them an immediate pleasurable sensation; 80 percent reported that this "high" returned when recalling the helping act. Helping others increased their sense of self-worth and calm; they reported fewer episodes of flu and colds, less overeating, faster recovery from surgery, less insomnia, fewer migraines and fewer stomachaches. Even those with lupus reported fewer pains. Nine out of ten respondents claimed to be healthier than others of their age. Because perception of health predicts future health and longevity, this perception of being healthier becomes important.[205]

The therapeutic power of helping others thus finds wide support in the literature. The old adage 'it is better to give than to receive' finds support from a recent study. People who reported providing no help to others were more than twice as likely to die over the five-year period of the study compared to people giving help to others.[206] Receiving help from others did not reduce the risk of dying over the five-year time period.[207] It's what you give in a relationship that benefit you, more than what you receive.[208] People who are helpful to others reduce their risk of dying by nearly 60 percent, compared to peers who provide neither practical help nor emotional support to relatives, neighbors or friends.

> It's what you give in a relationship that benefits you, more than what you receive.

Who joins a self-help group?

To the extent that illness or crisis embarrasses or stigmatizes, it isolates or sets the afflicted apart from others. Yet this very condition propels them toward others with similar challenges for support and help. Crisis or illness may cause anxiety but this is not sufficient for seeking support outside one's social network. But if the present network is weak or fails to provide sufficient support *and* the illness/ crisis socially marginalizes them (embarrasses or stigmatizes), then the individual becomes more likely to seek solace from others with the same problem. Connecting with these peers can help restore calm, reduce the isolation and increase understanding of the problem. By sharing, they learn practical tips and gain inspiration from managing their illness or crisis.

When people meet others undergoing similar challenges, they generally feel rapport in a "New-York minute."[209] When asked why they joined a self-help group, most members cite a crisis or personal problem (41 and 47 percent). Of those joining because of a crisis, most (85 percent) claimed the group helped them through it and nearly all (95 percent) felt encouragement from their group.[210]

Not all experiencing a crisis or chronic illness join a self-help group. Among those diagnosed with a chronic disease, only one in five join a self-help group. Women diagnosed with breast cancer join in higher percentages (35 percent) than men diagnosed with prostate cancer (12 percent).[211]

Those joining a group differ from those going it alone. Joiners are more motivated to change, possess a greater sense of personal control, are more educated and socially more competent than non-joiners. Individuals without family support more often join self-help groups than those with more family support.[212] People who join a self-help group make greater use of social support than people not joining.[213] Women are more likely than men to join. Most members are between the ages of 35 to 55. Self-help groups offer a pragmatic approach to solving one's problems with the group's collective experiential knowledge.

Self-help Group Participation Increased Dramatically in the 1990s

In 1991, 500,000 self-help groups were operating with approximately 10 million members according to a Gallup poll. The average group consisted of twenty members and had been meeting for more than five years. Most groups met once a week for more than an hour (40% for 2 hrs, 60% for one and a half or more hours).[214]

A 1992 survey in California identified nearly 4,000 self-help groups operating with nearly half dealing with physical illness. Newsletters and speaker bureaus were common with these groups.[215]

During the 1990s, the number of people participating in self-help groups increased by as much as 50 percent.[216]

A representative survey of self-help groups in Kansas found 57% of local groups had a formal relationships or affiliation with a national organization (eg, Emotions Anonymous International, National Multiple Sclerosis Society); 75% reported affiliation with a local organization or agency such as a hospital, social service organization, church or other community organization that provided a meeting place. The average group had been meeting for 8 years.[217]

Three Factors Fuel the Growth of Self-help Groups

During the last decade, the number of people participating in self-help groups increased dramatically as noted in the box above. Three major factors fueled this growth: increased life changes; increased accessibility of self-help groups; and erosion of stable support systems.

People face more life changes and transitions. Transitions and crises disrupt more lives today than 50 years ago. Over half of all marriages end in divorce[218] and half of all adults endure one or more chronic illness. Job instability and corporate downsizing unsettle lives, as do mental illness and increased incarcerations. Approximately 85 percent of adult Americans have struggled through some stressful experience in the last five years, as an increasingly complex world causes more transitions and stress. Half of adult Americans experience mental illness or depression some time in their lives, with the most common illnesses being depression, dependence on drugs or alcohol and anxiety.

Self-help groups are more visible and accessible. Self-help books, the yellow pages and the Internet all have raised the visibility of self-help groups. Clearinghouses (two national and 65 regional) for self-help groups now operate on the Internet, providing easy access to information about where and when local groups meet. The Internet multiplies the capacity of the clearinghouses to link people to numerous others suffering from similar life shocks or chronic conditions. The American Self-Help Clearinghouse supplied information to over 800,000 self-help groups in 2000.[219] Over 2 million web sites operated in February 2001 at Lycos.com for "consumer health groups," which includes both on- and off-line networks. As people are helped, they tell others, and some of them stay involved to "pass it on" to others. This word-of-mouth process enables self-help groups to grow in strength and number.

Stable support systems are eroding. Self-help groups provide support in ways that were once provided by large, extended families and stable communities. Today, because of a decline in marriages, more divorces, fewer children per couple and more geographical and social mobility, people spend more years living alone and with less stable support systems. People change their address on average every five years. A 55 percent divorce rate results in changes in family ties. For these and other reasons, the look and feel of one's social landscape becomes less familiar. The family and community are unable to provide as much buffering and support with life's transitions as fifty years ago. Clearly, social institutions provide fewer relationships with which to buffer and absorb the stress resulting from crisis.

Given the sagging levels of support derived from family, neighborhoods and churches, it is not surprising that more Americans are turning to self-help groups. Just as nature abhors a vacuum, people can't tolerate a social vacuum and so cultivate friendships and social support. Wherever they go, joining a self-help group brings a caravan of resources that helps the individual feel connected and supported.

Banding together to solve common problems is a distinctive American trait observed by Alexis de Tocqueville over one hundred fifty years ago. Bringing diversity into associational networks helps cultivate a "civil culture" and democracy. We exhibit the same tendency of banding together but today's modern concerns also involve chronic illnesses, loss, mental problems, parenting and other vehicles for self-help groups.

Self-help Groups are Modern *"Transition Assisters"*

All cultures use group activities and rituals of recognition to help their members traverse the major transitions in life, such as birth, coming of age, marriage and death. Americans today have fewer long-term support systems to guide them through these transitions. If life-threatening illness and crisis are "life-transformers," then self-help groups become "transition-assisters," helping members reframe how they "see" their problem. From the experience of hearing others tell their stories at group meetings, members forge new ways to cope with their problems and to refocus their lives for greater success.

Groups provide a forum for exploring the meaning and purpose of one's life, thereby helping transcend pain through a broader interpretation and understanding. Pain often shatters the mask of materialism, opening the door to the spiritual. After refocusing, many describe their problem or crisis as a gift that brought about their spiritual awakening. Becoming open to the spiritual side of one's challenge provides consolation to the sufferer and can strengthen three kinds of relationships: a vertical relationship with a "higher power," a horizontal relationship with other people, and an internal connection to the *self* within. This process shrinks pain and impairment to a more manageable size.

As modern "transition assisters," self-help groups are havens of authenticity, spontaneity and story-sharing in which people seek and often find answers to such questions as, "Why is this happening to me?" and "Is there some larger purpose to this?" In subtle ways, they incline members toward the positive and supportive, with rules that minimize criticism within the group. Thus, they articulate rules like these: "no one is here to *fix* anyone else," and "focus on the light, not the lampshade dimming the light."

Though small, self-help groups do not depend upon spontaneity completely. Most have formal leaders and all have both formal and informal rules. Most are governed by codes of conduct with such rules as: "listen respectfully," "offer support when you can," and "honor personal disclosures by not taking it outside the group." These rules encourage members to feel safe sharing in the group setting.

Relationships with others and with the spiritual are intimately intertwined with the human need for meaning and a life-purpose. Meaning stabilizes life, motivates living and enriches health. A person who finds meaning in life adapts to change more easily. Herbert Benson, M.D., of Harvard University and author of *Timeless Healing,* contends that religious faith and spiritual beliefs reduce stress and provide hope. He wrote: *Our bodies are wired to believe; prayer and other exercises of belief are healing.*[220] Meaning serves as a compass, providing direction through the daunting maze of change brought on by a crisis.

Crises precipitate shifts in consciousness, which often are shaped and guided by relationships, according to Rhea White.[221] Crisis often raises consciousness and cements a connection and greater intimacy with others.

Many survivors of serious illness write deeply moving accounts of their ordeal, explaining how it transformed them spiritually and taught them about life. Christiane Olsen's response to first losing her eyesight and then being diagnosed with multiple sclerosis (MS) illustrates these themes. She concluded, *there was a reason for this illness in my body- it wanted to tell me something.... Disease was my catalyst that helped me change negative patterns and actions.*[222] Illness and crisis ended up being a spiritual gift as they helped her refocus her life. Losing her sight enabled her to gain insight.

Similarly, Kat Duff relates how illness—in her case chronic fatigue syndrome and immune deficiency transformed her. Illness became an initiation and an awakening. She contends that conventional medicine, being rooted in technique and materialism, ignores the spiritual level because:

> *Modern medicine banishes that knowledge by insisting that suffering is without meaning, unnecessary, because pain can be technically eliminated. Symptoms are divorced from the person who has them and thus treating them as secularized mechanical mishaps, stripping them of their spiritual ramifications and meaning.*[223]

Chronic physical disease becomes a spiritual gift for many—a clarion call to reassess, refocus, and redirect, as illness leads many to spiritual truths. Betty Iams, for example, after receiving a diagnosis of MS, began to meditate for 30 minutes twice each day. She claims to have tuned into the infinite part of herself, which she believes connects to Universal Intelligence or God. From that vantage-point, she became convinced that *her body contains its own innate intelligence, separate from the conscious mind that knows what is wrong and how to correct itself.*[224]

A series of bizarre and frightening events triggered a transformational change for Raima, involving a three-year period of transformation. A very successful chemist and department head at a major university, Raima's transformational change began with a sudden unexplained, excruciating pain in her left arm that forced her to look inward for its source. Eventually she discovered that the pain held information—memories of physical and sexual abuse. She wrote:

> *I felt very much like a caterpillar in a cocoon. Everything I had come to believe and understand about myself and my life up to the point when I fell apart. I entered a cocoon the way a caterpillar's body melts into a chaotic soup of mole-*

cules and cells as it undergoes the process of metamorphosis as it changes into a butterfly. I discovered a great internal healing power capable of absorbing hurt...capable also of forgiving even the unforgivable. I was forced (by my body) to confront repressed feelings of rage and pain stemming from a childhood marked by physical abuse and emotional neglect...Relationships now take center stage in my life and loving others is my purpose.[225]

Table 4.3 Books Connecting Crisis to Transformation

Book Title	Author / Publisher / Year
A Whole New Life	Reynolds Price, Scribner, 2003
Alchemy of Illness	Kat Duff, Harmony 2000
Cancer as a Turning Point	Lawrence LeShan, Plume, 1994
Change you Mind and Your Life will Follow	Karen Casey Conari Press, 2005
Dying Into Life	Marion Woodman, Viking Compass, 2000
Excavating Your Authentic Self	Sarah Ban Breathnach, Warner Books, 2000
Finding Well-Being Despite Illness	Blair Justice, Blair Justice, 1998
From Crisis to Personal Renewal	Joann Lemaistre, Ulysses Press, 1995
Healing Dreams	Marc Ian Barasch, Riverhead Books, 2001
My Journey to Wellness	Claire Musickant, Peanut Butter Publishing, 1999
Journey to Wholeness	Barbara Marie Brewster, Four Winds 1992
Learning to Live With Chronic Illness	Sefra Kobrin Pitzele, Workman Publishing Company, 1986
Seven Principles for Meeting the Challenge	Linda Topf, Fireside, 1995
Using the Wisdom of Your Body/Mind	Jon Kabat-Zinn, Delta 1990

Suffering and pain strengthen empathy for others with similar problems while deepening the willingness to help others. Self-help groups build on this desire to help the similarly afflicted. In contrast to feelings of isolation, participation in a group provides an opportunity to share "life-lessons" and to develop a new life-sustaining vision.

Groups also connect their members to the spiritual by creating rituals that strengthen feelings of solidarity with the group and a sense of the sacred. By transcending the everyday and mundane, rituals nurture, empower and celebrate values that bridge the invisible and the visible. Groups patterned after Alcoholics Anonymous have their own 12-step rituals of assessing, owning up and surrendering to a higher power.[226]

While many self-help groups are secular in orientation, significant numbers create through rituals a spiritual component meaningful to their members. The chronically mentally ill who become involved in the GROW organization often experience changes in their spiritual worldview. Many feel closer to their God and believe that God does not judge them for having limitations. Members of 12-step organizations experience similar changes.

The sense of spiritual transformation need not be religious in the traditional sense. Even agnostics describe the constructive emotions and beliefs generated by the group as spiritual. When changed perspectives bring more joy and meaning to life, people often refer to this as *spiritual*. By creating a circle of support, all self-help groups potentially enrich members' spiritual lives—however they interpret "spiritual."

The Self-Help Groups as Lay Referral Systems

Self-Help is one of the most popular sections in bookstores. As noted in Chapter 3, books and manuals on self-help and health abound. Members of self-help groups become a lay referral system, sharing information on what therapies they found helpful. For example, more than nine out of ten patients using alternative therapies with breast cancer recommended their therapies to their friends and group members.[227]

The Internet facilitates those searching for health support networks and self-help groups. In addition to information about their illness, people consult the web to find support and understanding from others with the same problem. Self-help groups enhance the use of complementary therapies; both grow from the Internet. This information highway directs traffic to both self-help groups and CAM therapies.

The growth of both self-help groups and CAM therapies was slow until the late 1980s when the Internet joined in to create a healthcare triangle. Their intersection greatly accelerated the expansion of all three. When seeking to join a self-help group, many increasingly consult the Internet. When exploring a CAM therapy, many consult both the Internet and their self-help group members. The reasons for using complementary treatments were to maximize quality of life, seeking a natural approach to healing and staying well.[228]

The popularity of CAM grows from both the Internet and self-help groups—each functioning as a lay-referral system for use of CAM therapies for specific problems. Fitting together like three sides of a triangle—self-help groups, CAM, and the Internet—they synergistically direct energy and forge a new approach to managing disease and promoting health.

Online groups are especially helpful for those who are shy, easily intimidated, homebound, busy or live in isolated or small towns. People with illnesses such as multiple sclerosis (MS) find a natural home online because traveling to a group is difficult. The use of online groups was most popular among those suffering from MS in a survey of 20 common disease conditions but 16th among the face-to-face support groups.[229] Online groups are open 24 hours a day, can accommodate large numbers, and provide maximum anonymity.

Other online networks operate message boards, newsgroups, bulletin boards, chat groups, discussion mailing lists and similar online services. Of those seeking health information on the Internet in 2000, one in four (24 million) used digital chat rooms and 36 percent (33 million) searched for support groups, such as a breast cancer support group.[230] The website Support-Group.com, for example, connects people who wish to share their health and relationship experiences with a galaxy of over 200 message boards. This website also provides links to other support-related information with more than 125 of these helping efforts using support in their name such as alt.support.abusepartners and alt.support.turner.syndrome.[231]

The most active support groups at www.Support-Group.com in January 2001 included:			
• Anxiety/panic disorder	• Bipolar disorder	• Borderline personality disorder	• Child abuse
• Cushing's syndrome	• Depression	• Eating disorder	• Fibromyalgia
• Graves disease	• Loneliness	• Marriage	• Migraine
• Obesity	• Personality disorder	• Self injury	• Women's issues

Perhaps, the greatest strength of these web sites is with connecting people whose condition or concern is rare. The American Self-help Clearinghouse website provides a keyword-searchable database of over one thousand self-help support groups for any specific illness, disability, addiction, bereavement situation, parenting issue, caregiver concern, abuse or other stressful life situation. In addition, they list local non-profit self-help group clearinghouses worldwide and even give suggestions for starting both community and online groups. Through the clearinghouses, people can find the right person or group with which to communicate, no matter where they live.

The capacity of the Internet to provide specialized services is truly remarkable. For example, the online Air Craft Casualty Emotional Support Services offers peer grief support networks for those surviving or grieving loved ones lost in an air disaster. The web site "Anonymous One" claims that one can find more than fifty thousand 12-step meetings (averaging 1,000 in every state) and fifteen thousand treatment centers for addiction. Such web sites facilitate locating similarly-challenged others online and off-line. The capacity of groups to specialize grows. Some provide support for overweight persons with a particular sexual orientation (e.g., the National Organization for Lesbians of Size) or victims of abuse by ethnic background (Asian Institute on Domestic Violence) or alcoholics who are fundamentalist Christians (Alcoholics Victorious), Catholics (Calix Society), women (Women for Sobriety), or medical doctors (Caduceus Club).

Self-Help Groups Create a Sense of Community

The self-help movement is altering American society by changing our conceptions of "community," therapy, and health. In *Health Online*,[232] Tom Ferguson describes the creation of new online support groups, which he dubs as a self-help community. Self-help groups attracted participants in unprecedented numbers in the 1990s. The numbers contacting the American Self-help Clearinghouse increased nearly 18 fold after it went online in 1989, from 17,000 telephone callers to over 300,000 visits to their web site![233]

Building community via the Internet contributes to healing for many. One man diagnosed with a rare cancer of the blood turned to the web for emotional support during his chemotherapy treatments. Without family nearby or supportive doctors, he wrote: *I needed it to deal with the fear and the loneliness I was feeling.*[234]

Not only can the Internet substitute for face-to-face interaction, it can increase frequency of contact. In an experimental study, pregnant women who abused drugs were encouraged to share their experiences and challenges with one another. Half met biweekly in a face-to-face group meeting and the other half used an electronic voice bulletin board. Those using the electronic system were eight times more likely to participate actively than those in face-to-face meetings. Their sense of solidarity increased and more of the electronic communication was emotionally supportive, resulting in significantly lower usage-rates of the outpatient clinic.[235]

Online support groups serve unmet needs of many people. Sixty-eight percent of those with a chronic or disabling condition using an online support forum claimed the online support enhanced their ability to cope and live successfully.[236] One man who found support in the Disabilities Forum on CompuServe wrote:

> *When I suddenly became disabled due to a stroke, I sought out this Forum and found many friends, one in particular, who helped me adjust to the physical and mental aspects of 'being disabled.' This Forum was a lifeline for me, as I became isolated socially after leaving my job because of the stroke. I could not have coped without all the wonderful*

people in this Forum and all the helpful support and informa-
tion. Almost four years later, I still seek out support here and
try to help others. [237]

Another account attesting to the power of online support comes from a group that has 12 members with various disabling conditions. A woman named Georgia, who coordinates their weekly self-help group meetings, is both deaf and blind. While online in cyber space, its members discuss common challenges, exchange practical information and give emotional support, much like the other approximately one million self-help groups operating in the US. These members never leave home to attend meetings. Even though some live thousands of miles from one another, they all are part of a computer network, with some having a special computer keyboard for the disabled. By bringing these people together for heart-to-heart sharing online, the participant's limitations become less limiting.[238]

People with some types of illnesses are more likely to benefit from online support groups. Of the 20 illnesses studied in a recent survey in four large US cities, individuals with MS were the most likely to seek "cyber support." The next most likely to seek cyber support was individuals with chronic fatigue syndrome, followed by breast cancer, anorexia, lung cancer and colon cancer. Individuals with diabetes were also frequent users.[239] Some 40,000 online diabetic support group members participate according to one study.

The online group is the only support group with which some people interact, but for others, the online support group supplements an off-line or local face-to-face group. In fact, for some the online group serves as an introduction to an off-line local group.

Self-Help Groups, Not a Panacea

While self-help groups do not spend all their time emphasizing strength over pathology or cooperation over conflict, most do much of the time. And because self-help groups are democratic, they are not all the same. The "therapeutic effect" of self-help varies from group to group, from person-to-person, and from one time period to another. In this way, self-help varies as with any other therapy.

Occasionally, some local groups fail as a support system. Perhaps they lack a sufficient critical number to be self-sustaining. Further, any given self-help group dealing with the same issue, may be unsuitable for a specific individual. For example, there are three general approaches taken by self-help groups dealing with alcoholism—a spiritual approach that insists on abstinence, a non-spiritual approach that insists on abstinence or a non-spiritual approach that does not request abstinence.[240] Only one of these may be best for any one individual.

Two problems may undermine the effectiveness of a specific self-help group for the individual: disagreements with other members and infringements of their privacy.[241] Most disgruntled individuals can leave that group and locate another to retain their individuality without experiencing conflict with other strong-willed people. Disgruntled participants can and do quit because of conflict with other members. But, when many choices exist, individuals can find another group that supports and encircles them. Any given self-help group is not appropriate for everyone.

Summary

The growing participation in self-help groups is effectuating a quiet revolution in America. These small groups are enriching our understanding of the healing power of supportive relations and the role of spirituality. Self-help groups are also providing a nurturing environment for CAM therapies—a setting in which the latter not only survives but thrives. Small groups are transforming consciousness and shoring up new beliefs and lifestyle choices.

Research shows that shifts in worldviews occur within networks of people who are grappling with similar problems and questions. Thus, just as it takes a village to raise a child, it takes a group to nurture and change a paradigm—in this case, a change from a medical to a health paradigm. An isolated or solitary person may gain an insight, but the group affirms, nurtures, and sustains a new vision of the world over time, despite the mobility and mortality of its members. Participating in self-help groups is similar to joining a religious group or another type of identity group. Like a religious community, these networks provide a safe haven, tools for coping, social support and meaning.

CHAPTER 5.
THE LURE OF FAST-FIX CURES
UNDERMINES HEALTH

Perfection of means and confusion of goals seems to be our main problem.

Albert Einstein

America is something akin to a chronic disease factory producing diseases of affluence. We overeat and under exercise. Our diets contain overly processed foods with chemicals added along with more fat than 30 years ago. The diseases of affluence or over-consumption include cancer, coronary heart disease and diabetes. Every 24 hours, 3,000 Americans experience a heart attack. Forty percent of us will die from heart problems. Cardiologist Robert Elliot, M.D., describes our current situation as:

a medical system waiting at the bottom of a cliff for people to fall off. When we suggest building a fence at the top of the cliff to prevent people from falling, the answer from the bottom is, 'We can't afford it. We're spending all our money down here.[242]

We're spending all the money down here. We can't spare any money for prevention up there.

America is a "pathogenic society" declares DeGraaf in his book *Affluenza*.[243] Many institutions undermine health by marketing quick-fix solutions and over-consumption. The symptoms of this "cultural disease" include stress, anxiety and waste. We make ourselves sick with overwork and credit card debt in our compulsive drive for more. We take an increasing number of drugs to alleviate stress, depression and high blood pressure claims Peter Whybrow, MD, in his book *American Mania*. Affluence undermines our physical, mental and social health. We *sleep less, work longer and spend less time with our families in the manic rush to earn more money to buy more goods*.[244] The same tools and technologies that enabled America to achieve affluence are also eroding its social fabric. Social relationships are being fractured by our pursuit of self-interest as we pollute our bodies, our minds and our environment. The external environment mirrors the internal ecology of our bodies. Dis-ease abounds!

Virtually all our industries and occupations play their part, however unintentionally, in our epidemic of chronic illnesses. Most of us contribute to the generation of health problems when we shop, work in our jobs, feed our families and even as we swallow the prescribed drugs eagerly sought from our physicians. Even when well-intentioned people perform their everyday roles, they often unwittingly contribute to the rising prevalence of chronic disease.

To adequately understand how Americans became so fat, so stressed and so dependent on prescription drugs, we must cast a wide net to catch all the culprits. Americans must not only change their lifestyle choices, but also some institutional practices, if we are to reverse the spreading epidemic of chronic disease.

Numerous institutional factors undermine well-being and constrain healthy lifestyle choices.[245] Too many Americans believe marketing ploys that suggest happiness can be found outside themselves in the form of commodities that are marketed and sold in a package. These beliefs, commodities and practices create a pathogenic lifestyle that leads to dis-ease and a lower quality of life.

How the American Food Industry Promotes Poor Eating Habits

Health and well-being depend upon nutrition. Food affects mood, level of energy and future prospects of health and disease-resistance. The Surgeon General's Report on Nutrition and Health contends that 68 percent of all deaths are caused by diet/activity-related diseases, as shown in Table 5.1. The diet/activity nexus is summarized with a simple equation: caloric input should match caloric expenditure via exercise. Exercise brings many benefits including helping circulate fluids through the lymph system to avoid toxic buildup into a cellular cesspool that produces illness.

Table 5.1 Leading Causes of Death Related to Diet in the U.S.

Diet Related	Cause of Death	Rates (per 100,000)	Years of Potential Life Lost Before age 75 (per 100,000)
Yes	Heart Disease	271.6	1,396
Yes	Cancers	201.6	1,755
Yes	Stroke	59.7	240
Alcohol	Accidents	35.7	1,079
Yes	Diabetes Mellitus	23.4	175
Alcohol	Suicide	11.4	381
Yes	Kidney disease	9.5	281

See US National Vital Statistics Reports, 1999, US Dept of Health and Human Services.

Affluence has banished hunger for all but a few Americans. Most have enough to eat yet our diet is not healthy. Not only do we consume far too many calories, we eat the wrong foods, which leave us vulnerable to chronic illnesses. The primary culprit is the American food industry, especially fast foods, that promotes the consumption of high-calorie, high-fat convenience foods that are highly processed. Highly processed foods—especially carbohydrates with a high glycemic index—along with smoking contribute to heart disease and a long list of other chronic diseases.

The rise of fast food came with such restaurants as McDonalds, Wendy's, Burger King, Taco Bell, KFC, Pizza Hut and the like. But many 'fast food' products are also prepared foods sold at the supermarket and consumed at home. Whether eaten outside the home or in, the appeal of fast food is its ease and speed of preparation and its chemically engineered taste, smell and color to seduce our senses. Fast food restaurants moved into cities and neighborhoods across the US, targeting lower socio-economic areas two and one half times more often than the highest socio-economic neighborhoods.[246]

The American fast food industry brought four changes

The fast food industry has greatly changed our diet. The current American diet is overwhelmingly comprised of high-fat, high sugar, but low-fiber foods: hamburgers, French fries, tacos, fried fish and chicken, cokes, milkshakes, ice cream and pizza to mention some of the more popular.

With the advent of fast food, our diet has undergone four major changes. We consume: more meals outside the home; more processed foods; substantially more calories on an average day than we expend; and more chemicals in our foods. This transformation in diet is as deleterious as it is dramatic. Indeed, the overall change in our diet wrought by fast food rivals the change created by the prosperity of the Industrial Revolution. The latter banished hunger; the fast food revolution is undermining health. Where once many were malnourished, today over 60 percent are overweight and eat unhealthy foods. If "you are what you eat," those who rely on fast food become "fast and easy" which is *fast* to undermine health and *easy* prey to acute and chronic disease.

Eating out versus preparing food at home

About half the adult population in America on an average day visits a restaurant with approximately half of these (one out of four Americans) opting for a quick and easy meal at a low-cost, fast food restaurant.[247] In 1970, Americans spent about $6 billion on fast food, an expenditure that skyrocketed to more than $110 billion in 2000. The fast food industry popularized eating out, providing the menu and taste that pleases the palate. Only a generation ago (1970), three quarters of the money used to buy food in the United States was spent on ingredients for meals prepared at home. By 2001, only half the money was spent on ingredients for home-cooked meals. People are eating at restaurants twice as often as in 1970.[248] More than half of this 50 percent, or one-fourth of all "food money," is spent at fast food restaurants.[249]

Today French fries, not apple pie or the hot dog, are America's favorite food! The typical American consumes approximately four orders of French fries every week.[250] In 1960, the typical American ate 81 pounds of fresh potatoes, but only 4 pounds of frozen French fries as shown in Table 2. In 2000, Americans each ate 51 pounds of fresh potatoes every year and more than 60 pounds of frozen French fries—mostly purchased at fast food restaurants. There are now more than 130 different types of fries.[251] We eat more potatoes but more of these are in the high fat form of French fries.

Table 5.2 Percentage of Potatoes Processed Increased

Year	Fresh Whole Potatoes (pounds)	French Fries (pounds)
1960	81	4
1971	56	30
1981	46	41
1991	50	51
2000	51	60

Adopted from Laurent Belsie "World wants 'fries with that'" in *Christian Science Monitor* Jan 2, 2002.

The hamburger is the runner-up (as well as loyal companion) to the French fries. The average American eats three hamburgers each week, and more than two-thirds of these at a fast food restaurant.[252] The young eat even more per week—6.2 for those in the 7 to 13 age group; and 5.2 each week for those 13 to 33.[253] Even with all the hamburgers that are eaten each day, French fries are still the "fast-food king."

More Processed Foods

A revolution swept through the food preparation industry over the last forty years. Food is not merely packaged to keep it pure and to preserve it from spoiling on the shelf; it is transformed by processing, rendering it less healthy and wholesome. Indeed, little of what we eat is completely natural because of processing: bleaching, colorizing, freezing, dehydrating, cooking and adding chemicals which are the hallmarks of processing. Thus, in this mechanized metamorphosis into "convenient" food, the nutritional value as well as the appearance of the food becomes altered.

Food is now designed by scientists and manufactured for consumer taste, convenience, and appearance. The American diet has shifted from one dominated by fresh, whole foods to one in which 70 to 75 percent of all foods are extracted, refined or processed. This destroys fiber, nutrients and enzymes. A full 90 percent of all money spent on food in America is used to purchase processed foods for in-home consumption or out—items that have been canned, frozen, dehydrated and/or chemically treated.

> Ninety percent of all money spent on food in America is used to purchase processed foods.

The "golden age" of food processing arose in the 1950s with the marketing of refrigerators, freezers and other kitchen appliances.[254] One new processed food after another debuted with great advertising fanfare and a promise to simplify the lives of American housewives. Many of us can recall the advertising campaigns for such products as Cheese Whiz, Jell-O salads, Miracle Whip, TV dinners and Tang to mention but a few.[255] By 1996, about 320,000 packaged foods were available in the US marketplace. And about 15,000 new food products were introduced each year from 1993 to 1995 for an average growth rate of 8-percent per year.

Food processing almost always drains vital nutrients from foods as it seeks to improve taste and the companies' profits. Processing results in a nutrient loss of 20-25 percent in fruits and vegetables while destroying most beneficial fiber. When processors remove a whole grain's outer layers to create a bleached, white grain or flour, they remove 80 percent of 14 nutrients and nearly all the fiber. Many processes typically use synthetic substitutes and call the result "enriched" flour after removing the fiber and natural nutrients.

Today's food production system systematically reduces nutrient content, strips it of fiber and infuses it with an estimated 5000 chemicals to preserve shelf life, color or enhance taste.[256] Consequently, many Americans are becoming chronically deficient in nutrients and afflicted with illnesses from anemia to cancer, or suffering from fatigue, anxiety, headaches, nervousness, depression, eating or drinking disorders.

Americans have become accustomed to eating highly processed foods that come in a package. The very definition of food is being transformed by a $500 billion-a-year food processing industry. The term "processed whole foods" is an oxymoron. Whole grains include items such as brown rice—not Uncle Ben's white rice—or plain oatmeal—not Cheerios with added sugar and salt.

People who mostly consume a diet of preprocessed foods virtually starve their bodies of enzymes which are no longer in the food. Furthermore, if food is eaten without much chewing, the food reaches the stomach without the benefit of enzymes in saliva that facilitates the digestion process. To compensate for the lack of pre-digestion, stomach acids are over-produced, often bringing acid reflux in the esophagus. In addition, virtually all people who primarily eat processed or cooked foods develop an enlarged pancreas by age 40. Eating fresh, uncooked foods and taking time to chew food puts much less stress on the pancreas.

Fast food restaurants ushered in the era of processed foods. The current methods of preparing even simple fare like cheeseburgers and French fries are driven by research on the use of artificial chemicals to enhance taste and efficiency. Most products served at fast food restaurants contain processed ingredients, adding chemicals and then delivered frozen, canned, dehydrated or freeze-dried. The recipes don't come from grandma's cookbooks but from techniques gleaned from high-tech trade journals such as *Food Engineering and Food Technologist.*

More Calories Consumed—Sweet Seduction[257]

Eating out not only changed what we eat, but how much we eat. Restaurant meals tend to be high in fats and calories. The average meal contains 288 more calories than its at-home counterpart. When children eat in restaurants, they consume twice as many calories as when they eat at home.

> We eat more calorie-dense foods and we eat larger portions, which leads to our distortion.

The striking increase in caloric intake arises from two changes in our diet—we eat more calorie-dense foods and we eat larger portions. People who dine outside the home consume 16 percent more calories per meal and a five percent higher percentage of fat calories than those eating at home. This higher caloric intake can result in 30 extra pounds a year if they are not more active than those eating at home.[258]

Americans eat larger portions than the French. In a comparative study of Philadelphians and Parisians in their selection of food portions, Philadelphians ordered meals 20 percent larger in restaurants and bought 15 percent larger frozen dinners at the supermarket than Parisians. Even though Parisians ordered smaller portions at McDonalds than Philadelphians, they took one third more time to dine at the fast food place.[259]

A survey from US Dept of Agriculture shows eating out is becoming more popular. According to Catherine Woteki, Ph.D., USDA Under-Secretary for Food Safety, nearly six out of ten Americans (57 percent) in 1997 consumed meals and snacks away from home on any given day and consumed nearly half their total recommended daily caloric and fat intake outside the home.[260]

Even most hospitals serve unhealthy foods in their cafeterias according to a 2005 survey.[261] Less than one-third of the hospitals offer either a daily salad bar or a daily low-fat, cholesterol-free entree. Many entrees described as healthy by hospitals are actually very high in artery-clogging fat. Sixty-two percent of these "healthiest entrée" offerings derived more than 30 percent of calories from fat, and a few derived more than 50 percent of calories from fat.

We Americans (adults as well as children) on average consume 200 pounds of refined sugar and artificial sweeteners each year—one-third of it consumed in "soft drinks." And many were purchased at fast food counters. In 1821, the average American consumed 10 pounds of sugar a year but since 1900, sugar intake has soared, especially in the 1970s. In 1993, sugar intake rose to 147 pounds per person per year with another 50 pounds of sweeteners, such as Aspartame and high fructose corn syrup.[262] Most of these extra sugar calories in foods are destined to hang on the nation's expanding waistline. Sugar is added to a wide range of products, so that a full 25% of refined sugar is consumed in such unlikely foods as hamburger buns. In all, 14% of sugar is consumed in baked goods; 10% in fruit drinks; 5% in candy; and 4% in breakfast cereals. The average American consumes 20 pounds of snack foods each year. We are eating many more French fries, pizza, and other fast-food items loaded with hidden fat, sugar and calories.

Refined sugar is dead food, suppressing the immune system, leading to obesity and a host of other problems. Consuming refined sugars is fingered for hyperactivity in children, kidney damage, mineral deficiencies (especially chromium, calcium and magnesium), osteoporosis, migraines, and increases in liver and kidney size. It causes cyclical swings in the levels of insulin and sugar in the blood, leading to diet-induced Type II Diabetes.[263] This disease previously associated with the elderly now occurs in adolescents and even children. *Lives are cut short 20 years by a largely preventable disease* writes Francine Kaufman, a pediatric endocrinologist.[264] Type II Diabetes affects nearly 10 percent of the American population, over 18 million diabetics. A 2000 study estimated that roughly 1 in 3 children will develop diabetes in their lifetimes.[265] The prevalence of Type II Diabetes nearly doubled between 1990 and 2002 and the number of obese Americans expanded 57 percent.[266] Anyone at high risk for Type II Diabetes could virtually eliminate their risk by changing their eating habits, losing weight and exercising. Reducing sugar intake would decrease caloric intake and probably reduce weight.

Refined sugars are more than "empty calories." Such sugar cannot be digested properly as it deactivates digestive enzymes. Sugar, such as that in soda pop, has a greater effect on triglycerides than other carbohydrates and may promote heart disease in "insulin resistant" individuals.[267] Sugar also lowers bone density. In one study, subjects who consume high levels of sugar (as much as 20% of their diet, on average) had much lower bone density than other individuals.[268]

Corn is the principal source of sweeteners in the American diet. The use of high-fructose corn syrup has increased more than 4000 percent.[269] Subsidized corn sweeteners have pretty much taken over from sugar. They are in soda pop, candy, pretzels and even in some hot dogs.

Soda pop is America's single biggest source of refined sugars. Per capita consumption of carbonated soft drinks more than quadrupled over the past forty years in the US.[270] In 1997, Americans spent over $54 billion on soft drinks. Our collective intake is estimated to be 576 12-ounce servings per year or 1.6 cans (12-ounce) per day for every man, woman and child.[271]

Soft drink consumption is fueled by their ubiquitous presence. Coca-Cola Company's soft drinks, for example, are sold at two million stores, more than 450,000 restaurants, and 1.4 million vending machines and coolers.[272] The extent of access is reflected in the eating habits of the young. In 12- to 19-year-olds, soft drinks provide nine percent of boys' calories and eight percent of girls' calories. Those percentages tripled from 1977 to 78 for boys and doubled for girls.

Children start drinking soda pop at an alarmingly young age, and consumption increases through young adulthood. Twenty percent of one- and two-year-old children consume soft drinks. Those toddlers drink an average of seven ounces, nearly one cup per day. Almost half of all children between 6 and 11 drink soda pop, with the average drinker consuming 15 ounces per day. This represents a 25 percent (12 ounce) increase from 1977 to 1998.[273]

Fast food restaurants clearly contribute to the rising consumption of soft drinks, primarily because fries and burgers are typically packaged as "combo" and "super-size" meals. The average size of the most common soft drink order at a fast food restaurant increased from 8 ounces in the 1950s to the present 16 ounces. In more ways than one, soda pop is a growth industry. In the 1950s, Coca-Cola sold only a 6½-ounce bottle. That grew into the 12-ounce can, which is now being supplanted by 20-ounce bottles and then there's the 64-ounce, 600-calorie Double Gulp.

Chemists Add Color and Spice so it is Nice

Chemists are replacing family tradition and grandma's recipes with "techno-foods" by adding chemicals for taste, color, vitamins and minerals.[274] Techno-foods need not be healthy, only tasty and profitable! An industrial army of chemists specializing in the science of flavor, aided by the services of nutritionists, agronomists and psychologists are employed to concoct more palatable and enticing processed food.

New companies now specialize in the manufacture of food flavorings. As often as not, the wizards of this new science, called flavorists, have PhDs and work in impeccably equipped laboratories provided by such companies as International Flavor and Fragrances. This "flavor industry" is behind much of the use of the 5,000 plus chemical additives in our foods and beverages.[275]

The aroma of a food is responsible for as much as 90 percent of its flavor.[276] Chemists and food scientists are using new technologies to inject memorable color, odor and taste into processed foods stripped of their nutrients, texture and flavor. These food scientists even study childhood memories of particular aromas and tastes. Knowledge gained from consumer research gives the food "alchemists" the ability to seduce the shopping public.

With the use of such high tech tools as the aroma-spectograph, this new science generates findings of great value to the food processing industry. The aroma-spectograph identifies the chemicals involved in different aromas, thereby capturing the secrets involved in seductive smells and tastes. Food scientists also use the gas chromatograph and spectrometers—machines capable of detecting volatile gases at very low levels. The aromas of coffee or roasted meat may contain volatile gases with nearly 1,000 different chemicals while strawberries are relatively simple with only 350 different chemicals.[277]

Does this science of food contribute to the bottom line of the fast food industry? Clearly, it does inasmuch as "the proof of the pudding is in the eating." People flock to fast food. Still, serious concerns remain. Allan Spreen, MD contends there are over 20 food-linked diseases or syndromes associated with ingesting chemical additives, including allergies, arthritis, colitis, Crohn's disease, constipation, adult diabetes, fatigue, headaches, obesity, hypoglycemia, kidney disease and liver disease.[278] Research has firmly linked chemical additives to many of these diseases.[279] Not surprisingly, people who are sick can recover and get well by avoiding the offending chemicals. For example, in nine studies on children with typical ADHD, the behavior of many children who were put on an additive-free diet returned to normal.[280]

No simple or quick and easy solutions exist for this problem. The new foods are remarkably popular and most people are unwilling to change their diet when chronic illness hits them. Most seek relief from chronic conditions with medications. But often this attempt at managing symptoms fails, because medicines have chemicals that either simply mask symptoms or even create new problems.

Fast Food and Portion Distortion Contribute to Illness

Government data show more than 64 percent of American adults are overweight, with 30 percent of these being obese. Adult Americans gained an average of ten pounds during the decade of the 1990s and 25 pounds since the late 1970s.

The percentage of overweight school age children jumped from five percent in 1964 to over 20 percent in 2001.[281] Obesity rates among our children are twice as high as in the late 1970s and tripled among adolescents.[282] In the 1990s alone the obesity rate among children rose eight percent. Obesity nearly tripled in the past two decades among adolescents.

> Most dieters fail or are derailed by holding a negative goal of avoiding junk foods which creates stress. This in turn creates the craving for "comfort foods."

At any given moment, 35 percent of Americans are attempting to lose weight (45 percent of women and 25 percent of men) with only five percent achieving and maintaining their weight-related goal. Americans spend in excess of $33 billion on weight-loss products and services a year but most dieters fail or are derailed by holding a negative goal of avoiding junk foods. This in turn creates the craving for "comfort foods."

> As weight goes up, life span goes down by as much as 13 years among the obese.

Obesity puts people at risk for cardiovascular disease and increases the risk of stroke, diabetes, hypertension and certain types of cancer. Obese individuals have a 50 to 100 percent greater risk of premature death from all causes compared to individuals without excess weight. As weight goes up, life span goes down by as much as 13 years.[283] According to the US Surgeon General, obesity is directly related to some 300,000 deaths per year. Obesity can also take an emotional toll, leading to a poor self-image and depression. Obese individuals experience nearly twice the chronic health problems as people of optimal weight. Obesity is a more significant risk than health problems caused by poverty, daily smokers or heavy drinkers.[284]

Overweight individuals are 35 percent more likely and obese individuals are 100 percent more likely to develop kidney cancer than those of normal weight.[285] Medical care for obese individuals costs an average 37 percent more than for people of normal weight. The treatment of illnesses related to overweight and obesity costs $93 billion a year. Medical costs connected to obesity and smoking account for nearly 9 percent of all medical expenditures.[286]

Fast food clearly contributes to the epidemic of overweight and obesity. The super-sizing of meals and portion distortion at restaurants contributes to the super-sizing of our population. Not only has the size of soft drinks ballooned from 8 to 20 ounces, but the largest serving of McDonald's French fries has grown from 200 calories in 1960 to 320 calories in the late 1970s to 450 calories in the mid-1990s to the present 610 calories in this new century.[287] Even government officials have taken notice. In TV interviews, Health and Human Services Secretary Tommy Thompson has publicly pressed the fast-food industry "to do what is right for Americans," such as offering low-calorie meals and tips on healthier living.

> The super-sizing of meals and portion distortion at restaurants contributes to the super-sizing of our population

The consumption of high fat and high calorie meals is related to the nation's growing weight problem and to the concomitant higher rates of obesity-related diseases such as Type II Diabetes, hence the word *diabesity*, linking obesity and Type II Diabetes.[288] Fast foods are especially popular with the young, and the earlier a person begins to carry excess weight the greater the impact on their future health. Obesity rates more than doubled among children age six to ten in the past forty years according to government statistics. Forty percent of all newly diagnosed cases of what was once typically adult-onset Type II Diabetes now occur in children.[289] Lifestyle-induced Type II Diabetes grew 17 percent among 30 year olds from 1980 to 2000. Many Americans are well down the road to chronic illnesses by the time they turn 40.

Why are Americans adopting these eating habits?

Why do Americans dine so often on fast food and pre-processed food? No definitive answer exists. Convenience certainly fits into the American lifestyle and explains part of its popularity. Good taste also helps explain the grip of fast food. But even more importantly, eating choices are governed more by emotional rather than rational factors.[290] Early childhood memories and habits persist through time into adulthood. During periods of stress and emotional upset, we turn to foods that comforted us in childhood which was/is often the high fat, high sugar kinds. Frank, a member of Overeaters Anonymous, proclaimed: *When I was five years old, a very emotional conflict between my mother and father caused me to withdraw into the kitchen to eat and it was then that I began to stuff my feelings with food.*

Eating choices are governed more by emotional than rational factors.

Over half of those surveyed in a recent study cited emotions as triggering the craving for a particular food—almost double the number citing hunger. We use food for relieving stress, for diversion when bored, for comfort when anxious, and as a reward for achieving tasks. Hunger is only one among many reasons for eating. Emotional factors primarily motivate the decision of when and what to eat, not rational, conscious reasons for most individuals most of the time.

Emotions also greatly influence when and what we eat! Stressful situations increase the consumption of "comfort foods." Surveys find individuals commonly giving the following reasons for craving a particular food: it "gives me a good feeling," "takes my mind off the problem," "reminds me of good times in the past," "makes me feel safe" and "reminds me of my mother and home life." Women more often than men turn to comfort foods particularly during times of stress and relationship strain.[291]

Falling Serotonin

Most dietary preferences and eating habits are established early in life by parents who model habits for their children. Most children maintain these habits into adulthood. Sarah Leibowitz, a neurobiologist, contends that frequent eating of fatty foods may change brain chemistry and lead a person to crave even more fat. When high-fat diets are eaten, a brain signal (a neuropeptide) increases and stimulates the appetite to eat more. A high fat diet increases the level of lipids know as triglycerides. These triglycerides stimulate the production of neuropetides that interfere with the brain's ability to feel full.[292] Dieting is sabotaged by these changes in brain chemistry. When the body stops receiving the accustomed fuel, serotonin and beta-endorphin quickly fall and the person feels tired, fatigued and depressed.[293] These feelings spur the search for comfort foods which causes a person to consume excessive caloric intake and gain weight.

Changes in family life and the economy also contribute to unhealthy changes in diet. American families have more disposable income to spend on food prepared outside the home since food costs as a percentage of household expenditures fell from 13 percent in 1980 to 10.7 percent in 2000. Fast foods and convenience foods tend to have more fat and calories. These foods are pre-processed by large corporations with profits in mind. They know the public will buy high fat, sweet and high calorie foods. In giving us what we want, they help us undermine our own health. The economic constraints of years gone by which kept us out of the restaurants and delis may have been good for our health after all.

Another reason for the poor quality of the American diet is the time pressure that many women face on a daily basis. Now that women (the cooks in traditional homes) work many more hours outside the home, they have less time for cooking.[294] With women having little time to prepare meals, eating has acquired a spur of the moment habit ruled by impulse. Because many more mothers are not home at the dinner hour, most adolescents (80%) don't eat with their parents, and three out of four adolescents select their own foods. Market research shows that 60 percent of Americans don't know what they will be eating 30 minutes before hand, and as a result, two thirds of these will eat out.

> For every $1 the government spends on nutrition education, the food industry spends $10 in advertisements.

Often American choices are guided by the siren songs created by the $30 billion spent on advertising.[295] With more processed foods to choose from, it's easy to select only those foods we like, not necessarily the healthy foods. Advertising effectively steers us toward sweeter, richer foods and over time many of these choices subvert our health. For every $1 the government spends on nutrition education, the food industry spends $10 in advertisement.[296]

Advertising, fast food enterprises and time constraints on working couples, all work to change the nation's eating habits toward eating processed and convenience foods. They do so as surreptitiously as a stealth bomber passing undetected through a radar screen. One reason for this unforeseen effect on our dietary behaviors is that food choices are inherently complex, and motivated by attitudes, values and environmental influences (family, workplace, school, grocery stores, community and mass media). In a social atmosphere that promotes convenience and taste, consumer choices are not likely to be healthy unless positive nutritional messages are effectively communicated. But few companies perceive a potential profit by providing and promoting healthy food.

If we are to successfully change our diet, intervention by governmental and workplace leaders must deal with the full range of these complex influences. At the very least, nutrition education must offer sustained and consistent messages starting in the primary and secondary schools, messages that can be delivered in multiple ways over the long term with sufficient breadth and depth to compete effectively with the countervailing seductions of the food industry.[297] It may also be necessary to change the incentives that confront producers and consumers, a theme discussed in the next chapter.

The Sedentary Lifestyle

Caloric intake alone rarely leads to weight gain when the person with a high-calorie diet is physically active. Exercise enhances health by helping to remove toxic buildup in the lymph system, by burning calories to maintain weight, and by increasing the ratio of muscle to fat in the body. Exercise helps protect against heart disease, osteoporosis, diabetes and many other physically debilitating conditions. Muscle mass increases metabolism, which burns more calories in the course of a day. Exercise is good for you!

But American society discourages an active lifestyle as much as it encourages overeating; and this deadly combination spawns chronic illnesses. Two out of three adults are under active. Compared to work in agriculture and manufacturing, modern service sector jobs impose few physical demands. Many of us sit at a desk or stand behind counters all day long. Our work requires very little lifting and walking which does reduce the rate of job-related injuries but it has also lessened physical movement, diminishing the overall health of the workforce. The engineering of the postindustrial workplace ensures safer, softer jobs compared to our parents and grandparents; but we expend fewer calories at work and elsewhere while over-consuming calories.

If we compare the caloric intake of the average adult American with a typical adult Amish farm community member, the Amish consume more calories per day, (2,850 vs. 2,600) but he/she also expend much more energy. The Amish work-load is the equivalent of walking eight miles/day compared to three miles/day for most Americans. This high expenditure of energy results in a very low percent of the Amish community being obese compared to other American adults (4% vs. 30%).[298]

Like work, transportation has become mechanized, requiring less physical energy. Few Americans walk to work or to the bus stop or to the train. Instead, we walk 20 feet to our automobile and drive to the parking lot next to our workplace. Suburbia, as much as the service sector economy, subverts the expenditure of energy. Unlike the old urban neighborhoods, few stores and other destinations in the suburbs are within walking distance and many merchants even provide drive-through shopping.

The declining reliance on public transportation feeds the epidemic of obesity and Type II Diabetes. Few Americans take a bus or train to work. Though rarely acknowledged, public transportation requires walking at least part way to the traveler's destination. In this way, public transportation enhances public health. Recent studies show the significance of public transportation. The sprawling and automobile-dependent cities of the South and Midwest have the highest levels of obesity for they are the very cities in which workers least rely on public transportation or walking to work.

Do suburbs make you fat? Exercise and Mobility is the solution.

Obesity expanded with the decline of public transportation. Compare the automobile commute of a suburbanite to the walk and ride of a transit-using urbanite. The transit-user walks to the bus, rides and then walks to the workplace. At night, he or she repeats the process. A quarter mile spent walking at each end of the journey adds a half-mile of walking in the morning and then again that evening, that is a one mile walk each workday. Under these conditions, the urbanite would walk 240 more miles per year than the auto-riding suburbanite. Over the course of a year, this would burn enough calories to shed 7 pounds. Over the years, this alone could be the difference between a healthy and an unhealthy weight. Researchers at the CDC found that suburban dwellers weigh an average of 6.3 pounds more than central city dwellers and also have higher blood pressure.[299]

Our planned suburban environments foster inactivity, weight-gain and chronic illness, without intending it. In suburbia, fewer people walk to work, to the store or to church. Many suburban streets lack sidewalks. But even if they have sidewalks, few residents would walk to their preferred destinations, whether near or far.

Television, Exercise and Foods

Television also promotes an inactive lifestyle, eating more junk food and gaining weight. Our spud-like shape forms by watching television and eating snack foods like a "couch potato." Nearly half our high school population is immobile, watching television for an average of three hours a day. Average viewing time in 1991 increased 40 percent over that in 1960. Heavy use of TV contributes to *exercise deficiency syndrome* and the growth of obesity, now 15 percent among children and 30 percent among adults. When the child's motor activity is limited in the first years of life, it causes postural muscle problems, which can cause later learning disabilities.[300]

Watching more TV leads to consuming more unhealthy foods, both because of the sedentary activity and TV ads. The average

American child spends 22 hours a week in front of the TV where they are bombarded with 385 commercials per week or 20,000 a year. Most of these ads are for foods of an unhealthy variety such as soft drinks, breakfast cereals, candy, chips and fast-food restaurants. In the last ten years, such marketing has increased more than 55 percent.[301]

TV fails to stimulate the senses beyond the visual. Some even suggest that TV has changed our children's learning patterns. Studies show a decline in academic performance since television was introduced. TV reduces sense modality coordination and may increase failure in school.[302] Television also undermines participation in social activities that promote intimate ties and social support systems.

Stress in America

Herbert Benson, MD, an expert on stress claims that stress is America's number one health problem. Stress related problems account for 60 to 90 percent of all US medical visits. Stress plays a role in most chronic disease, including heart disease, stroke, high blood pressure, diabetes, cancer, asthma, herpes, cirrhosis and headaches. The source of stress can be physical, mental or emotional. Stress can be internally generated (envy, fear, hate and jealousy) as well as externally provoked by excessive job demands, responsibility without control or excessive noise or heat. Different people perceive different situations as stressful and bring different resources (mental, social and economic) with which to manage and adapt. People who stress at work or fret over paying their bills or in relationships experience more illness.

Stress related problems account for 60 to 90 percent of all US medical visits.

Work creates stress for most Americans as illustrated in Table 5.3.[303] Work is the primary source of income, power, time pressures and regimentation. A Gallup survey in 2000 found 80 percent of workers feel stress on the job and nearly half want help in learning how to manage stress.[304] Between 60-80 percent of industrial accidents result from stress, including such notorious events as the Exxon Valdez oil spill and the Three Mile Island nuclear disaster. Twelve percent of workers have called in sick because of job stress, four out of ten job turnovers result from stress and medical care expenditures are nearly 50 percent greater for workers who report high levels of stress.[305] An estimated 1 million workers are absent on an average workday because of stress related complaints. Not surprisingly then, the market for stress management programs, products and services grew from $9.4 billion in 1995 to $11.31 billion in 1999.

Table 5.3 National Job Stress Surveys[306]

- Over half the working people in the U.S. view job stress as a major problem, double that of a decade ago
- 40% of workers reported their job was "very or extremely stressful"
- 75% of employees believe that "workers have more on-the-job stress than a generation ago"
- 29% of workers felt "quite a bit or extremely stressed at work," the highest in the pollster's history
- 26% of employees said they were "often or very often burned out or stressed by their work"
- Job stress is more strongly associated with health complaints than financial or family problems.

The "New Turbo Capitalism" as Stress-Generator

The new economy with heightened international competition of companies generates stress. This heightened competition brings more job insecurity from downsizing and job layoffs, more hours and responsibility with less autonomy and often less job satisfaction.

Paradoxically, while America's 10 trillion dollar Gross Domestic Product steadily grew over the past 30 years, and the number of wives working jumped dramatically, the average family's income rose very little. Without the steady inflow of married women into the workplace, the average American family would have lost buying power. The wages of workers with a high school education or less dropped in real terms. Amazingly, even wages for college grads fell 1.5 percent in 2002 so the average worker brings home less money today than in the 1970s.[307]

The quality of life on the job is also a paradox. Fewer Americans perform hard physical labor so there are fewer work-related injuries and deaths. Yet the amount of work-related stress has risen as more employees are monitored and their output is measured in the computerized workplace. Stress rises with the total number of hours worked. Many Americans are working more hours each week. In fact, many low skilled Americans are working two, even three jobs.

Married female workers are especially vulnerable to time pressure as many also are overloaded with household tasks. The entry of women into the workplace brought many positive aspects, but it often injects new forms of stress into families by allowing less time for the children and other household tasks. While many women choose fulltime employment, others feel compelled to work outside the home to maintain the family's standard of living. American parents spent 40 percent less time with their children in the 1990s than parents did in the 1960s. And despite dramatic economic growth from 1958 to 1980, Americans reported feeling significantly less well off in 1980 than 22 years before!

No futurist predicted that industrial productivity would rise, factory wages would fall and more hours would be worked per family.[308] The connection between productivity and wage growth has been severed. Productivity grew 46.5 percent between 1973 and 1998 while the actual wage of a typical worker fell.[309]

Low income Americans experience more stress and illness because they frequently cannot pay their bills at the end of the month. The threat of illness stresses many, especially the 15 percent of Americans without medical insurance, many which are employed in low wage or temporary work that offers no such benefits.

Workplace Insecurity: Many Americans are experiencing a dramatic change in their relationship with their employer. Employment in the private sector is less unionized, less long term and less secure. The American corporation routinely offers new employees low wages and short term, tenuous employment.[310] From the ranks of middle managers down to the shop floor, employees are increasingly vulnerable to layoffs, wage cuts or part-time employment and outsourcing. Employers restructuring their organizations create great insecurity by resorting to such wage-lowering practices as contingent and leased employment, or even sending more work overseas. Today's organization is haunted by employment insecurity, constant change and instability.

Corporate executives attribute these changes to increased competition in a global economy. Three out of four executives cited increased economic pressures from competitors as the reason for corporate restructuring and downsizing.[311] Much of this intensified competition arises from world trade that grew dramatically. Since 1960 the share of the US economy comprised of imports has nearly tripled. Many changes arise from deregulation of the economy from trucking to airlines, telecommunications and financial services. Whatever the source, the scope of change is vast. The number of company failures increased eightfold between 1970 and 1996.[312]

The pace of change in the corporate world is quickening. One example is shortening lifecycle of products. The time from conceiving a new product to its production and marketing phase has quickened across a wide range of products such as cars and telephones where the time is cut by half.[313]

In this hyper-competitive atmosphere, bankruptcies and mergers occur with regularity with workers scrambling for new employment. Plant closings and downsizing are common, even among companies that survive the competition. The challenge of managers in today's corporate environment is described by the dean of management theorists, Peter Drucker, as "managing in turbulent times."

All Americans are buffeted by these gusts of change, but workers are affected more than others. One study concluded: *Older, non-college, blue collar, and unionized employees...find themselves disproportionately located in companies that have cut their workforces through a host of actions.*[314] By the time the turbulence in corporate suites reaches the shop floor it has grown to hurricane size, with a storm surge that sweeps away entire occupations from the economic landscape. Upper level managers usually reach high ground, while workers and middle mangers are swept away.

Managers tend to depreciate the value of workers as well as machines over time. With increasing regularity, older workers are released and younger workers with new skills are recruited as the former products, capital equipment and older employees become obsolescent. Thus, the utility to management of many workers depreciates more rapidly than ever, along with the marketability of the products they make and the value of the capital equipment they use.

Cutting cost has reduced the number of permanent employees over the last 30 years. In virtually all industries, management contracted out for contingent workers. Management increasingly uses new technologies and related management information systems to eliminate even middle managers.

Many of the temporary, contingent employees have no medical insurance. This in itself stresses many because medical costs can bankrupt a family. In 2002, the fear of devastating illness created job-lock for one in four American workers where they stayed in a job longer than they desired for fear of losing their medical insurance benefits. Only 17 percent felt job-lock in 1993 rising to 25 percent in 2002.[315]

Stress Undermines Health

Stress doubles the risk of death from heart disease.[316] Job strain (defined as high work demands and low job control) and effort-reward imbalance (defined as high demands coupled with low security and few career opportunities) each doubled the risk of cardiovascular death among initially healthy employees.[317] In a similar study involving over 25,000 employees, workers with little control and high stress in their jobs were 50 percent more likely to die over a ten-year period than workers with *more control* in high demand jobs.[318] Stressful work conditions without much control are especially unhealthy.

> Job strain and effort-reward imbalance each doubled the risk of cardiovascular death.

Workers in less autonomous jobs compared to workers in more autonomous jobs missed work nearly three times more often during the previous year. Workers in less autonomous jobs were six times more likely to exhibit symptoms of depression, were nearly seven times more likely to report cardiovascular symptoms of chest pain and shortness of breath. Almost all workers in less autonomous jobs said they felt stress.[319]

Credit Card Debt: Buy Now and Pay Later

America is a shopper's paradise and a lender's goldmine. Our shopping malls are filled with goods, lenders extend easy credit and advertising entices more spending. The profusion of new products, easy credit and intense marketing conspire to create record levels of consumer debt and record numbers of personal bankruptcies. Currently more than 641 million credit cards circulate in America. Over three out of every four families held a credit card in 2001 with over half (55 percent) of these families carrying a revolving monthly debt. This represents an estimated 115 million Americans. The average credit card debt among American households more than doubled over the past decade and seven million filed for bankruptcy in the last five years.

In *Credit Card Nation*, Robert Manning argues that banks consciously sought to alter American values to increase their own profits. The average saving rate of Americans fell precipitously from about 10 percent of our income in 1980 to zero in 2000. Rather than waiting until we can pay for it, credit card ads assert "buy now and pay later." *We are replacing the traditional mantra "a penny saved is a penny earned" with marketing mantras such as "you deserve it today" and "you are worth it."* Credit cards enable spending by making it easier to buy and forget the amount spent. The willingness to spend more for a specific product increased 100 percent when credit rather than cash could be used in a recent study.

During the 1990s, the average amount of credit card indebtedness tripled. This debt reached $743 billion in 2004. If you stumble in paying the minimum on time, the new rate soars to 29 percent. Such high interest rates cause many to sink into financial quicksand. On average, we paid 13.3 percent of our total income on revolving debt on our credit cards. One in every 67 households in America filed for bankruptcy in 2003 because of job loss, a health crisis or divorce. One in three families in bankruptcy owes an entire year's income on their credit cards.

Debt-counseling services are skyrocketing. More people file for bankruptcy each year than obtain college degrees. Debt crisis in the family affects more children than a divorce.[320] Debt generates financial insecurity. Seventy percent of American families who hold revolving debt claim this makes their life stressful and unhappy.

What do people do when juggling so much stress? They often turn to quick fixes such as mind-mellowing drugs or pain relievers.

A Quick Fix with Rx Drugs

Americans like quick fixes and popping a pill all too often becomes the first response to unpleasant symptoms or pain. There are pills for headaches,[321] for sleeping, to lower fever, to quiet coughs, and to clear the sinuses. With pills, Americans attempt to lose weight, relieve heartburn, control Type II Diabetes and relieve the psychic ailments that afflict humanity—anxiety, depression, and inattentiveness/hyperactivity.

Each year, Americans take over 5 billion doses of tranquilizers to calm down (mainly benzodiazepines), another 5 billion doses of similar drugs to unwind and sleep, and another 3 billion doses of amphetamines either to perk up, suppress appetite or treat attention deficit disorder. In our un-winnable "war against symptoms," modern drugs are the primary weapons in the arsenal, deployed again and again.[322] Americans buy more prescription medicines than people in any other country. The pharmaceutical industry served up more than $250 billion worth of sales in 2004 or $850 for every American.[323]

The number of prescriptions has swelled by two-thirds over the past decade to 3.5 billion yearly. In 2001, the total cost was $180 billion or just over $60 dollars per prescription. American pharmacies filled 1.9 billion prescriptions in 1992 or 7.3 for every man, women and child in the United States. In 2001, the average person filled 12 prescriptions. Prescription drug sales have pushed upward by an annual average of 11 percent over the past five years.

This industry-wide growth in demand and price also applies to over-the-counter (OTC) medications. Currently there are more than 600 drug products in the OTC market that were available only by prescription ten years ago. This relaxation in the regulatory process is known as the Rx-to-OTC switch. Disingenuously presented as a form of patient empowerment, this dramatic change reflects the industry's desire to market directly to customers, with a $4.9 billion dollar market in year 2000, and expected to become $12 billion by 2005.

Drugs used for chronic conditions potentially undermine health in three ways: by creating dependency, leaching nutrients from the body during the process of metabolizing and producing side effects that create new problems—even death.

Drugs Create Dependency: For every ill, there is a pill.

Drug companies and many doctors are selling a message that creates dependency on a 'McQuick-fix' menu of drugs and expressed with the mantra: *For every ill, there is a pill.* Drugs are one means of countering concerns from acid reflux to depression to high cholesterol and hot flashes. The indirect message is that drugs are wholesome and safe, helping people live a rich and satisfying life. This message being sent on television, on radio, and in magazines helps cultivate the consumer expectation for a quick-fix pill, rather than exploring a lifestyle change. Simple exercise and diet are as effective as drugs for heart disease, diabetes and a host of other chronic conditions while being safer and cheaper.

Nowhere is this more alarming than the use of drugs on children; 13 million children in kindergarten through 12th grade take medications at school. Most common are behavioral and mood-regulating medications that may cause permanent changes in brain chemistry and "learned helplessness." In the US, up to five percent of children are diagnosed with attention deficit disorder or ADHD. ADHD is defined by the inability to concentrate, difficulty in organizing, and impulsive behavior that persists for more than three months. A large proportion of those diagnosed with ADHD are prescribed Ritalin, a stimulant that increases dopamine in the brain. Higher dopamine levels in the brain cells may cement the connections during development.[324] Experimental research suggests that these changes in brain chemistry are associated with a significantly higher degree of 'learned helplessness,' a condition marked by depression and withdrawing when faced with a challenge.

Neil Bush, brother of President George W. Bush, described his own seven-year ordeal with his son who was diagnosed with ADHD at age 10. In Neil's testimony at a congressional hearing in August 2002, he said: *There is a problem in this country where schools are often forcing parents to turn to Ritalin. It's obvious to me we have a crisis in this country.*

Prescriptions for Ritalin increased five-fold in the past decade. Spending on prescription drugs for children through age 19 increased by 28 percent from 2000 to 2002. Because the FDA approved the use of Prozac for the treatment of depression and obsessive/compulsive disorder in children aged 7 to 17, the use of antidepressant drugs in children increased by 124 percent from 1995 to 2002. Parents now spend more annually on drugs to treat behavioral disorders like attention deficit disorder and depression than they do on antibiotics and asthma medications.

I'm not nearly as happy as the people in the drug ad. I may need a greater dosage of this drug.

Our reliance on drugs has cultivated more dependence. Medical professionals are cultivating our dependence on drugs and medical care. Dependence on quick-fixes has caused an estimated 6 million

Americans to abuse medical drugs for pain relievers (2.6 million), sedatives and tranquilizers (1.3 million), and stimulants (0.9 million).[325]

Lifestyle change as a therapeutic response to chronic illness is ignored by most physicians. A change in lifestyle could benefit the vast majority of those with chronic ailments. The number one cause of death in America is the diet/exercise factor which includes smoking cigarettes. Nearly 40 percent of Americans are physically inactive, with nearly two thirds being under-active.[326] Approximately 22 percent of our adult population smoke cigarettes and 61 percent are overweight. The number of Americans who could benefit from new health habits is huge.

In his book, *The Drug Lords...America's Pharmaceutical Cartel*, Tonda Bian contends that the pharmaceutical industry plays a central role in creating demand and keeping us over-medicated. Drug advertising and marketing until the 1980s was directed toward doctors in the form of samples, continuing education of physicians, and advertisements placed in medical journals. The FDA lifted the total ban on direct to consumer drug ads in the 1980s.

Working with physicians, the drug companies and the Food and Drug Administration (FDA) have successfully blocked alternative therapies. The lucrative cancer treatment area illustrates the suppression of alternatives with "medical cops." Drugless alternatives were generally suppressed and even outlawed by the medical establishment and the FDA. The book *Cured to Death* provides an inside look at the cozy relationship between drug manufacturers and the government.[327] Also, Don Haley's book *Politics in Healing* gathers over 10 accounts of medical outsiders to show how the American Medical Association (AMA), the FDA, and big pharmaceutical companies conspired to prevent new ideas from entering medical research and practice. His stories include Andrew Ivy, who advocated the anti-cancer drug Krebiozen, Harry Hoxsey, herbalist with his Alternative Cancer treatments), Gaston Nassens, blood researcher with his Alternative Cancer treatments, Royal Rife, builder of a light microscope to see viruses, and Stanislaw Burzynski, the anti neoplastin researcher. In addition to these fairly well known persecuted medical investigators are less well known cases like William Koch, developer of the anti polio drug Glyoxylide.

Haley contends that many of his subjects were victims of drug companies and organized medicine's turf war of protecting their profitable prescription drug trade against outsiders. The use of laetrile for cancer exposed the crisis of public confidence in conventional scientific medicine. Public use of laetrile put the medical establishment on the defensive against the charge that monopoly powers were withholding possible cures from the public so as to protect lucrative sales of approved therapies that were ineffective.[328] Haley calls for more citizen involvement and action to support legislation that permits freedom of choice in the form of Access to Medical Treatment Act. See www.citizen.org for more information.

Creating Demand and Cultivating Habits

Direct advertising to consumers escalated in the 1990s after the FDA relaxed its restrictions as long as the ads included a brief summary of indications, side effects and who should not use the drug. In 1997, the FDA dropped the requirement that contraindications be listed. This brought a dramatic explosion of short sound bytes of televised drug advertisements. The amount of money the industry spent annually on direct-to-consumer drug advertising skyrocketed with a ten-fold increase from $250 million in 1994 to $2,500 million in 2000, with 62 percent of this being spent on TV.[329]

The money spent on promotion and marketing rose from $5.5 billion in 1995 to $10.5 billion in 2000.[330] The dramatic expansion in marketing drugs coincides with the use of TV ads to "educate" the public on which pill can best treat their illness. Earlier the pharmaceutical industry directed advertisements to doctors only, but now they spend a large percentage of their budgets directly appealing to consumers. Advertising also promotes many drugs whose patent has expired and are now permitted to sell them over-the-counter (OTC). Whether prescription drug or OTC, these ads seek to induce use by creating the "first medical opinion."

In addition to those with chronic conditions, drug companies are prospecting for more customers among the healthy middle-aged.

One pharmaceutical company, for instance, ran an advertisement in national magazines, showing an attractive woman of approximately 35 years of age. The headline under her picture asks: "Has your arthritis started yet?" It suggests that she begin using a medication in hopes of preventing a condition that has yet to develop.

Similarly, another ad showed a despondent mother sitting in an empty house after her grown children had left home, while a concerned voice informed the audience of a medication to treat the despondency of "empty-nest syndrome." This open invitation to use drugs is not unusual.[331] Nightly, we are barraged with ads suggesting medications for any number of conditions from hyperactive children to unfocused seniors, to men with erectile dysfunction.

Direct-to-consumer advertising hits its intended targets with the accuracy of a smart bomb. Prescription drug sales are soaring for depression, allergies, arthritis, high cholesterol, erectile dysfunction, and gastrointestinal problems. Prescriptions for Allegra and Nasonex both increased 38 percent within a three-year period; Lipitor and Zyrtec increased 29 percent and Viagra rose 26 percent.[332]

Many Americans are seeking immediate gratification in their health according to the Natural Marketing Institute. Whether for losing weight, treating acid reflux or lowering cholesterol, we want instant results and the trend may be strengthening. Americans treating high cholesterol with prescription drugs rose 21 percent from 2001 to 2005 and the numbers using prescription drugs for acid reflux/heartburn increased 10 percent.[333]

The quest for drug profits may be distorting the practice of medicine and creating a "fast-fix industry" with McQuick-fix menus ready to prescribe relief from a long list of symptoms. Direct-to-consumer advertising creates many a patient's first opinion for their symptoms and the doctor's visit is reduced in status to a second opinion. Among consumers who both saw a drug ad and visited a doctor, one in four (25%) asked for this drug and most (70 percent) obtained a prescription for that drug. Only half of these patients were tested to confirm a diagnosis and most never learned from the physician about other possible treatments for their condition.[334] Patients who formed their first opinion from drug ads obtained compliance half of the time without tests from their 'second-opinion' doctor, and usually without hearing about other options.[335] By marketing drugs directly to consumers and creating demand, drug companies are "de-professionalizing" doctors by providing fast-fix drugs for an assembly-line treatment system.

> Twenty-five of the most heavily advertised drugs accounted for half of the increased drug sales.[336] Much of this new spending is wasteful. Of the ten drugs most heavily advertised directly to consumers, eight are classified by the World Health Organization as less essential.[337] Most of these drugs have low-cost generic alternatives. For example, Celebrex, a heavily advertised drug with little or no advantage over ibuprofen costs $188 for a standard month's supply while ibuprofen costs $18 for the same amount.

The largest part of the marketing strategy still remains directed toward physicians. Pharmaceutical firms spend on average $14,000 per year on each physician as presented in Chapter 2. Drug companies send salespersons to visit physicians often, sponsor all-paid "educational programs" in exotic vacation spots, and lucrative support for medical lectures.

> Pharmaceutical firms spend on average $14,000 per year on each physician.

Dispensing drugs to cultivate habits and seed profits

The army of drug sales workers grew from 42,000 in 1996 to almost 88,000 in 2001.[338] The pharmaceutical industry spent more than $16 billion on marketing in 2000, with nearly $10.5 billion of the $16 billion spent on dispensing free samples. The doctors give these pills to their patients, who, if they like them, frequently ask the doctor to prescribe the drug for their ailment. Showering physicians with free samples is a good investment, as many physicians play a critical role in turning patients into dependable drug consumers by dispensing "starter-kits."[339] This tactic is especially true for chronic disease medications, which must be taken daily with no end date. From the pharmaceutical industry's standpoint, the perfect consumer is one who never gets better and never dies. They are the "cash-cows," addicted within the legal drug trade.

Drug makers spend millions studying the prescribing behavior of specific doctors. Drug companies know whether doctors are switching specific patients from one drug to a competitor within days of its occurrence.[340] Brand-name drugs dominate the U.S. market and account for more than 90 percent of total drug spending and about 60 percent of prescriptions filled.[341] Dispensing free pills to doctors sows seeds for a bountiful harvest. Clearly the public ultimately pays, as the combination of advertising and free samples increases the cost of disease care treatment with drugs. The average Medicare recipient spends on average $2,300 on drugs each year, or over $190 per month. The new Medicare drug bill is a cornucopia for the pharmaceutical industry that will cost the tax payers dearly.

> From the pharmaceutical industry's standpoint, the perfect consumer is one who never gets better and never dies but keeps coming back for more.

We are one nation, under-medicated, at liberty to produce enough drugs for all!

Drugs Leach Nutrients

Virtually all prescription drugs "rob Peter to pay Paul" by taking nutrients from the body to metabolize the prescribed drug. This depletion stresses and imbalances the internal ecology of the body and its biochemical processes, potentially impairing health in new ways.[342]

As presented in Chapter 2, drugs undermine the absorption of nutrients from food.[343] Antibiotics for example, destroy both good and bad intestinal tract bacteria, undermining the ability to metabolize and absorb food nutrients. Drugs that inhibit stomach acids significantly decrease absorption of vitamin B-12, one of the primary vitamins needed to prevent anemia. Inhibiting stomach acids increases the chance of developing pneumonia. Many of the prescribed medications on the market deplete nutrients. They include antibiotics, antidepressants, anti-inflammatory, blood pressure medications, cholesterol-lowering drugs, estrogen, and tranquilizers all can strip valuable vitamins and minerals from the body. When any of these drugs are combined, the risk of anemia increases.

Many drugs deplete the body of nutrients and imbalance the internal life of the gut, thereby inducing disease. Blood tests reveal significantly lower serum levels of critical nutrients like alpha-tocopherol, beta-carotene, potassium and co-enzyme Q-10 among patients taking specific drugs such as statin drugs to lower cholesterol. These low levels are associated with a greater susceptibility to disease.

Drugs Produce Side-Effects

Prescription and over-the-counter drugs often produce results other than those intended or desired.[344] Adverse reactions are both common and costly. Some reactions are minor while others are serious, requiring another visit to the doctor, the emergency room, the hospital, a long-term care facility or even death as shown in Table 2.1 in Chapter 2. Adverse drug reactions requiring hospitalization account for one in every 20 admissions. The additional total cost of adverse drug reactions was $177 billion in 2000.[345]

With well over 3 billion prescriptions filled in the US in 2002, tens of millions of patients suffer from drug side-effects each year. One out of every four people taking prescription drugs experiences adverse side-effects according to a 2003 article in the *New England Journal of Medicine*. The use of four prescription drugs taken simultaneously ensures a drug interaction. Though many side-effects are only a minor inconvenience, many are catastrophic, causing nearly 200,000 deaths each year, the third leading cause of death in the US.[346]

For every 100 admissions to the hospital, seven patients suffer hard-to-foresee adverse drug reactions and another three suffer outright drug mistakes. This translates into 3.6 million drug misadventures a year.[347]

Three types of widely used drugs pose the highest risk of side effects. These drugs are: selective serotonin-reuptake inhibitors or SSRIs; beta blockers; and non-steroidal anti-inflammatory drugs or NSAIDs such as ibuprofen. Both NSAIDs and SSRIs were among the most frequently prescribed drugs during doctor visits in 2002.

Selective serotonin-reuptake inhibitors (SSRI), such as Prozac and Zoloft, are used to treat depression. From 1995 to 2002 antidepressant use among adults increased by 48 percent, and during this same time period use increased by 124 percent for children.[348] The side effects of SSRIs commonly include nausea, headache, nervousness, insomnia, fatigue and sexual dysfunction. When directly questioned by a physician, 60 percent of adult patients taking an SSRI reported experiencing sexual dysfunction—decreased libido, delayed ejaculation and difficulty achieving orgasm.[349] One in four males with erectile dysfunction developed this condition from using prescription drugs.

Beta-blockers such as Inderal and Lopressor are prescribed to treat hypertension, congestive heart failure and abnormal heart rhythms. Beta-blockers mask the signs and symptoms of hypoglycemia and prolong it. Patients complain of extreme tiredness, fatigue and mental "clouding" with beta-blockers.

Ulceration develops in up to one in every four traditional NSAID user, causing more than 107,000 hospitalizations and 16,500 deaths per year in the U.S.

Non-steroidal anti-inflammatory drugs (NSAIDs), such as aspirin and ibuprofen products, are used to treat joint pain and headaches.[350] From 1995 to 2002, NSAID use grew by 10 percent. NSAIDs are the most problematic because they are available without a prescription and are known to cause serious liver and kidney impairment, painful gastrointestinal conditions like ulcers and bleeding and an increased risk of hypertension. Ulceration develops in up to one in every four traditional NSAID users, causing more than 107,000 hospitalizations and 16,500 deaths per year in the U.S. NSAID-induced gastro-intestinal complications cost approximately $4 billion a year.

The right balance of risk and benefit is difficult to strike for many of the heavily promoted drugs that treat common, persistent, daily life conditions: anti-inflammatories, antacids, and pills for allergy, depression, premenstrual problems, waning sexual powers and impulsiveness in children. *Americans are taking far too many drugs for dubious or exaggerated ailments* declares Marcia Angell, MD, former editor of the *New England Journal of Medicine* and author of *The Truth About the Drug Companies.*

Summary

Many of our institutional practices in America undermine health. The point is not that people should never take prescription drugs or eat French fries. Nor should our economic institutions be turned upside down to eliminate all sources of economic and job insecurity. But we should not ignore those aspects of our way-of-life that undermine health with stress, dangerous drugs and poor nutrition. Nor should we ignore the institutionalized obstacles to healthy choices. We cannot expect people to ignore all the temptations and restraints created by their social and economic environment. A quick fix rarely enhances health. Speed kills.

Health is a matter of public policy as well as an individual private choice. Surely, if we are to improve eating habits of Americans we must encourage the food processing and fast food industries to offer more healthful products. One step in this direction would be a law requiring fast food establishments to print the calorie and fat content of each item on their menus next to the item's description and price. Consumers must also be educated and enabled to choose the more healthful items. Similarly, if people are to exercise routinely, cities must be designed with walking and bicycling in mind. Employers also have a role to play by motivating healthier eating habits, programs for stress management and exercise. If healthier habits are encouraged through organizational arrangements and designs, fewer people will develop chronic diseases and disease care expenses. Medical care expenses can be lowered.

Increased income security, exercise, eating habits, and stress management must be built-into our institutions. Taming today's "turbo-capitalism" along with redesigning transportation systems to enhance health require long term strategic thinking and reengineering.

More than education is needed to improve health. Chapter 6 suggests a variety of tax and other financial incentives for food producers and consumers alike, incentives that reward the production and consumption of more healthful foods.

There are counter trends seeking to combat unhealthy consequences discussed in this chapter. The complementary and alternative health movement is one response to the dependence on disease care. The "slow-food" movement arose in response to the fast food movement, the ecological movement and shift toward "voluntary simplicity" and "naturalism." Another is the rise of small self-help groups. Self-help groups counteract the dependency on medical experts and the erosion of social support system at work in our society.

CHAPTER 6.
BUILDING THE FOUNDATION FOR HEALTH PROMOTION

Early to bed and early to rise, makes a man healthy, wealthy and wise.
Benjamin Franklin

A man traveling across the country in a hot air balloon realized he was lost. Spotting a man at work in a field, he lowered his balloon and called out *"Where am I?"* The man on the ground answered *"You're in a hot air balloon about 30 feet above ground."* The man in the balloon yelled down *"You sound like a scientist."* *"I am, but how did you know?"* asked the man on the ground. The balloonist answered *"I know because what you've told me is technically correct, but of no use to me."* The scientist on the ground answered *"You sound like a policy maker."* The balloonist in the air responded *"I am a policy maker, but how did you know?"* The scientist on the ground replied *"I know because you are too high above the ground to know where you are, where you're going and you're blaming me for being lost."*[351]

This story, told by US Surgeon General David Satcher, illustrates the big gap between research on health and health care policy. Scientists study treatment of disease and prevention, but their studies do not necessarily result in health improvements. Public health policy seeks to change unhealthy behaviors to improve health and reduce costs, but few changes occur and the costs only increase.

The Center for Practical Health Reform documents the waste and inefficiency resulting from treatment of preventable medical conditions after the fact with expensive drugs that merely mask symptoms.[352] Our medical system swallows one out of every seven dollars in the American economy and consumes a larger share every year. Yet, our "healthcare system" operates without a health orientation. Medical insurance policies are based on outdated risk models and without incentives to control escalating costs. Consumers are insulated from the costly consequences of their lifestyle choices as they clamor for unlimited services. None of the above parties accepts responsibility for the waste and inefficiency they each contribute.

Our "healthcare system" operates without a health orientation.

This chapter examines the big shift away from treating disease after it occurs toward preventing disease and promoting health. This shift is being forged by political and business leaders who are using incentives to change unhealthy behaviors. The rising cost of chronic illness is inspiring the creation of programs for identifying health risks and promoting healthy change. Taken together, these programs are building the foundation for health promotion.

Many political and business leaders recognize the importance of health promotion. The Secretary of Health and Human Services, Tommy Thompson, for example, recently stated: *I am willing to consider the unconventional to...get Americans to take better care of their health. This may wind up as tax breaks for people who stay in shape.* Shifting the focus from a disease care to a health promotion system, Thompson launched a new $20 million dollar program in 2002, called Healthy Communities to support community-based measures for lifestyle changes.[353] He pointed to a debilitating cluster of health problems: the rising incidence of chronic illness, the obesity epidemic, over-reliance on prescription drugs, the skyrocketing costs of high-tech medical treatment and the growing number of deaths due to drug reactions and mistakes in the hospital.

Health promotion springs from the simple truth that most disease, including as much as 89 percent of chronic disease, is preventable and others can be postponed through changes in lifestyle.[354] Health promotion improves both quality of life and longevity. By promoting health, we avert diseases, prolong life[355] and shorten the time and severity of disability. Healthy habits compress chronic conditions into a shorter time period near the end of life so one can experience quality of life until they die. The financial payoff for a healthy lifestyle is impressive. Enriching health can reduce the amount now spent on treating diseases by more than 50 percent.[356]

> By promoting health, we avert diseases, prolong life and shorten the time and severity of disability. Healthy habits compress chronic conditions into a shorter time period near the end of life so one can experience quality of life until they die.

Financial Benefits of Health Promotion

Smoking

Smoking kills 440,000 Americans each year. Smokers consume a large percentage of the total medical care expenditures ($75 billion in 2004) each year in the United States.[357] On average, men who smoke shorten their lives 13.2 years and female smokers lose 14.5 years.[358]

Each person who quits smoking reduces medical care expenditures by hundreds of thousands of dollars. This is a large return for the relatively modest cost of $1600 per person for most smoking cessation programs.[359] Other programs that reduce exposure to cigarette smoke can also generate big savings from modest investments. The *Community Guide* found that restrictions that eliminate second-hand smoke in nonresidential buildings bring a net benefit of $42 to $78 billion nationwide.[360] Cigarette smoking presents a direct risk for lung, throat and mouth cancers along with increasing the risk for hypertension, heart disease and stroke.

Obesity

Americans' extra weight and obesity costs the country $117 billion annually in medical bills and related costs such as reduced productivity, increased absenteeism and higher medical and disability insurance premiums.[361] In the last 20 years, obesity rates increased by more than 60 percent among adults, raising hospital costs threefold from 1979 to 2000 according to the CDC. Annual spending on medical care for the overweight is approaching the level spent on smokers.[362] Obesity alone causes over 330,000 deaths a year in America.[363]

A group of large employers (The National Business Group on Health) created the Institute on Cost and Health Effects of Obesity and announced a campaign to encourage overweight workers to slim down as a way of improving both their personal health and their corporation's bottom line.[364] In 2003, the Institute released its first tool-kit for employers, highlighting the best practices and strategies in workplace weight management.

Promoting health brings a return on investment of over five dollars for each dollar invested and that is a 500 percent return![365] Health promotion avoids huge disease-care expenditures. Table 6.1 summarizes the results of cost saving programs that reduce impairing conditions such as alcohol abuse, arthritis, birth defects, diabetes, heart disease, hypertension, obesity and stress.

Table 6.1 Promoting Health and Savings Money

- Each $1 spent on diabetes outpatient education saves $2 to $3 in hospitalization costs.

- The cost of preventing one cavity through water fluoridation is about $4 compared to $64 for a dental restoration.

- For every $1 spent on preconception programs for women with preexisting diabetes, $1.86 can be saved by preventing birth defects among their offspring.

- Participants in arthritis self-help courses experienced 18 percent reduction in pain at a savings of $267 in medical care costs per-person over 4 years.[366]

- Hysterectomy patients who used guided imagery prior to surgery compared to those not using guided imagery experienced less anxiety and had 4.5 percent lower hospital charges; they also had 8.4 percent lower pharmacy charges ($18 saves $654 per participating member, or a $1:37 ratio)[367]

- A worker-based committee, in conjunction with General Motors, promoted a screening for alcohol problems, incorporated into a larger program that provided a cardiovascular health education with risk assessment and confidential counseling about heart disease risks; 60 percent of the work force participated. After the program, 42 percent of the plant's at-risk drinkers became "safer level" drinkers and nearly 90 percent of employees with high health risks showed improvement three years later. GM's medical costs dropped 13 percent, or $453 per employee.[368]

- Smoking cessation programs bring a return on investment of $6.70 for every $1.[369]

- Body massage reduces cost of treatment of patients with traumatic spinal pain by 20 percent compared to conventional treatment.[370]

- The five-year new savings resulting from adults over 65 taking a daily multivitamin is $1.6 billion.[371]

- Dean Ornish's program for reversing heart disease with a low-fat diet, exercise, stress management and group support saves over $17,000 per enrollee for a return of over $3 for $1 invested.

Shifting Toward Health Promotion

Over fifty percent of what causes the onset of chronic disease comes from lifestyle behaviors, with environmental factors and genetics each explaining 20 additional percent increase, while access to medical care services explains less than 10 percent. One's DNA is not one's destiny when it comes to disease.[372] Personal choices are twice as important in explaining the onset of chronic disease.

The US Preventive Services Task Force summarized the conceptual foundation for health promotion over 20 years ago when they asserted:

- Individual choices and behaviors are central to reducing death and disease.
- Individuals must assume greater responsibility for their own health to be healthy.
- Preventive services should be integrated with disease care services.
- Improving health relies more on patient education and counseling than on diagnostic testing. [373]

In the 1980s the CDC started pushing prevention and health promotion,[374] with research evidence to support the shift toward health enrichment.[375] They focused on the causes of disease in the population, their environmental context and predisposing personal factors with an epidemiological approach. Their research pushed medical intervention toward disease prevention and health promotion, but organized medicine and most physicians resisted.

Two epidemiologists at the CDC examined the ten most common causes of death and disease. While the "official" causes of death were heart disease, cancer, stroke and chronic obstructive pulmonary disease, the actual causes were primarily smoking, diet, lack of exercise and stress. The ten most common causes of death are largely preventable, yet medical practice simply treats diseases after their onset rather than helping prevent them by treating their behavioral causes. These diseases are preventable if people's unhealthy habits are identified, treated and changed. If individuals are to remain healthy, they often need help with identifying unhealthy behaviors and social support for change to occur. Drugs and surgery are expensive options and involve an increased risk of mistakes and side effects that might kill them.

Only three percent of adult Americans follow all four key health goals of exercising regularly, maintaining proper body weight, eating fruits and vegetables (five or more servings each day) and not smoking. The results seem to be more positive when examining each health goal separately: 77 percent don't smoke, 40 percent maintain proper body weight, 23 percent eat five daily servings of fruits and vegetables and 22 percent exercise regularly.[376]

We must create an environment and a set of incentives where it's easier to follow these guidelines. You can't make people adopt healthy habits. For example John Q had emphysema and required oxygen from a tank. One evening he accidentally set his oxygen tube and himself on fire while lighting a cigarette. Even this did not convince him to quit smoking!

The CDC, the Department of Health and Human Services and alliances of large employers are all targeting lifestyle behaviors that cause chronic disease so as to prevent chronic diseases from developing and bankrupting the system with mounting medical care costs. This research shifts the emphasis toward earlier intervention with smoking cessation, exercise, weight-loss and alcohol abuse programs.

A first step toward health is enhanced by the creation of data sets such as:

- Behavioral Risk Factor Surveillance System (BRFSS),
- Health Enhancement Research Organization (HERO),
- Health Plan Employer Data and Information Set (HEDIS)
- US Department of Health and Human Services (HHS), a 2-year demonstration project.

The Behavioral Risk Factor Surveillance System (BRFSS) was developed in the 1980s by the Center for Disease Control and Prevention, working with state health agencies.[377] The BRFSS is the primary source of scientific data on risk behaviors that endanger health, providing information that enables health promoters to design programs for helping people change their disease-inducing habits. Planners use BRFSS data to compare state and city health promotion programs over time within the same program. These data were used in monitoring the nation's progress toward the goals set by Healthy People for the years 1990, 2000 and 2010. A related program, funded by the 107th

Congress, called the Environmental Public Health Tracking Grant, identifies where and when chronic diseases will occur and links them to possible environmental and individual choice factors.[378] Since the BRFSS was developed, over 50 other risk assessment instruments have been developed, many for use in the public sector, giving rise to the "modern era" of risk assessment in the early 1990s.

The Health Enhancement Research Organization (HERO) arose in 1993 as an alliance of thirteen large employers. HERO is a consortium of industrial and scientific experts committed to evaluating the cost-effectiveness of health promotion programs. With over 46,000 employees in its database, the consortium tracks health risk information, biomedical screening, medical plan enrollment, medical use, and cost claims. Many studies are evaluating the effectiveness of preventive and risk reduction programs by using the HERO data set.[379]

The Health Plan Employer Data and Information Set (HEDIS) provides a type of standardized performance "report card" that assesses medical insurance plans' effectiveness for employers to use in their purchasing decisions. HEDIS, developed by The National Committee for Quality Assurance (NCQA) in the mid 1990s, compares the performance and quality of managed care plans in the following areas:

- plan's use of best practices,
- plan's usage of preventive and well care services, and
- level of patient satisfaction with the plan.

Nine out of ten medical plans in 1999 measured their performance using HEDIS data and more than half the nation's HMOs participated in HEDIS. Care plans with higher HEDIS scores are more effective in keeping workers and their families healthy, thus reducing sick days and disability.

The US Department of Health and Human Services (HHS) in February 2003 authorized a 2-year demonstration project to test a new coding system (the ABC codes will be discussed more fully in Chapter 7) for billing the preventive and health promotion services of CAM and nursing services. This enables CAM therapies to be compared on their quality and cost-effectiveness with conventional medical approaches when treating patients of comparable age and risk factors. This also enables research on quality and cost comparisons by highlighting best practices among all approaches to care, not just disease-based/conventional medical care.[380]

The development of HEDIS, HERO and HHS demonstration project facilitates the study of treatment costs for patients with different risk factors and lifestyle behaviors over time. By identifying the incidence of different chronic diseases, this will facilitate cost effective health promotion programs so as to counter unhealthy behaviors.[381] These data sets are fostering health promotion as they document the cost effectiveness of CAM as a health enhancing set of therapies.

Research on Health Promotion

A 3-year study of over 8,000 workers compared the effect of a high-risk health promotion program on medical care costs of those who participated and those who did not. At the outset of the study, medical expenditures were nearly identical (two percent apart) but after three years, the medical care costs were nearly one third higher for those not participating in the health promotion program; those promoting health had significantly lower medical costs ($392 per person), when compared to those not participating. Participants had lower inpatient costs, fewer hospital admissions, and fewer hospital days of care when compared with non participants.[382]

The Healthy Foundation conducted a scientific study in 40 states to determine the impact of vitamin intake on at-risk youth and their school performance. Half of all parents participating reported that their children were sick less often since taking daily vitamins. One third said their children earned higher grades. More than 20 percent experienced a marked improvement in energy, appetites and self-image.[383]

Research is tracking the rise in screening services and health promotion programs.[384] One dramatic example of countering behavioral causes is Dean Ornish's alternative by-pass plan for heart disease. After 25 years of research, Dean Ornish's Preventive Medicine Research Institute in Sausalito, California offers people with cardiovascular disease an alternative to surgery by using diet, exercise, group support and stress management. Without treatment, over three fourths of those selected for treatment would experience a cardiac event within a year.[385] The Ornish program greatly reduces the number of such events, saving lives as well as money—more than $17,000 per participant in averted high-cost invasive procedures, hospital bills and cardiac rehabilitation.

Errors: Over Treatment—Under Assessment

The search for improved quality generally focuses on three measurable problems: errors, over treatment,[386] and under assessment.[387] The use and improvement of these measures will improve the quality of health care. The focus here is primarily with under assessment which is the failure to screen for risk factors and to promote health. I have previously discussed the errors and over treatment.

The most comprehensive study on preventive care included nearly 7,000 adults in 12 metropolitan areas: they reviewed medical records and rated preventive care and management of 30 common medical conditions.[388] Evaluating 439 clinical indicators of care for conditions such as asthma, diabetes, colorectal cancer, heart disease and pneumonia, researchers found that adults were not receiving recommended care nearly half the time. People with diabetes received 45 percent of the health maintenance basics and only 25 percent of them had their blood sugar levels measured regularly. Patients with coronary artery disease received 68 percent of recommended care, while only 45 percent of heart attack patients got medications to reduce their risk of another attack. On average, patients received less than optimally recommended care for their conditions: pneumonia patients received 39 percent of the recommended care, colorectal cancer patients received 54 percent, and patients with high blood pressure received 65 percent. Overall, patients received general preventive care 55 percent of the time; for acute and chronic conditions, they received recommended care 54-56 percent of the time as shown in Table 6.2.[389]

Table 6.2 Percentage of Patients Receiving Recommended Care for Acute, Chronic and Preventive Care

Diseased Condition	Recommended Care
Acute	53.5%
Chronic	56.0%
Preventive care	55.0%

Another national survey in 2000 found similar results. Individuals with a diagnosed chronic illness received risk reduction interventions only half the time for such behaviors as smoking, alcohol abuse, and lack of exercise.[390] Half of these patients surveyed didn't receive condition-specific tests. Of patients with coronary heart disease, one in four still smoked, and only half said they had been advised by their doctor to quit smoking. Nearly four in ten people with chronic lung disease or emphysema still smoke, as do nearly one in four with asthma, and nearly one in five with diabetes.[391] Four in ten individuals with hypertension claim they were not advised to limit salt intake or control their weight; four in ten suffering from diabetes were still confused about how to manage their illness and half were uncertain about eating right.[392] Among individuals suffering from depression, nearly six in ten were not treated at all, while one in five received ineffective treatment.[393] Currently, preventive care is a "hit and miss" service. While screening and preventive care is improving within medical care plans, much room for improvement exists.

Medical care improved in 2001 by using more preventive services according to the *State of Managed Care Quality Report: 2003* from the National Committee for Quality Assurance. They used audited data on medical care provided by 273 commercial organizations that collectively cover 63.3 million lives. The report gauges medical care delivered against treatment protocols that are widely considered best practice for specific types of patients. Screening rates for cervical cancer and cholesterol were up significantly, as was the percentage of patients treated for high blood pressure. Nine out of 10 heart patients received beta-blocker treatment, thereby helping prevent a second heart attack.

This shift toward health promotion is resulting from the efforts of political and business leaders to craft programs for motivating healthier choices. Political leaders are seeking cost reductions associated with public (Medicare and Medicaid) and private sector medical costs. Large corporate business leaders seek to lower their medical insurance costs so as to remain internationally competitive. The motives of the leaders across sectors differ, but all seek a medical care system that produces healthier outcomes (preventing chronic disease and disability) at affordable prices.

Political Leaders Seek To Reduce Costs

The federal government pays for over 40 percent of all medical care delivered to patients in the United States through Medicaid, Medicare, the military and other local, state and federal employees. Managed care and other recent reforms have increased the overall efficiency of the system because they managed cost more than medical care. But with medical costs on the rise again, it appears that popular opposition to the controls within managed care limits the ability to significantly contain the surge in the demand for care.

Realizing the necessity to control costs, elected officials and policy specialists are turning to health promotion as a likely solution to the emerging funding crisis. In a 2001 survey of the US Congress, 65 percent of the respondents said that health promotion programs are a "very high" priority. Eighty percent felt funding for health promotion and disease prevention should at least double by 2003.[394]

Cross-sectional surveys of Americans show greater support for health promotion relative to finding new treatments for disease:

- 44 percent think research on preventing disease is more valuable than research on curing.
- 32 percent feel research on curing and treating disease is more important than promoting health.
- 20 percent believe they are equally important.[395]

Health promotion for the elderly has been an important priority of the federal government as early as 1995 when the White House

Conference on Aging proposed several health promotion programs. The Conference on Aging proposed that older adults take a daily multivitamin within an insurance framework because the savings to the system are greater than the cost of providing the benefit. The five-year estimate of savings is approximately $1.6 billion relative to the risk of medical costs of $3.9 billion for coronary artery disease, hip fractures and lower immune function as compared to the expense of $924 million. A daily multi-vitamin could help many avoid hospitalization, nursing home stays, and home health services for infections.[396]

The cost of medical care is the number one issue for Americans, declared Tommy Thompson, then Secretary of the Department of Health and Human Services (HHS) back in 2003. Secretary Thompson incorporated many health promotion goals as official policies of his 12 HHS agencies. *We spend $270 billion a year to treat diabetes, obesity and the effects of tobacco use. Yet all three conditions can be controlled and handled by individuals*, Thompson declared. He called on private insurers to promote healthy lifestyles among their members with incentives and programs.[397]

The Secretary of HHS used his position as a "bully-pulpit" to admonish business leaders to focus on health promotion in 2003. In his report, *The Impact of Poor Health on Businesses,* he states: *More businesses need to recognize that poor health means lower productivity and higher medical insurance costs. Smart business leaders increasingly are finding that it is the right decision to promote health education, physical activity and preventive benefits in the workplace.*

Secretary Thompson advocates health promotion. As former governor of Wisconsin, he was an early advocate of reforming welfare and the culture of dependency. Now he seeks similar change in the culture of dependency on doctors, drugs and the entitlement to health insurance without personal responsibility. In a 2002 speech given in Chicago, Thompson called medical care plans wrong for not doing more to promote health before expensive maladies develop. He appealed to physicians and medical insurance plans to create incentives for more healthy life styles.[398]

Passage of The National Health Promotion Resolution in 2002 by both Congressional bodies (H.RES.115 & S.CON.RES.11) clearly suggests that the momentum for health promotion grows. Advanced by a nonpartisan coalition of 400 health scientists, health providers, association representatives and employers, The National Health Promotion resolution is designed: (1) to enhance the scientific base required for effectively promoting health and preventing disease; and (2) to encourage the development of strategies to integrate health promotion programs into national policy. The ultimate goal is to make health promotion an integral part of American society in schools, workplaces, families and communities.

The Health Promotion Advocate, a nonpartisan group, introduced the Healthy Lifestyles and Prevention (HELP) Act in 04. This legislation is the first ever comprehensive wellness and disease prevention legislation to focus attention on wellness and disease prevention. Many new health-related initiatives were funded in the omnibus appropriations bill for the following programs in 2005:

- research at the National Institutes of Health into the causes and cures of obesity
- programs that address nutrition, physical activity and obesity
- tobacco prevention and cessation activities
- public health research at the CDC
- implementation of the YMCA's new Activate America initiative for developing community-wide approaches to wellness and disease prevention.

This legislation helps reorient our approach to health care in America—to reorient it towards prevention, wellness and self care. When it comes to helping people stay healthy, we fall woefully short. We don't have a health care system in America; we have a 'disease care' system. It costs us dearly both in terms of health care costs and premature deaths.

Supporters of CAM in the 2001 US Congress formed the bipartisan Complementary and Alternative Medicine and Natural Foods

(CAMNF) Caucus to elevate CAM issues. Leadership was shared by Representatives Dan Burton (R-IN), and Dennis Kucinich (D-OH) and Senators Tom Harkin (D-IA) and Orrin Hatch (R-UT). The caucus's mission is to learn about CAM practices and their role in improving the health of Americans.

School boards in many towns and cities are beginning to reverse the troubling trend of placing vending machines in schools to raise money. These have facilitated the sale of soda and other junk foods to teenagers, who often substitute cokes and chips for a healthy lunch. School boards are also recommending that meals be made more nutritious. Presently, many are heavily laden with fat and calories.

The CDC is also active in the drive to increase our physical activity. It has developed the Active Community Environments Initiative in which CDC partners with communities, agencies, and nonprofits to promote the development of accessible recreation facilities. The following exemplify their activities:

- A partnership with the National Park Service's Rivers, Trails, and Conservation Assistance Program to promote the development and use of neighborhood parks and recreation facilities,
- The development of a guidebook for public health practitioners to use in partnering with transportation and city-planning organizations to promote walking, cycling and neighborhood recreation facilities,
- CDC's Kids Walk-to-School Program encourages children to walk to and from school in groups accompanied by adults, and
- The Greenstyles Survey, developed by CDC and EPA, assesses the effects of environmental, social and personal variables on walking and cycling.

Examples of a few reforms to encourage health promotion and more vigorous lifestyles include:

- Local governments are passing zoning rules requiring sidewalks in residential and commercial areas in the suburbs and the design of "walk-friendly" commercial and residential projects. For example, parking lots are placed on the edge of downtown areas to encourage walking to stores and offices.
- School boards are beginning to reverse the troubling trend of placing vending machines in schools to raise money that have facilitated the sale of soda and other junk foods to teenagers. School boards are also recommending that meals be made more nutritious than most of the present foods which are heavily laden with saturated fats.

Incentives to Encourage Health Responsibility

The American lifestyle undermines health on many fronts. Reports of a growing debacle are disturbing—fewer than one quarter of our schools require physical education; growing numbers of money-starved school districts contract with soft drink companies to make non-nutritional soft drinks readily available in schools for a percentage of dollars returned to the school district; children spend on average 22 hours per week watching TV, more hours than getting physical exercise; 15 percent of our children are obese along with 20 percent of our adults. More than six out of ten adults are overweight and the same numbers fail to exercise enough for good health.

Moderate physical activity enhances health, vitality, mood, creativity and longevity. Exercise is central to promoting health and averting disease and disability. Exercise reduces serum low-density lipoproteins and glucose; it reduces stress effects and improves muscle mass, metabolic rate and respiratory efficiency. *Higher levels of activity protect against functional decline and postpone disability approximately by 7.75 years* as noted in chapter 2.[399]

Motivating people to walk, ride a bike, swim and engage in any physical activity will reduce medical care expenditures. Researchers at the CDC compared medical care expenditures of the physically active with the inactive. People who exercise for 30 minutes three times per week can dramatically lower overall spending for medical care. The physically active individuals consumed $865 dollars less care per person each year than their inactive counterparts. They had fewer hospital stays, fewer physician visits and used less medication. The greatest difference in direct medical costs was among women 55 and older. It was estimated in 2000 if all inactive American adults took up physical activity, the nation could save $76.6 billion dollars.[400] Medical insurance companies can improve health by building incentives into their insurance packages that encourage people to participate in programs designed to enrich health (e.g., programs for smoking cessation, exercise, stress management and weight loss). More medical insurance plans are offering financial incentives to promote physical activity among their members. Most people want to add life to years, not just years to life. Half of the medical plans offer discounted health club memberships and/or health education classes.[401] The employees who adopt healthy lifestyles could be rewarded with a reduction in their share of the insurance premium, the employer's cost of the premium for the employee could be lowered, or both could see reduced costs. To encourage more healthy lifestyles, some corporate employers are motivating employees to reduce their health risk by discounting their medical insurance premiums if they quit cigarettes or lose weight. If employers can't charge people extra for their unhealthy habits, they can reward those who reduce their health risks.[402]

Most people want to add life to years, not just years to life.

For health promotion to succeed, government legislation must fix a key problem in medical insurance membership that undermines the profitability of health promotion—the high turnover rates each year in a medical plan. The current system permits individuals to change insurance plans every year and that undermines continuity of care and also longer-term health promotion efforts. High turnover rates in medical insurance membership encourage a short-term orientation that leaves patients without health promotion programs.[403] A typical commercial medical plan in the 1990s experienced turnover rates of 24 percent a year.[404] With a quarter of their membership leaving every year, insurance/managed care organizations will not invest in promoting healthy lifestyles.[405] Why offer, for example, smoking cessation as a free benefit when so many members will leave the care plan in the next few years? While investments in promoting health save money in the long run, they rarely yield savings in one or two years. Some health promotion efforts only materialize after one year, some after two years, others after three years, and some not until more than a decade. Medical insurance companies are unwilling to spend money to prevent future heart attacks for enrollees who may leave the plan the next year before they realize any benefit.

Lengthening the enrollment time period would encourage long-term investment in health promotion and reduce future disease-care costs. Federal legislation for a mandatory 3 to 5 year minimum enrollment period would encourage more long-term strategic planning and health promotion as an investment.[406]

Business Initiatives: Health Promotion and Managed Care

Larger employers have become prime supporters of the shift to health promotion because most American companies provide medical care insurance for their employees. Two out of three Americans under 65 get their medical insurance through their employer which translates to 163 million Americans get coverage at the workplace.[407] Medical benefit spending accounted for 42 percent of total compensation in 2002, up from 26.6 percent in 1980. Medical care has become a critical and costly business issue.[408]

> Medical benefit spending accounted for 42 percent of total compensation in 2002.

Medical care costs are spiraling out of control.[409] With an aging population and an increase in chronic disease, employers are being hit with run away medical costs. Not surprisingly, employers in the 1990s initiated cost containment strategies by turning to health promotion and case management of those employees most at risk.[410] In the late 1980s, Lee Iacocca wrote: *The price of a new car at Chrysler includes more than wages and more than steel, rubber, and glass.... Hidden in there is the price of employee health-care costs, run-*

ning about $600 a car.[411] The employee medical cost per car rose to $1,000 in 1992 as he decried at a shareholder's meeting: *Health-care costs are bleeding us white.... That's nearly three times what some of our competitors [in other countries] have to pay! So how can we be competitive?*[412] In 2004, the cost of employee insurance added $1,300 onto an average mid-size car.[413] General Motors spent $5.6 billion on 1.1 million workers and retirees which added $1,500 to their vehicles in 2004.

Employers are scrutinizing the return they get on the cost of their medical insurance plan. They are requiring that medical care insurance include more preventive regimes. The cost of a medical care plan *per se* is not the only concern to employers. The health and vigor of the workforce contributes most to the bottom line.[414] As Helen Darling, President of the Washington Business Group on Health said:

> *Few business decisions are worse than buying poor quality medical care, because the indirect costs of poor care go beyond just the premiums. First, you pay the premium, then you pay to replace workers when they get sick, and then you pay a third time when productivity drops.*

More employers are pushing for health promotion and case management. When the move toward health promotion began in the 1990s, the largest employers led the charge, motivated by the financial "bottom line." Poor health not only costs more in direct medical care expenditures and future insurance premiums, poor health also increases indirect costs via lower productivity, higher absenteeism and replacement costs. Direct medical costs represent only about one-third to one-half of the total cost of poor health, with the remaining indirect costs resulting from lower productivity, more sick days and training replacements, as shown in Figure 6.1.[415] Because chronic diseases lower the productivity of 90 million adult Americans, employers are adopting health promotion and disease management.[416]

Figure 6.1   Distribution of Total Costs of Poor Health to Companies

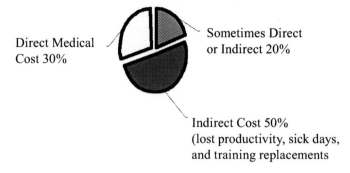

Direct Medical
Cost 30%

Sometimes Direct
or Indirect 20%

Indirect Cost 50%
(lost productivity, sick days,
and training replacements

Employers are seeking cost effective ways to help their employees improve their health and fitness. Employers gain financially and strategically by promoting health in several ways:

- Promoting health reduces overall costs in the long run according to quality improvement studies. Preventing problems is cheaper than fixing them after they arise so they "build quality in."[417]
- Healthy workers are more productive and less costly with fewer absences, fewer disabilities and fewer retraining costs to replace disabled workers.
- Employers can create a culture of health in the workplace by using incentives within a stable network of relationships. If for example a low fat menu is wanted in the cafeteria, the employer can create it. Employers can choose to hire only nonsmokers and, in some states, can refuse to hire the overweight.

Linking employee health and well being to organizational outcomes (productivity, absenteeism and sick-day expenses) is the vision of "American's Healthiest Companies," an elite group of 146 awardees. The management of these companies believes that cultivating health must become "built into" their corporate culture.[418] Employers invest in health as they institute wellness programs that cultivate or maintain health. The return on investment in terms of improved worker health and productivity reduces total costs for poor health by as much as 10 to1.

Employers are taking a more strategic approach to employee health by lengthening their planning cycles of medical care needs over longer time-periods.[419] Employers also are viewing medical insurance plans as both an expense as well as an investment in worker productivity.

Medical insurance plans with the lowest unit-price don't necessarily deliver the lowest-priced total performance. Short-term emphasis on the lowest cost often leads to costly long-term consequences as was discovered in a six-year study of 19 care systems in a Minnesota business coalition. The lowest unit price resulted in being more costly because prevention and screening were not used. The direct medical cost increased due to actual use and payout by employers, along with higher indirect costs of absenteeism and lowered productivity. The short-term unit price is like a lure that entices the bite, but reeling in the best buy requires finding a plan with a longer-term, outcome-based plan for lowering the total cost of poor health.[420]

Ninety-five percent of the largest corporations offered some form of health promotion in 2002, with nearly half using financial incentives and disincentives to encourage employee behavioral change.[421] A 2005 survey revealed that 90 percent of companies now have lifestyle incentive programs within their organizations or have plans to implement in the future.[422] Yet, wellness programs only comprise one to two percent of a company's medical care benefit package. While such programs may initially involve a higher direct cost, indirect costs shrink over time. Companies can employ a variety of insurance-related [423] and more proactive, outreach strategies to keep costs manageable.[424]

Consumer-directed health plans (CDHPs) are a top concern for employers seeking to lower their premiums. Nearly four in ten employers plan to add CDHPs to their benefits packages in the next two years and more than half are looking to their current carrier to provide the product according to the 2005 Benefits Strategy and Technology Study. More than half of employers said that an integrated health spending account and rollover provisions for employees' health savings accounts were extremely important.[425] The number of large firms offering health savings accounts has grown dramatically since 2004 from one in four to one in three in 2005.[426] The number of health saving accounts is projected to top six million by 2008.[427] Another estimate is that the 2.7 million enrollees in 2005 will grow to 12 million by 2007.

Health promotion is a smart policy that contributes to a company's healthy bottom line. Changing an individual employee's behavior is difficult so companies are harnessing two practical strategies for improving the health of their workforce:[428]

- creating cash and non-cash incentives to promote healthy changes,[429] and
- case or disease management to limit demand and promote health.[430]

Creating Incentives to Promote Healthy Changes

Employers are creating a variety of cash and non-cash incentives to promote healthy lifestyle changes for reducing the risk of disease in their employees.[431] Their operating assumption is that employees will change their unhealthy behavior if the right incentives are used. Thus, employers are developing their own health promotion programs and/or buying insurance packages that encourage healthy behaviors for those individuals at risk of disease, e.g., weight loss programs, programs for reversing heart disease,[432] smoking cessation, asthma, lifestyle change buddies and exercise programs for those with Type II Diabetes.[433] Under these incentive programs, individuals who lose excess weight to reduce their risk could pay less for their share of the medical insurance premium. In some plans the employee who adopts a healthy lifestyle is rewarded with a reduced share of their premium. The city of Virginia Beach, for example, offers its school and city employees reimbursements if they enroll in smoking cessation programs. Such programs are cost effective almost immediately, because nonsmokers develop far fewer colds and respiratory infections and miss fewer days of work than smokers.

Programs with incentives to encourage healthy behaviors in their employees are illustrated by Quaker Oats' "Live Well, Be Well" program.[434] Employee participants can earn up to $600 in cash for a flexible benefits account which includes $150 for completing the health risk assessment, and $50 for taking part in the free, on-site health screenings (cholesterol, height/weight, BP, coronary risk profile). In addition, they receive $50 each for pledging to avoid tobacco, refraining from abusing or misusing alcohol or drugs and promising to exercise a minimum of 20 minutes three times a week. This successful incentive program has an 80 percent participation rate, and saves Quaker Oats approximately $2 million per year in medical expenses because many formerly high-risk employees lowered their risk classification and thus the company's premiums.

The Nebraska Health System, an Omaha-based hospital and medical center, uses WellBucks, to motivate employees to adopt healthy choices and goals. By engaging in approved activities—exercise, healthy eating, prevention, screenings, flu shots, blood pressure checks—employees accumulate WellBucks, that can be used for "buying" passes to the zoo or the movies, a $20 gift certificate to a mall, or a paid leave-day. Such rewards, although small, generate large effects—participation rates are 75 percent after ten years of the program's operation.

Northeast Utilities offers a WellAware program to employees and their families to reduce lifestyle-related health risks. The program includes a health-risk assessment and targeted follow-up efforts, such as smoking-cessation counseling and rebates for purchasing smoking-cessation aids. During its first 24 months, the program reduced claims related to lifestyle and behavior choices by $1.4 million.[435]

Many incentive programs are based on measurable goals for employees such as:

- Trigon Blue Cross Blue Shield employees save money on medical-care premiums if they avoid smoking and maintain healthy weight, blood pressure and cholesterol levels.

- Providence Everett Medical Center's "Wellness Challenge" pays eligible employees up to $375 in cash if they meet four of six wellness criteria. These criteria include healthy eating (the five-a-day fruits and vegetables challenge), exercise (12 days per month, accumulating at least 30 minutes per day of some form of exercise or physical activity) and not missing work. Providence's 10-year-old Wellness Challenge averages a 65 percent participation rate. The 10-year return-on-investment rate averages $3.50 on the dollar, an estimated $2 million saved in medical care spending.[436]

Businesses are discovering that managing health risk and promoting health makes sense and yields dollar savings.

Case Management to Control Cost and Promote Health[437]

Most medical insurance claim dollars are spent on relatively few patients with chronic conditions. Since chronic conditions are not managed effectively by most medical plans, these individuals develop new medical problems that can consume mounds of money in additional medical care. Preventing unnecessary and avoidable expenses presents a great opportunity for cost savings. Three fourths of all medical care dollars are used by less than 10 percent of medical plan members.[438] A few large claims consume most of the money spent.[439] Epidemiologist and consultant Bruce Kelley contends that the typical medical plan spends about 97 cents of every claim dollar on treating 15 different conditions. Only three percent of claims dollars are spent on the well or on those at-risk to forestall future expenditures.[440]

> Three fourths of all medical care dollars are used by less than 10 percent of medical plan members.

Seventy percent of disease-care expenditures for workers are preventable according to CDC epidemiological data.[441] Health promotion programs empower individuals with response-abilities. Often they target unhealthy behaviors that cause heart, kidney, lung and Type II Diabetes diseases. Proactive disease management programs identify people most likely to use large amounts of services—usually those with high-cost chronic conditions like heart disease and diabetes. Disease management programs restrain costs by teaching skills for controlling an illness and promoting health.[442] Teaching skills and healthy choices can save money, improve quality of life and increase longevity.[443] When insurance plans educate the chronically ill and monitor their adherence to a prescribed regimen, disease management programs prevent many catastrophic events and their attendant costs. Relatively small outlays of $2,000 to $4,000 per employee can save $40,000 over a three-year period. The return on investment brings over $10 for each dollar invested in case management.[444] Motorola claims they get as high as an eight dollar return for each dollar invested in their program for managing 12 diseases.[445] The caseworker becomes coach and cheerleader.

We spent over $1.8 trillion on medical care in the US in 2004 and 75 percent of that total went to chronic disease care. The annual cost of cardiovascular disease is about $352 billion, for diabetes it is $132 billion, for obesity $117 billion and for smoking more than $75 billion.[446] An estimated 18 million people have diet-induced diabetes nationwide.[447] Each dollar invested in diabetes management brings from $2.30 to over $10 in savings.[448] Table 6.3 illustrates the potential of management programs for improving quality of life for workers and returns on investments for corporations.[449]

Table 6.3 Disease Management Programs

- Disease management for congestive heart failure patients cut total days in the hospital by 36 percent and readmissions by 44 percent
- A pediatric asthma program produced a 400 percent return on investment
- Diabetes management cut annual costs by 12 percent
- Reducing risks saved $53 per employee per year for 1000 employees at GM
- Controlling high serum cholesterol levels of workers with heart disease brought $2 return on investment [450]
- 22 million sick days could be avoided per year if "best practice" were adopted by all providers for just five conditions (depression, diabetes, asthma, heart disease, and hypertension) [451]

Disease management lowers costs by minimizing unnecessary use of medical services through teaching self-care skills or by providing more health-enhancing providers (e.g., a nurse). At present, many patients see a physician for minor illnesses that they could treat effectively at home. Teaching self-care skills reduces the need for many physician visits. A large two-year study demonstrated that a low-cost program for promoting self-care and management could improve health while reducing medical care costs of patients with diverse chronic diseases.[452] Since over one in four (28%) Internet users have participated in on- or off-line behavioral modification programs, disease management programs are using the Web to gain greater adherence to medical regimens.[453]

Patient education also places less strain on the system as it relies on less expensive providers—nurse practitioners, nutritionists, health educators and other CAM providers.[454] Such providers are vital to the success of disease management because the average primary-care physician would need 7.4 hours of every working day to provide patients with all the preventive health services recommended by the federal government, according to researchers at Duke University. Both disease prevention and health promotional services are provided more effectively by CAM practitioners.[455] The increasing use of non-physicians for health promotion services is presented in Chapter 7, Table 7.3.

Psychological illnesses, like depression, also affect productivity. Nearly 15 percent of adult Americans suffer from at least one personality disorder according to a recent article in the *Journal of Clinical Psychiatry*.[456] Nearly ten percent of employees suffer from some form of depression at any given time, yet six out of ten of these individuals go untreated. Nearly 9 out of 10 workers with depression have at least one concurrent physical symptom and nearly half have six or more physical symptoms. Depression costs employers dearly in absenteeism and decreased productivity. Reduced productivity and increasing treatment expenditures for psychological illness cost employers $44 billion a year, according to an article in *The Journal of the American Medical Association*.[457]

Prompted by widespread employer interest, the medical insurance industry added disease management and patient education programs to their medical plans. Half the managed care plans had disease management programs in 2003, rising from virtually none in the early 1990s.[458] For serious chronic diseases, more than three out of four (76%) of managed care plans instituted patient management programs.[459] Teaching enrollees who are at high-risk to care for themselves before they get seriously ill can limit the ballooning of future medical costs. Substantial cost reductions arise from managing diabetes, obesity and high blood pressure.[460] Harvard Pilgrim's chief medical officer estimates that one percent of their enrollees are high-risk patients who consume 25 percent of their medical costs.[461] Harvard Pilgrim hired hundreds of trained nurses to work with high-risk patients and monitor their adherence to treatment regimens. Nurses both educate and motivate the chronically ill, with the result that patients improve, thereby preventing future medical problems. Case management of the chronically ill increases the likelihood of patients improving their diet, exercising, taking medication at the right time and in the correct dosage. Only half the patients with chronic illness on average adhere to their medical regimen resulting in both financial and health consequences.

The federal government is also tapping into disease management programs and counseling services for their cost-saving potential. HHS funded a three-year demonstration project to offer disease management services to Medicare patients with chronic conditions, such as congestive heart disease, diabetes and stroke. Medical providers receive a fixed payment for each beneficiary enrolled in their programs. The Centers for Medicare and Medicaid Services, (CMS) which is overseeing the demonstration project, expects the programs to use evidence-based care, to promote multidisciplinary care, and to improve patient outcomes.[462] Providers can now be reimbursed for prevention services and Medicare coverage has been expanded to pay for nutritional and physical activity counseling and smoking-cessation programs.[463]

The Community Guide helps spread the word about effective programs in demand management and incentives. This new organization provides solutions for employers in (a) negotiating with medical plans, (b) helping employees take an active role in their health at the worksite, and (c) working within local communities to encourage prevention investments by and for the community. These strategies help employers maximize their current investments in medical care and disease prevention.[464]

A model program of collaboration between the public and private sectors is the California WorksWell program for state employees.[465] They began in 1997 with their first of two health risk assessments.[466] They launched a major educational effort, starting with a monthly wellness newsletter followed by seminars on nutrition, exercise, weight management, hypertension, allergy relief, and stress management. They also started a walking program with walking clubs around the state.

A shift toward more health promotion and risk reduction is clearly visible. Health maintenance organizations (HMO) in California in 1996 offered comprehensive preventive care benefits and health-promotion programs. They also reached out to citizens in the community, making health-promotion programs available to more members of the public.[467] More medical care plans are offering financial incentives or programs intended to promote physical activity among their members. Half the medical care plans in a recent survey offered financial incentives for healthy living, such as discounted health club memberships and health education classes. And a fifth of these plans provided grants to support community-based fitness activities.

Some HMOs are forming significant partnerships with public health agencies. These collaborative efforts are often centered on clinical preventive services such as immunization, outreach, education, and HMO-sponsored public health fairs. Even large companies are joining in collaborative efforts to improve medical care delivery within local markets.[468]

Conclusion: The Shift Toward Health Promotion

The American medical care system has been in crisis for over 30 years by specializing in disease care services rather than promoting health and preventing diseases.[469] By treating preventable chronic diseases after they develop with high-tech interventions that merely mask symptoms is wasteful and dangerous. The disease care approach to chronic illness benefits the medical industrial complex more than consumers. The big shift toward health promotion came from researchers, government and business leaders.

- Over 20 years ago, the conceptual foundation for health promotion and the central role of individual involvement in their own health was established. The CDC identified the primary cause for chronic disease was individual behavior—two and one half times more important than both genetics and environmental factors in the onset of such life-style diseases. Health enhancing behaviors lessen disease, prolong life and compress disability time into a shorter period at the end of life. Nearly 90 percent of chronic disease is preventable according to the CDC. By building a health promotion program before the onset of disease, medical care costs can be cut in half. Treating preventable diseases with costly measures that are ineffective is pushing both government and business leaders to shift the focus toward health promotion.

Consumers need more information on their risk factors and social support to change, not symptom suppressing drugs and surgeries. More effort is being given to risk assessment, skill-building and social support for changing lifestyles.

- Large private sector employers are on the front line of pushing medical care from "doctoring disease to promoting health." Because the indirect cost of poor health to the company costs from two to two and one half times more than the direct cost of medical care services, promoting health becomes a cost-saving measure that improves both the worker's health and the company's economic health. By promoting health in their workforce as "quality improvement," employers lower their direct medical cost as well as indirect costs by lowering their unit cost of productivity. This enhances the company's competitiveness in world markets. Most large companies have health risk assessment programs and incentives and disincentives for employees to enroll in smoking cessation, diabetes and stress management, exercise and dietary change for reversing heart disease. Companies are cultivating health so it will become "built-into" their corporate culture.

- Because the government pays for well over 40 percent of the medical care delivered in the US, political leaders are also seeking to reduce medical costs by emphasizing more health promotion as well as case management of workers with expensive chronic diseases. The White House Commission on CAM envisioned an important role for complementary therapies in promoting health. Complementary therapies may be the most effective way of achieving 14 of the 26 major health objectives of Healthy People 2010. CAM therapies are moving into the mainstream as they are being integrated into many clinics around the country as I show in Chapter 7.

We are on the cusp of change in the delivery of care. Strong forces are pushing medical insurance and workers toward health enrichment. America's large employers are providing leadership and incentives to shift from doctoring diseases to promoting health. The prospect of profit and productivity are motivating these changes. Both the employer and worker stand to gain from this new vision and strategy.

CHAPTER 7.
HEALTH ENRICHING THERAPIES
GO MAINSTREAM

The only limit to our realization of tomorrow will be our doubts of today.
Franklin Delano Roosevelt

A bamboo curtain between alternative and conventional medicine is splintering declared George Lundberg MD, then editor of the *Journal of the American Medical Association.* Lundberg was announcing that a special edition of organized medicine's flagship journal in 1998 would be devoted to complementary and alternative medicine (CAM). This signaled that organized medicine was shifting its earlier policy of resistance and exclusion of CAM toward one of accommodation and inclusion. CAM was moving not only into a mainstream medical journal but into clinics and even medical school education.

Organized medicine had earlier ridiculed CAM therapies and exaggerated their risk in the 1960s and 1970s. They had denounced CAM therapies suggesting that no physician should ever refer patients to them and solicited state help to intimidate 'unconventional' therapists. Then in the 1980s and early 90s, they began to reassess and come to terms with the growing public disaffection with conventional medicine, the rise of consumerism and managed care. In 1987, the federal 7th Circuit Court found organized medicine guilty under the Sherman anti-trust law and slapped them with stiff fines for restraining chiropractic care.[470] Organized medicine suspected that the growing use of CAM might be related to the growing patient disaffection with modern medicine. By the early 1990s, the growing use of CAM was challenging the preeminence and cultural authority of the medical profession. Organized medicine abandoned its open resistance and began drawing CAM into the medical mainstream. The AMA also encouraged its members to become more informed about CAM while also insisting that these therapies be scientifically studied.[471]

Dramatic change was already coming in the 1990s as CAM therapies became more visible and accepted by more educated consumers. Indeed, the 1990s was the decade of CAM's public debut in America, as illustrated in Table 7.1. Not only was an Office of Alternative Medicine established within the National Institute of Health, beginning with a $2 million budget, but this office was upgraded to a full-fledged center in 1998. The budget of the new CAM center grew to $80 million by 2000. Passage of the 1994 Dietary Supplement Act enhanced self-care and access to herbs and vitamins by relaxing FDA restrictions. A White House Commission on CAM Policy was established in 1999 and recommended in its report that CAM be integrated into the mainstream.[472]

Table 7.1 CAM's Public Debut in America During the 1990s

- 1990　Federal Organic Foods Production Act passed
- 1990s　17 new scientific journals devoted to CAM therapies formed
- 1992　Office of Alternative Medicine (OAM) created with a $2M budget growing to $80M in 2000
- 1994　Dietary Supplement Act permitting sale of herbs without FDA control
- 1997　Acupuncture endorsed as a safe intervention by the National Institute of Health
- 1998　OAM upgraded to a center- the National Center for Complementary and Alternative Medicine
- 1999　White House Commission on Complementary and Alternative Medicine Policy was established.

Bringing CAM into the mainstream will help promote health and prevent disease. As its name suggests, CAM complements the current system's exaggerated concern with fighting illness. Increased use of CAM would shift the emphasis away from 'disease care' toward health promotion but drugs and surgery would remain in the medical toolkit. Only when health promotion mainstreams will we have a 'healthcare' system.[473]

CAM and Public Policy

The White House Commission's 2002 report on CAM foresaw a major role for CAM therapies in helping Americans[474] move toward healthier lifestyle choices.[475] CAM practitioners cultivate collaborative partnerships with patients, empowering individuals toward healthier lifestyles, preventing disease and saving money. CAM usage expresses a shift in values toward a more holistic view of health and a desire for safer, more natural therapies.

> CAM practitioners cultivate collaborative partnerships with patients, empowering individuals toward healthier lifestyles, preventing disease and saving money.

CAM practices, such as acupuncture, biofeedback, yoga, massage therapy, and tai chi, as well as certain nutritional and stress reducing practices, can help us achieve the nation's health goals."[476] CAM is especially well suited for health maintenance and disease prevention since it actively cultivates more individual responsibility. Moreover, CAM, unlike conventional medicine, works with the body's capacity to heal itself by enhancing its natural defenses. There are times when the skills of conventional medicine are appropriate, but promoting health requires a different set of skills and therapies than those used in fighting disease. Some therapies such as tai chi and yoga serve as both exercise and stress management as they absorb the person with concentrating on the mental management of muscle for movement.

CAM contributes most to the prevention of disease and to the treatment of chronic conditions by empowering patients to change toward healthier lifestyles. Healthy lifestyles protect and enhance the healing powers of the body. The authors of the White House Commission Report understand CAM's potential role for enriching health but were not suggesting it replace conventional medicine's role in acute disease, trauma and emergencies.[477] The CAM Commission wrote: *The effectiveness of the healthcare system in the future will depend upon making use of all approaches and modalities that promote health.*[478] Thus, CAM can contribute to the nation's health by:

- Preventing up to 89 percent of chronic conditions[479] and delaying the onset of others,[480]
- Reducing the severity of illness for some patients, and
- Enhancing the recovery for others.

The Commission recommends implementing CAM in many of the Federal and State funded medical care programs. The federal Health and Human Services department alone funds twelve medical care programs, including Medicare and Medicaid.[481] CAM can perform a role and support their mission.[482] For example, the Commission on CAM suggests that the US Public Health Service's Healthy People programs incorporate more CAM techniques and tools, especially in the schools. The schools should teach principles of a healthy diet, exercise and stress management techniques. Another example is the prison population; they could profit from tai chi because it is an exercise and relaxation technique that lessens hostility and distress as devotees' focus on the here and now by mentally managing muscles for movement.[483] CAM can also contribute to nutrition programs, to mental health programs, and to reducing injuries at work. The commission contends that CAM therapies may be the most efficient means of achieving over half the Healthy People 2010 objectives. Because 80 percent of Medicare beneficiaries have some form of chronic condition, 99 percent of Medicare dollars treat chronic conditions.[484] By ignoring CAM's ability to promote health and wellness, the nation misses an opportunity for improving health, reducing chronic disease, and extending the quality of life.[485]

Unlike conventional care, CAM focuses on the long term, cultivating consciousness and promoting health via lifestyle changes. People are attracted to CAM because it promotes and enriches health,[486] empowers the individual through more active involvement, views health holistically and uses more natural, gentler interventions (e.g. massage, meditation, herbs with fewer adverse effects.)

CAM succeeds at health promotion and prevention of disease by employing positive goals, rewarding experiences and the individual's involvement. Most conventional approaches to disease prevention use fear or scare-care. While fear may bring temporary compliance with doctor's recommendations, it fails to sustain motivation over time because fear is inherently unpleasant, causing its suppression. People thrive on rewarding activities, which reinforce the continuation of the behavior.

> People are attracted to CAM because it promotes and enriches health, empowers the individual through more active involvement, views health holistically and uses more natural, gentler interventions.

Pleasurable health practices reduce stress and provide sustainable long-term benefits. For example teaching people simple relaxation techniques such as diaphragmatic breathing and positive imagery can dramatically reduce anxiety and stress levels. Two research studies, summarized in Table 7.2, illustrate the efficacy of stress reduction techniques.

Table 7.2 Benefits of Stress Management for Heart Disease

- The effects of three types of intervention for heart disease were compared. Ninety-four men with established coronary artery disease were recruited and divided into three groups: stress-management training, regular exercise, and a drug therapy. The first group received one and a half hours of stress management training each week for 16 weeks. The second group exercised three times a week for the same time period, while the third group received medication and regular monitoring. All received annual check ups for five years to track their heart health. Over the follow-up period, the average five-year medical care costs were one-third less and nearly 40% fewer cardiac events for the stress management group than in the exercise and drug therapy group.[487].

- In a similar study, heart patients who use stress management techniques enhance their heart health. This study found a 75% drop in risk with patients using stress management. Heart patients (107) were randomly divided into three groups: a control group of patients received usual medical care; another group engaged in a vigorous exercise program for 35 minutes three times a week for 16 weeks in addition to their usual medical care; and a third group of patients (along with their usual care from physicians) participated in a stress management program that included weekly group sessions and muscle relaxation practice and biofeedback. Patients were taught how to monitor irrational thought patterns and to develop alternative interpretations of situations and thought patterns. They were also taught how to read the many faces of stress and manage moods such as anger and depression.

- Patients were tracked for the next two to five years for heart attacks, bypass surgery, and angioplasty. In the control group that received standard medical care, 30% had additional heart trouble compared to 21% in the exercise group but only 10% of the stress management group had further heart problems. The stress management training also lowered the levels of psychological distress, hostility, and episodes of ischemic chest pain.[488]

The disease-care system inadvertently promotes illness by cultivating dependency and over-reliance on medication and experts. CAM, in contrast, reduces the dependence on medication by promoting empowerment and healthy practices.

The Growth and Integration of CAM

Increasing numbers of Americans over the last 30 years are using complementary and alternative approaches. CAM therapies are both more natural and helpful with fewer side effects than conventional therapies.[489] Yet CAM continues to be stigmatized by many in the medical community despite the fact that it offers a sustained, healing partnership between the doctor and patient, and encourages greater patient participation in the therapeutic process. Complementary therapies are strong in areas where conventional medicine is weak; thus, CAM can be a marvelous support to overall health.

Some clinics are integrating the best of CAM therapies and conventional medicine by combining the insights of ancient healing systems with scientific advances to preserve health and speed recovery from illness. Integrative medicine is a holistic practice in which the patient, not the disease, takes center stage.[490] All appropriate healing modalities and providers are engaged in the delivery of care, using the safest, least invasive and most cost-effective approaches.[491] The full range of credentialed providers is utilized.

The infrastructure to support integrative medicine is growing. Some examples of this infrastructure include new CAM journals, Best Practice software, credentialing agencies for quality assurance and integrative networks of providers. Seventeen new journals devoted to CAM arose in the 1990s. Best practice standards arose in the 1990s that include both CAM and conventional therapies and are based on evidence-based outcome studies. By 2005, 9,000 CAM research trials were completed. Best Practice "infomatic" companies arose to provide on-line CAM-related Best Practices, e.g., OneMedicine.com, WholeHealthMD.com and Health Notes.[492] The Institute for Health and Healing (IHH) at California Pacific Medical Center in San Francisco started in 1994 with a focus on health education and spiritual counseling services. IHH broadened its continuum of care beyond wellness and self-care to chronic and life-threatening illness with integrative therapies such as massage and energy therapies. The number of patient visits from 1994 grew 60 times, the budget grew 16 times and the number of settings expanded into six additional locations.

TRIAD Healthcare, Inc. formed an integrated health-care network in December 1996 that grew into a nationwide network in 2003 with more than 6,000 integrated-health providers in all 50 states, connecting patient, payer and provider. Two other resource agencies, American Specialty of San Diego and American Whole Health Networks credentialed CAM practitioners and linked them to medical plan contractors. Whole Health alone claimed over 26,000 credentialed CAM providers in 2003.[493]

Medi-Merge, founded in 1999, launched a provider network called the Integrative Medical Network that includes 14 different types of CAM providers in addition to physicians. In 2004, they started with 30,000 network providers and expect over 40,000 in 2005.

CAM therapies are being integrated and moving into the mainstream as evidenced by the following:

- Over nine out of ten medical insurance plans offered at least one CAM therapy in 2002.[494]
- The Collaboration for Healthcare Renewal Foundation (CHRF) formed to promote integrated care across the entire medical care system.[495]
- Comprehensive cancer centers are integrating CAM practices into their services, e.g., M. D. Anderson in Houston, Memorial Sloan-Kettering Cancer Center and Columbia -Presbyterian Medical Center in New York City, and Duke University in Durham, North Carolina.[496]
- Integrative clinics are arising across the country, e.g., The Center for Integrative Medicine in downtown Chicago, which employs an acupuncturist, herbalist, psychologist and homeopath.[497]
- New "infomatic" companies are forming to provide on-line CAM-related information and best practices as noted above.
- Consumer spending on CAM is growing at a compounded 38 percent per year.[498]
- The National Integrative Medicine Council was formed to promote the philosophy of integrative medicine through legislative action at the state and federal level.[499]
- Integrative medical care was the lead story and on the cover of *Newsweek* December 2, 2002.
- The American Hospital Association and Innovision Communications has sponsored conferences on "integrated care" since 2002 bringing leaders together to grow the field of integrated care.[500]
- More than one in every four hospitals in the US offered some form of CAM therapy in 2003, up from only one in nine in 1999.[501]
- The Consortium of Academic Health Centers for Integrative Medicine formed in 1999 and now has 27 medical centers working to implement integration.[502]

There are 26 integrative clinics at major medical centers in 2005 as shown in Table 7.3

Table 7.3 Integrative Clinics at Major Medical Centers

Medical Center	Name of Clinic
Beth Israel	Continuum Center for Health and Healing
Columbia University	Richard and Hinda Rosenthal center for Complementary & Alternative Medicine
Duke University	Duke Center for Integrative Medicine
Georgetown University	Kaplan Clinic
George Washington University	Center for Integrative Medicine
Harvard Medical School	Osher Institute
Oregon Health and Science University	Women's Primary Care and Integrative Medical Center for Women's Health
Thomas Jefferson University	The Myrna Brind Center for Integrative Medicine
University of Arizona	Program in Integrative Medicine
University of California, Irvine	Susan Samueli Center for Integrative Medicine
University of California, Los Angeles	Collaborative Centers for Integrative Medicine
University of California, San Francisco	Osher Center for Integrative Medicine
University of Connecticut, Farmington	Health Center
University of Hawaii at Manoa	Program in Integrative Medicine
University of Maryland, School of Medicine	Center for Integrative Medicine
University of Massachusetts, Worcester	Center for Mindfulness
University of Medicine and Dentistry of NJ	Institute of Complementary & Alternative Medicine
University of Michigan	Integrative Medicine
University of Minnesota	Center for Spirituality and Healing
University of New Mexico	Health Sciences Center
University of North Carolina, Chapel Hill	Program on Integrative Medicine
University of Pennsylvania	Office of Complementary Therapies
University of Pittsburgh	Center for Integrative Medicine
University of Texas Medical Branch	UTMB Integrative Health Care
University of Washington	Department of Family Medicine
Wake Forest University	Holistic and Integrative Medicine

Integrative medicine is moving into clinics, hospitals, medical schools, government programs and support industries. Integrative medicine reflects a new industry, meeting a substantial demand from a large consumer base. The industry newsletter, *The Integrator* for the business of alternative medicine, is a subscription-based, monthly newsletter, continuously published since July 1996. It analyzes the latest business models and trends in integrative medicine.

Models of Integrating CAM and Conventional Medicine

Over the past few years, a growing number of major academic medical centers have integrated CAM into more of their education and clinics. Various models of integration are taking root that range from a complete merger of CAM and conventional therapies, to various degrees of collaboration between formally separate disciplines. Conventional and CAM practitioners work in some settings as equals where they collaborate in both the diagnosis and treatment of patient conditions within the same clinic. Other settings are more physician-centered where doctors are gate keepers to CAM practitioners within a clinic under the supervision of a primary care physician. Some physicians who support CAM are overcoming obstacles and successfully integrating both conventional and CAM therapies into their practices.[503]

A few conventional physicians have developed popular integrative programs based on their own research. Two notable examples are Dr. Herbert Benson's Mind/Body Medical Institute at Harvard University and Dr Dean Ornish's Preventive Medicine Research Institute in Sausalito, California.

Benson's Mind/Body Medical Institute integrates a number of new and ancient tools to relieve stress. The Institute utilizes the tools of his "relaxation response"— meditation, mental imagery, and breathing techniques—for a variety of specific medical problems. According to Benson, stress-related disorders are the source of 60-90 percent of patient visits to medical professionals. These stress-related problems include hypertension, chronic pain, infertility, insomnia, and cardiac disorders. Each year the Institute at Harvard offers courses for practitioners who seek mind/body expertise.

Dean Ornish's Preventive Medicine Research Institute integrates a combination of four CAM therapies for reversing heart disease. After conducting many studies, Ornish documented the reversibility of heart disease with a low-fat diet, small group support, aerobic exercise, and meditation. A mix of cardiologists, exercise physiologists, behavioral health specialists, nutritionists and others collaborate in providing patient care in his Heart Disease Reversal Program. The Ornish program now operates in at least six medical centers. His "alternative by-pass-plan" is a very successful integrative program covered by over 40 insurance plans.[504]

Oxford Health Plan, a Yale affiliate, integrated CAM with a dual-physician model. Prior to treatment, a patient sees both a naturopathic and a conventional doctor at the initial visit, After assessing the patient separately, the two practitioners meet to discuss possible treatments and present the patient with both conventional and non-conventional options. This model goes beyond the short-term focus on unit-price to the longer term total price, helping eliminate incorrect diagnoses and less effective therapies with a given patient. This dual-physician approach has lowered the cost of care.

Alternative Medicine, Inc. (AMI) of Chicago developed an innovative patient-oriented wellness care model for managed care plans to improve quality while cutting costs. AMI uses a reverse hierarchy approach to integrate alternative and conventional care within a network of hospitals based in Chicago. They start with the least invasive treatment with the fewest side effects. If ineffective, they move to the next least invasive treatment until the therapeutic goal is achieved. With most patients, this means first using CAM and non-pharmaceutical therapies such as craniosacral and massage therapy, spinal manipulation, acupuncture or herbal medicine. AMI has partnered with Blue Cross/Blue Shield of Illinois since 1997 to compare 800 patients using the reverse hierarchy approach with a similar group of patients receiving only conventional care. They found the patients treated by AMI with reverse hierarchy lowered hospital admissions by 69 percent, lowered drugs use by 56 percent and lowered the number of outpatient surgeries and procedures by 80 percent. Reduced usage of drugs and surgeries and hospital stays slashed overall expenses by more than 60 percent.[505]

Obstacles to Integration

The White House Commission on CAM in 2002 identified four major obstacles to integrating conventional and CAM practitioners: creating two-way referral systems; standardizing the education and credentialing of CAM providers; providing CAM insurance reimbursement; and funding more research to insure the safety and effectiveness of more CAM therapies. In an earlier benchmarking project in 1999, John Weeks, then editor of *The Integrator,* examined the first three obstacles.[506]

Creating Two-Way Referral Systems

Some 15,000 to 20,000 conventionally trained physicians who are primarily in primary care are integrating CAM in their clinics or practices.[507] These eclectic, holistic healers are growing in number and referring more patients to CAM. One in five CAM patients makes an appointment with complementary practitioners because of a medical referral. Six out of ten primary-care physicians recommended CAM therapies to their patients at least once according to a 1994 survey and the percentage of physicians referring patients to CAM is increasing.[508]

Pioneers in integrative medicine are people who feel secure within their own field and are open to different therapeutic approaches. These doctors must be able to work with and be open to both health promotion and disease-care practitioners. Both Herbert Benson at Harvard and Dean Ornish in San Francisco are examples of well-established physicians who have respect and obtain referrals from other more conventional physicians that help ensure the economic survival of their integrative programs.

The Center for Complementary Medicine, an outpatient, multi-specialty group practice in Park Ridge, Illinois illustrates how an early pioneer built bridges and gained referrals. Before opening the center, the medical director Donald Novey, a family-practice physician, spent a year laying the groundwork by building referral relationships with his medical colleagues. He went to the members of the Advocate Medical Group, a network of 260 physicians affiliated with Lutheran General Hospital, and asked if they wanted alternative therapies in their network and, if so, what kinds. Two-thirds of the physicians expressed interest in alternative therapies and one third said they already were referring patients outside the Advocate Medical Group to CAM providers.

Novey consulted with his medical colleagues to ensure that the Center's services wouldn't compete or overlap with his medical peers. He opened the Center for Complementary Medicine in the Fall of 1998 in the basement of a small medical office building in the shadow of its parent facility, the 555-bed Lutheran General Hospital. The Center started small with five practitioners—two massage therapists, one chiropractor, one homeopath and one acupuncturist. As referrals grew, the Center expanded to fifteen practitioners—five massage therapists, one physical therapist, two chiropractors, one homeopath, three acupuncturists, two clinical psychologists and a nutritionist, plus the medical director. By the 20th month of operation, the Center was breaking even.[509]

Many of the 700 patient visits per month to the Center come from their doctors' referrals after standard treatment fails. Some are in pain; others are seeking help with chronic conditions like arthritis or lupus. When there is uncertainty about a diagnosis, the whole team confers.[510] The Center draws patients from a geographic area that is almost three times larger than the hospital's service area.

The Center recruited CAM practitioners with working experience, the appropriate license or credential, a willingness to cooperate, and an awareness of their own limitations so they would refer problem cases best treated by others. CAM practitioners typically work on a contract basis and are paid on a flat rate of half the revenue they generate.

Referrals are part of the "life-blood" of any new service and half the directors of integrative clinics reported that they experienced significant pressure to achieve financial sustainability within two years.[511] Integrative clinics must become part of a two-way referral system to ensure growth. Well over half the respondents in patient surveys claim they would use CAM if their physician suggested it.[512] Of those patients already using CAM, most came initially by a referral from friends and family, not because of a physician's suggestion.[513]

Jane Guiltinan, a practicing naturopathic physician at the King County Natural Health Clinic in Seattle, says: *Having conventional physicians who are open to CAM therapies becomes essential for integrative care to grow.*[514] Her clinic offers acupuncture, Chinese herbs, naturopaths, and more conventional therapies.[515] This clinic became the first natural medicine clinic run by a local government.

The Integrative Medicine Department at Evanston Northwestern Healthcare System (ENHS) opened its doors in January, 2001, and achieved breakeven financially by the end of 2003. The caseload is growing, and the program now sees 350 patients per month. The staff includes three Chinese medical practitioners, six body workers, a nutritionist, an integrative licensed clinical professional counselor, a family systems therapist, an Ayurvedic practitioner and an herbalist. Karen Koffler, MD, director of the department, sees patients three days a week, most of them quite ill with chronic disease or cancer. The staff meets weekly as a team to discuss patients, performs team consultations, creates educational programs and learns together.

Initial funding came from ENHS and from its associated physician group, ENH Medical Group. The Integrative Medicine Department found space in a newly developed community center, paying an overhead fee to the hospital to cover the costs of space, lights and phones. About half the patients are physician-referred, most from the ENH Medical Group. The program also gets referrals from physicians and practitioners throughout the Chicago area, who have heard Koffler speak of the newly formed Integrative Medicine Department.

Table 7.4 Medical Mind-sets and Paradigm Paralysis

One obstacle to mainstreaming CAM is a medical mind-set. The inability to think outside a medical model causes misuse of language and confusion about what medical care delivers, whose codes are used on insurance forms, and whether insurance will reimburse for.

A cultural mind-set arose in the early 1900s with state medical practice acts establishing monopoly control by physicians. This mind-set is complicated further by misappropriating the term health. Health care is the practice of enhancing physical, mental, and social well-being. Medical care is the practice of using outside agents to counter disease and restore health after disease descends. In America, medical care is called healthcare, i.e., about doctors and services that restore health after the onset of a disease. By referring to disease-care as healthcare, no appropriate words are left in the "well-of words" to distinguish health enhancers from disease fighters. Until the 1990s, nurse practitioners were a notable exception, gaining the right in many states to diagnose and prescribe drugs under the protocol in the 1970s

Additionally, "health insurance" is about reimbursing disease-care specialists to restore health with "medically necessary" services. Health promoting practitioners are generally NOT reimbursed by the insurance industry in spite of the 47 percent increase in the total number of visits to CAM practitioners from 1990-1997. Only the more affluent are undeterred by out of pocket payments. Lack of insurance coverage keeps most people from using CAM.

The term health care somehow got misappropriated in describing medical or disease care services.[516]

While Koffler accepts Medicare, all other patients pay out of pocket. Increasingly, insurance companies reimburse their patient enrollees, so all are encouraged to submit their bills.[517] Two out of three medical insurance plans now reimbursement for acupuncture and massage.

Another early adopter in integrative medicine is David Edelberg M.D., co-founder of American Whole Health, a private, for-profit company operating six integrative centers around the country. Edelberg contends: *Many conventional doctors have the erroneous idea that alternative practitioners want to take their patients away from them, but our [CAM] providers know their limitations. The physician must understand that he doesn't know everything in the world. There are other healers who want to work with him without encroaching on his territory.*[518] Being open minded to alternative perspectives is important, as noted in Table 7.4. Pioneering an integrative medical clinic is not easy. Pioneers often get the arrows but settlers get the land.

One integrative clinic had initial difficulties in claiming an adequate revenue stream from referrals. The clinic found a market niche by moving into pain management and working with "Workers' Comp" carriers along with selling nutritional supplements and herbs. The Integrative Clinic became solvent and self-sustaining after 31 months. The clinic now uses 20 practitioners, including two family physicians, an internist, a naturopath, an acupuncturist, chiropractors, massage therapists, a dietician, an herbalist and psychotherapists.

Nearly twice as many patients are obtaining preventive services from non-physician CAM providers than from physicians.

Medical clinics across American are forging a new division of labor as suggested by recent surveys. Non-physician CAM providers are being used as educators for patients and for more preventive services as shown in Table 7.5 below. The numbers of patients consulting CAM providers increased by 20 percent from 1987 to 1997. More significantly, nearly twice as many patients are obtaining preventive services from non-physicians CAM providers than from physicians. Many non-physicians are working at sites where a physician also works, suggesting they are specializing in different roles. Fueled in part by state legislation expanding the scope of practice for CAM practitioners, this trend paves the path for more patient choice and more collaborative relationships.

Table 7.5 Shifts in Consumer Use of CAM Practitioners in the US

- The percentage of patients consulting a CAM provider increased from 31% in 1987 to 36% in 1997[519]
- The number of CAM practitioner-visits rose 47% from 1990 (427 million) to 1997 (629 million[520]
- Expenditures for CAM professional services increased 45% between 1990 and 1997[521]
- Patients use CAM providers for preventive services more than for acute services.[522]
- More consumers are seeing a CAM practitioner at clinics where a physician also practiced.[523]
- Two out of three medical group practices employed non-physicians in 2001, up from half in 1997.[524]

Acupuncturists, chiropractors and naturopaths are accepted and used as primary care providers by the public, joining nurse practitioners.[525] Acupuncturists, chiropractors and naturopaths combined represented 11 percent of all primary care providers in 1994, rising to 14 percent in 2002.[526] In 2000, there were 70,000 chiropractors, 14,000 non-MD acupuncturists, 1,400 naturopaths and 73,000 Nurse Practitioners.[527] The numbers of primary care CAM providers are expected to increase dramatically in the future.

Education and Credentialing of CAM Practitioners

CAM training,[528] licensing requirements and certification[529] are becoming more standardized as noted in Table 7.6. The CAM Commission believes the federal government should help states evaluate the impact of state licensure and legislate medical practice laws and access to CAM therapies. However, each state must decide the type of regulation they will use. Nationwide standards for licensing and credentialing of CAM providers would help lift their prestige, increase referrals to them and elicit clearer practice standards and minimize unqualified CAM providers.[530] The regulatory strategy should balance concern for protecting the public from dangerous practices while ensuring freedom to choose different therapies.[531]

The dramatic growth of consumer demand for CAM therapies has energized CAM practitioners to expand their scope of practice by pressuring state legislatures.[532] In response to growing recognition of CAM therapies by conventional medical practitioners, the Federation of State Medical Boards developed model guidelines for the referral and use of CAM therapies in their practice in 2003. This serves to protect conventional practitioners when they refer patients to safe CAM therapies.

> The regulatory strategy should balance concern for protecting the public from dangerous practices while ensuring freedom to choose.

Table 7.6 Standards Established for Selected CAM Providers

Profession	Accreditation Received	Standardized Exams	State Regulated	Practicing CAM Provider
Acupuncture	1982	1982	34	17,000
Chiropractic	1971	1963	50	70,000
Massage	1982	1994	30	250,000
Naturopathy	1978	1986	14	1,400

Adapted from David Eisenberg et al, *Annals of Internal Medicine,* vol.137: 965-73, 2002 and John Weeks, Integration Strategies for Natural Healthcare, Seattle, WA

The holistic training of CAM practitioners contrasts with the one dimensional physical focus of conventional physicians. Medical education focuses on physical disease and assumes that a given problem arises from the same biochemical causes. Medical education does not include emotional or mental causes for physical disease. To prepare physicians for potential referrals to alternative therapies and/or working with CAM practitioners,[533] medical education must insure physicians are knowledgeable. In the 1990s the American Holistic Medical Association (AHMA) established a board to certify competence in seven core areas: nutrition, exercise, environmental medicine, behavioral medicine, social health, energy medicine, and spiritual attunement.[534] This exam standardizes "holistic medicine" and establishes specialty areas for practitioner certification.[535]

At least two companies are providing best practice protocols with evidence based research that facilitates the integration of CAM. Two companies, OneMedicine and SaluGenecists, both provide primary care practitioners' and patients' information on best practice norms for specific medical conditions with advanced programs on CDs. OneMedicine.com offers a definitive, interactive database of medical conditions, herbs, supplements, drugs and interactions that displays both conventional and alternative treatments side-by-side. The database is cross-referenced for easy access and use. SaluGenecists provides an evidence-based expert understanding of integrative health by using a computerized system to identify each individual's underlying physiological dysfunctions and the steps to remedy them with natural health expert systems. By answering an individualized series of questions, the user provides information in their profile which cues the program into creating a map of his or her unique metabolic and functional needs. Customized knowledge solutions include whole-foods education at whfoods.com, dietary supplement efficacy database and disease education protocols.[536] SaluGenecists also features an easy-to-use Diet Analysis Tool, providing details on 138 different nutrients.

Networks of credentialed CAM providers arose in the late 1990s. The National Committee for Quality Assurance helped design standards for certification of those working in integrative clinics and CAM networks.[537] Table 7.7 below gives examples of CAM networks that offer services to their insured members at a discounted rate and their geographical location.[538]

Table 7.7 Selected CAM Networks and Their US Geographical Location

CAM Network	Geographical Location
American Specialty Health	Nationwide
Altercare	Oregon
Alternative Medicine Referral Services	Greater Washington, DC area
Consensus Health	California
Health and Healing Card	Greater San Francisco
Health and Healing Trust	NY, NJ, CT and Mid-Atlantic states
Infinite Health	Minneapolis and St. Paul, MN
Vitality Access	Denver and Boulder, CO

American Specialty Health Networks (ASH), based in San Diego, provides complementary health care networks, administrative services, and clinical management services for self-funded employers, insurance carriers, and medical plans. ASH Networks is the nation's largest specialty benefits company for complementary medical care and lifestyle management. ASH grew from seven million insured individuals in 2001 to over nine million in 2003 because they obtained licenses in 40 states, allowing them to administer benefits nationwide.[539]

The White House Commission on CAM suggested changes in training the next generation of both conventional and CAM practitioners to facilitate their working together collaboratively.[540] Both CAM and conventional practitioners need exposure to what the other does since the former promotes health and the latter fights disease. The best way to ensure this exposure is within each of their training programs. As a result of this exposure, conventional providers could better discuss CAM with their patients, provide guidance on CAM use, collaborate with CAM practitioners, and make referrals to them. CAM practitioners can communicate and collaborate with conventional providers more effectively and make appropriate referral to conventional physicians if they received this exposure in medical school. Presently, 50 of the 125 medical schools with classes in some aspect of CAM offer them only as elective courses; only 25 schools make CAM part of a required course.[541] CAM training programs generally require some anatomy and physiology classes but they need more courses in toxicology.

The White House Commission's report suggested a novel and far-reaching change: CAM and conventional medical programs should each offer their students training in self-care and healthy life-choices to improve their own health, to encourage their teaching abilities and to model their own healthy lifestyle to their patients. Living the practice ensures greater empathy from the practitioner and effectiveness with their patients. Some medical schools are moving towards a concept of maintaining wellness rather than just treating disease according to a report by the Association of American Medical Colleges.[542]

CAM Insurance and Reimbursement

Lack of insurance coverage of CAM represents the biggest obstacle to both patients and physicians according to consumer surveys. One in three physicians report they do not mention useful CAM therapies to patients when their medical insurance doesn't cover CAM because they presume the patient would not pay the added expense.[543] Six out of ten consumers express interest in using CAM if their insurance covers it.[544] Still most CAM users pay out-of-pocket which limits the demand significantly.

> Lack of insurance coverage of CAM represents the biggest obstacle to both patients and physicians according to consumer surveys.

Americans want the opportunity to choose from both conventional and CAM therapies.[545] Many people want increased access to CAM, along with conventional services because CAM focuses more on health and the latter on disease. Medical insurance generally covers only disease care services, not prevention or health promotion. However, Medicare and Medicaid extended chiropractic care coverage in the 1970s and more medical plans in the 1990s started covering acupuncture, naturopathy and massage therapies because of their cost effectiveness and popularity.

CAM is offered typically as a supplemental benefit rather than a basic benefit in medical insurance plans. Some include discounts for services provided by a network of CAM practitioners,[546] while others provide annual health savings accounts against which services may be purchased.[547]

How do insurance companies and managed-care organizations determine what medical care services to offer and whether to include CAM? The decision is similar to four people driving an automobile. The marketing director has his foot on the gas, knowing that CAM is a way to expand the insurance company's market share. The chief financial officer has his foot on the brake, fearing that CAM may cost more and undermine profitability. The actuary analyst drives the car by looking out the rear-view mirror as he bases decisions on what happened in the past. And the consumer is a back-seat driver, giving suggestions from the back seat. Both the accountant and the actuary request hard facts but evidence is still limited on the cost effectiveness of CAM because its ideas are new to the insurance companies.

> Are CAM services an add-on expense to conventional treatment, or do CAM services replace *or* lessen the need for some conventional therapies and services?

When insurance plans add CAM to their basic coverage, they must determine whether to charge the same fee, less or extra for CAM services. Are CAM services an add-on expense to conventional treatment, or do CAM services replace *or* lessen the need for some conventional therapies and services? Two in three primary care physicians believed CAM would be cost-effective in 1999.[548] Belief is fine but the actuary analysts want hard numbers for proof but such studies are now providing the numbers.

A four-year study comparing the experiences of one million medical plan members without chiropractic coverage and 700,000 members with chiropractic coverage revealed that patients with chiropractic coverage experienced 28 percent lower costs than patients without chiropractic coverage. Overall, patients with chiropractic coverage experienced 6.3 fewer inpatient stays per 1,000 patients than patients without chiropractic coverage.[549]

Patients using CAM therapies believe CAM decreased their medical need for conventional visits, drugs and surgeries by sixty percent.[550] Half the patients in Puget Sound, Washington who used acupuncture, naturopathic or massage benefits reported their use of CAM decreased their need for conventional medicine. Primary providers who offered a range of CAM therapies reduced their referrals and treatment costs.[551] The use of acupuncture for chronic headaches decreased medical visits by 25 percent and decreased prescription drug use by 15 percent.[552]

Tom, a schoolteacher in his fifties could no longer walk due to back pain resulting from a fall. Tom's fall occurred one year after having a medical operation to fuse several lumbar vertebrae together due to degenerative disk disease. The only option for maintaining his livelihood of teaching was to work in a wheelchair. After physical therapy, steroid injections, and doses of pain medication that provided little relief, Tom's neurosurgeon recommended additional surgery. Desperate, Tom inquired whether any other alternative therapies might help. The surgeon suggested that acupuncture might help, although he had no idea of where or how to find one. Fortunately Tom's wife was a nurse manager and worked with a nurse practitioner who regularly referred patients to acupuncturists, so she suggested several.

While Tom was skeptical, he made a 90-day commitment with a licensed acupuncturist. Within a month, Tom was able to walk again. In the following month, he experienced further relief and greater mobility with treatments starting at twice a week plus herbal therapy then tapering off to less frequent treatments. Though Tom had to pay out-of-pocket, the benefits exceeded the cost. While not totally pain free, John greatly reduced his pain medication and resumed work again. As Tom expressed it, *I don't understand how acupuncture works, but it helped me to walk again.*

The cost of Tom's intensive phase of pain clinic treatment was nearly $6,000 compared to the $1,500 for the acupuncture treatments and herbs. The maintenance phase of the pain clinic and drug medication was $375 per month compared to $320 for the acupuncture, herbs and reduced level of pain medication. Pain motivated Tom to explore an alternative. That alternative helped him walk away from his confinement in a wheelchair and Tom now enjoys a dramatically improved quality of life with fewer medications.

Over 400 patients who experienced chronic headaches (predominantly migraine) were recruited by physicians to test the relative effectiveness of drug medication versus acupuncture treatments for a one-year time period. Subjects were randomly assigned for drug and acupuncture treatments and each patient kept a diary, rating the severity of their headaches. Acupuncture patients experienced 22 fewer days with a headache, 25 percent fewer visits to the doctor and had 15 percent fewer sick days away from work at the end of the year.[553] Acupuncture users at clinics reported fewer office visits to medical doctors (84 %), use of fewer drugs (79%), fewer insurance claims (77%), avoidance of surgery (70%), and reduction in use of psychotherapy (58%).[554]

A recent report by the Institute of Medicine shows that practitioners on average spend differing amounts of time with their patients in large part due to what therapies they use. Visits to acupuncturists and massage therapists lasted nearly 60 minutes while visits to naturopathic physicians lasted 40 minutes, those to chiropractors lasted less than 20 minutes and a visit with conventional physicians lasted less than 10 minutes.[555]

Conventional medicine is more impersonal, standardized and less effective with behavioral change and building skills in patients.

More than six out of ten patients in another study used fewer prescription drugs for pain or other symptom management problems using CAM compared to those using conventional therapies for the same condition. Four out of five respondents rated acupuncture helpful compared to one out of five who rated their conventional care helpful for the same chronic condition at the end of the year.[556]

To determine if CAM therapies increase or lower cost by lessening demand for conventional therapies requires more research data over time similar to that provided by AMI of Chicago discussed earlier. Using comparable patients who either use only conventional disease-care services or CAM health enrichment services to examine the total cost of the services to each group over time will provide the necessary answers.

Independent practitioners use the Current Procedural Terminology or CPT™ coding system for insurance reimbursement. The CPT™ is a coding system for insurance payment of outpatient services that are "medically necessary" after the disease develops. If no disease or imminent risk exists, most insurance plans will not reimburse because health promotion or maintenance therapy codes do not exist. By failing to support health promotion, the cost of medical care increases and the patient's quality of life decreases.

The medical insurance industry, being disease-centric, largely ignores health promotion, regardless of practitioner type. Only a handful of CAM procedures are recognized in the CPT codes.[557] Only eight out of 8,000 CPT™ codes are for CAM therapies (four codes are for distinctively chiropractic services, two for acupuncture and two other services.)[558] The entire medical insurance industry is deeply rooted in a disease-centered focus. Medical 'mind-sets' impede the shift toward health promotion by failing to reimburse therapies other than what is "medically necessary" for a specific disease, (e.g., diet education for diabetics or cardiac patients).

Under-girding this control is the American Medical Association's (AMA) monopoly over the CPT™ billing codes used by insurance plans. The AMA gains tens of millions of dollars in revenue each year from the industry's use of these codes. The AMA controls the coding committee and has failed to create codes for enhancing health and CAM therapies other than the eight out of 8,000 codes mentioned above.

The CPT coding committee consists of 15 medical doctors, ten appointed by the AMA and five who are appointed by other disease-care interest groups such as the American Hospital Association and Blue Cross/Blue Shield. Since the AMA has been unwilling to expand a coding system for health promotion, most CAM therapies are excluded. Until insurance covers health promotion, the incentives will flow to disease care rather than promoting and enriching health.[559]

Pressure for change is growing. The experience of Melinna Giannini, who benefited from CAM therapies, illustrates the need for recognizing effective therapies. Ms. Giannini tells her story:

In 1992 I developed a very painful kidney problem which started as water retention and discomfort. By May of 1994 the situation had escalated to fluid retention, mental confusion, constant pain, and depression. I had had three rounds of tests that included sonograms, cystoscopy, and x-ray flow tests. No diagnosis was ever formulated in all that time. But I was given five rounds of penicillin. I kept getting sicker and sicker. Finally, a friend recommended that I try an alternative M.D. Within two weeks, I had lost 14 pounds of fluid, had gained control of my problem, and felt better than I had in over two *years. The holistic practitioner's entire course of treatment, including herbs, injections, follow-ups, and adjustment of dosages was less than $500.00. The previous two years had cost my insurance company $15,000. They happily paid for the tests, doctors, and drugs that did not improve my condition, but were unwilling to pay for alternative treatments.*[560]

Giannini's positive experience with alternative therapies, combined with her insurance background, inspired her to develop a new coding system for insurance reimbursement—the Alternative Billing Concept (ABC). She and six business partners developed the ABC Codes and patented them in June 1999. These codes are compatible with the existing conventional medical care system and facilitate third-party reimbursement for CAM therapies.[561]

The CPT medical codes severely restricted CAM practitioners. Giannini provides a simple reason for why new codes were needed.

CAM practitioners must use codes developed for conventional therapies. Providers send claims to insurance companies but commonly experience problems getting reimbursed because they are using codes that do not adequately describe the services they provide.[562]

The approximately 4300 codes in this new ABC system incorporate the specific treatments and therapies provided by 13 different types of CAM practitioners.[563] However, CAM practitioners experienced two major obstacles: 1) the AMA's control of the CPT codes used for insurance billing and reimbursing outpatient professional services, as discussed above,[564] and 2) the limited research on CAM's cost effectiveness. Instituting a new set of billing codes and documenting CAM's cost effectiveness are an inter-related "Catch-22"problem.[565] You can not accomplish either without implementing both.

Instituting a new set of billing codes and documenting CAM's cost effectiveness are an inter-related "Catch-22"problem.

The AMA's stranglehold on the insurance billing codes was broken in January 2003 when HHS Secretary Thompson accepted the Advanced Billing Concept system (ABC Code) for use in a two-year demonstration project in all federal programs. The stimulus was the 2003 phase-in of the Health Insurance Portability and Accountability Act (HIPPA), which simplified and standardized the processing of medical insurance claims. This two-year project allows HHS to test modifications of the existing code set and will permit policymakers to draw upon a more complete dataset in analyzing the cost effectiveness of therapies, not just from disease-based models of care. The Secretary of HHS will oversee three concurrent reviews of ABC codes, positioning these codes to become a HIPAA standard if cost benefit data show positive results.

The lead applicant, Melianna Giannini, in using the ABC codeset declared: *This is a huge step in helping measure alternative approaches to quality and cost-effectiveness while comparing them with mainstream approaches.*[566] This could bring improvements in claims processing, management of clinical practice and insurance coverage in the near future.[567] Use of ABC codes reflects the adoption of electronic data standards and reliance on evidence-based outcomes.[568]

A new medical insurance plan, MediMerge, integrates both health promotion and disease care benefits. This plan integrates different providers who perform these services. They incorporate the services of a Certified Health Advocate™, a registered nurse, whose purpose is to help members and their providers develop an integrative approach to health promotion, prevention and disease care. The MediMerge model identifies at-risk individuals, intervenes through proactive risk prevention and health advocacy programs, uses ABC codes, and emphasizes evidence based best practice protocols.

MediMerge creates baseline data for plan sponsors and improves health outcomes by reducing risk factors with early identification and intervention with a Certified Health Advocate.[569]

The Healthy Lifestyle and Prevention Act of 2004 reimburses for the first time prevention services. Tommy Thompson initiated the government's reimbursement of nutritional and exercise counseling for Medicare recipients who are at-risk.

A visionary stance arose from the Hawaii 2003 Conference on Integrative Pain Management. This conference identified both alternative therapies and conventional therapies that resulted in the best patient outcomes. National experts on pain management addressed the best techniques and tools for pain management, cost effectiveness and the role of evidence-based outcomes in an attempt to develop chronic pain management protocols. They formulated recommendations to insurers in support of chronic pain management.[570]

A growing number of large private employers are incorporating CAM providers in their insurance coverage plans. These plans generally offer chiropractic care (94%), and growing numbers cover acupuncture (67%) and massage therapy (70%). But when CAM is in the plan, coverage often limits the number of visits and restricts the clinical applications of CAM.

> A growing number of large private employers are incorporating CAM providers in their insurance coverage plans.

The medical insurance industry is not yet an active player in promoting health because they primarily serve as "actuarial intermediaries" who market their service to raise money for investing in the stock market and real estate.[571] Insurance companies are similar to banks in terms of investing money and earning 3 to 4 percent on premium dollars before paying out claims. Since as much as 95 percent of their profits may result from "outside" investments, medical insurance premiums rise soon after the stock market drops and remain high until stock prices rise.[572] Robert Hunter of the Consumer Federation of America, and a former insurance commissioner in Texas, testified in 2001...*the current spike in premiums is clearly a function of the insurance cycle, where premiums rise when insurers' investment income in the larger market falls.*

More Research on CAM Needed

CAM's widespread use adds urgency to examining the safety and effectiveness of CAM. But bringing CAM into the mainstream requires more research to establish its place in the best practice protocols. The White House Commission on CAM recommended more research, demonstration projects and evaluations on CAM's safety and cost-effectiveness.

CAM can not be integrated into the insurance system until standardized codes are used and studies show their cost effectiveness. Data must establish the cost effectiveness of CAM therapies compared to conventional therapies when comparable patients are studied over time. Small data sets and non-standardized codes are easily discredited as anecdotal or flawed methodologically. Both standardized codes and a large dataset are two legs joined at the hip, each requiring the other to move forward.

> Both standardized codes and a large dataset are two legs joined at the hip, each requiring the other to move forward.

Conventional medicine carries the mantle of having scientifically-based therapies, yet only 30 percent of their procedures had undergone rigorous scientific analysis in 1990 as documented in Chapter 2.[573] So the majority of reimbursable conventional procedures described in the CPT™ codes were derived from "established medical practices" that were not scientifically established. Evidence-based outcome studies arose in the 1990s in part to limit the challenge of CAM.

Many CAM therapies require more scientific evaluation to meet the higher standard that conventional medicine mistakenly assumed it already had for its validation. Many CAM procedures had time-tested medical practices over three thousand years in China, India and elsewhere. The White House Commission on CAM and others called for these therapies to be tested for their efficacy.

Most articles referenced in Western medical literature do not include CAM therapies. Only ten percent of all scientific medical journal articles referenced in Medline from 1966 to 1996 were on

CAM therapies.[574] To correct this problem, the Cochrane Collaboration was formed to conduct controlled trials of CAM therapies and modalities. The Cochrane Collaboration is an international organization of more than 9,000 contributors from more than 80 countries who must follow the highest methodological and scientific rigor. More than 9,000 controlled trials of CAM therapies are completed and accessible from the Cochrane Library based at the University of Maryland Center for Integrative Medicine.[575]

Comparing the scientific evidence base from randomly controlled trials for conventional and CAM therapies showed that conventional therapies were no more likely to have a positive effect than CAM therapies (22.5% vs 24.8%), 4.2 times as likely to have no effect (20% vs 4.8%) and over 11 times more likely to be harmful than CAM therapies (8.1% vs .6%). Many conventional and CAM therapies have insufficient evidence to know their effect (21% vs. 56.6%) but more CAM therapies require research than the conventional.[576]

> Conventional therapies were no more likely to have positive effects than CAM therapies (22.5% vs. 24.8%) but with over 11 times more likely to be harmful than CAM therapies (8.1% vs. 6%).

Systematic outcome studies are needed comparing conventional and CAM therapies on patients with similar risk conditions over time. At this time, no large actuarial data set exists with which to demonstrate definitively the effect of CAM therapies in averting costs of disease-care by reducing patient risk conditions. Overcoming barriers to coverage and reimbursement will require first, collecting data to determine the benefits and cost-effectiveness of CAM and, second, giving equitable, impartial consideration to those practices and products demonstrating safety and effectiveness. Insurers need outcome studies of patients who have comparable risk factors at the outset where some use only CAM, others use only conventional therapies and a third group uses both CAM and conventional practitioners. Such studies will show their cost effectiveness over time.[577]

The Policy Institute for Integrative Medicine was formed in September 2002 to support the integration of CAM therapies with research and education. Their mission is to determine which alternative therapies could substitute for other kinds of care and to support federal investment in integrative medicine.[578]

The National Center for CAM continues to research the safety and effectiveness of CAM therapies and products that are unable to be patented and are unlikely to attract private research dollars, e.g., herbal therapies, massage and energy therapies such as Reiki and healing touch. Big pharmaceutical firms dominate the research process because they have the $200- to $300M required to go through the FDA testing process from their lucrative sale of drugs with patent protection against competition. More natural and energy therapies, which cannot be patented, need federal support to ensure that treatment options have a chance against those with deep pockets to go through the expensive process of FDA testing.

Future Prospects for CAM

By any measure, Americans spend more money on medical care than any other industrialized nation, yet our life expectancy is ranked thirteenth among nations and years-of-disability is longer than most other countries. More than fifteen percent of our people are uninsured and often forego needed treatment.[579] Meanwhile, thousands are killed or injured by intrusive modern high-tech medicine. Many who derive some benefit from their prescribed drugs and treatments find only temporary or limited relief from their chronic ailments. Paradoxically, we over-treat many patients with drugs and surgery, while under-treating over half our adult population at high-risk. Patients at high-risk need more help to understand that their unhealthy habits cause their illnesses and disabilities. Behavioral change strategies must use social support systems for motivating and reinforcing lifestyle changes that enrich health.[580]

CAM can not solve all our healthcare problems but it can enrich the people's health in a variety of ways by partnering with patients to treat unhealthy habits. CAM is finding its place in many mainstream settings such as the hospital, medical centers and integrative clinics. In fact, individual physicians are referring an increasing number of patients to complementary and alternative treatments in spite of the AMA's exclusionary policy.[581]

Perhaps the most revealing sign of physician acceptance is their willingness to use CAM therapies themselves. In Florida, 52 percent of a medical school faculty had used some form of alternative therapy. In Washington State and New Mexico, the medical school faculty usage rate was 47 percent. Research shows that physicians who have used CAM are seven times more likely to recommend CAM to their patients. Younger physicians, female and family practitioners are more favorable toward CAM.[582]

One futurist envisions medicine in the next 20 years being more energy-based, decentralized, and promoting health and wellness. Much less emphasis will be on invasive interventions. The bulk of care will occur during three periods: in early life from fetal origins into early childhood; during adolescence to early adulthood; and at the end of life. All modes of intervention will be housed under a single roof. Treatments would include dietary interventions, energetic interventions (Reiki, healing touch and others), movement therapies, and supplements that may include medications. Auxiliary wellness stations would be located at workplaces, schools and faith-based institutions. Insurance coverage would be based on wellness care.[583]

Time will tell which scenario best describes our future, but change is certain. We can and do create futures by our present actions and aspirations.

AFTERWORD
MEDICINE FOR THE NEW MILLENNIUM

The cell is a machine driven by energy. It can be approached by study-
ing matter, or by studying energy. In every culture and in every medical
tradition before ours, healing was accomplished by moving energy.
Szent-Gyorgyi (1967)

All systems are regulated not only by known energy and material factors
but also by invisible organizing fields.
Barbara Brennan

This book is about a cultural shift from doctoring disease to enriching health in America. The increasing use of alternative therapies
expresses this shift from a disease centric to a health centric model.
This shift is from a fear-based fixation on disease toward a positive
goal of health promotion. America is shifting from a dependency on
a pill for every ill and experts who dispense such quick-fixes toward
patients seeking more natural therapies and more personal 'response-
ability.'

What about medicine in the new millennium? I believe CAM will
continue to integrate but the segment of CAM that will expand most
dramatically will be Energy Medicine. These therapies are not only
less intrusive and more enriching of health but many engage self-help
and lay healing. The Energy Medicine model is based on the princi-

ples of physics. Both practitioners and patients are using more energy therapies that range from acupuncture to therapeutic touch therapies. Gerber asserts: *energy medicine is part of an emerging revolution in health care that will take us to the leading edge of discovery by blending ancient healing wisdom with modern-day insights.*[584]

Energy therapies range from high-tech tools to low-tech therapies such as healing touch techniques that are similar to ancient practices of laying-on of hands. Laying-on of hands creates a "natural" bio-circuit by holding two points on or over a person's body to create a flow of energy between areas where more energy needs to flow.

Energy matters because it is the foundation of life and health as it taps into subtle, solar, geomagnetic and atmospheric energy systems. Richard Gerber, MD, in his book *Vibrational Medicine*, examines the dynamic chemical, electrical, light based, bio magnetic and subtle energy systems that must work together to maintain harmony and health.

The human body is a bio-electrical system that can be altered, strengthened and balanced through the use of energy.

In *The Scientific Basis of Integrative Medicine*, Leonard Wisneski, MD, contends that modalities of subtle energy medicine are cutting edge. Wisneski discusses acupuncture, applied kinesiology, healing touch, homeopathy, polarity therapy, prayer/spiritual healing, QiGong, Reiki, therapeutic touch and Thought Field Therapy.[585] Our bodies are absorptive, reflective and generative of informational energy fields.[586] The human body is a bio-electrical system that can be altered, strengthened and balanced through the use of energy.

James Oschman summarizes the extensive research on the emerging energy model.[587] Oschman shows that the body is suffused by a network of channels that carry energy and signals to all parts of the body. Cells and internal organs all generate electrical currents. The heart alone produces 1.5 watts of power that is 50 times stronger than that of the brain. Each organ has its own frequency but the heart is an electromagnetic means for regulating the body. The magnetic fields generated by these currents within the body extend beyond the skin and can be measured by sensitive instruments such as the Superconducting Quantum Interference Device or SQUID. Kirlian photography also captures the textured colors of this electromagnetic field called the human aura.

Advocates of the energy model contend that illness is not only caused by germs, viruses, chemical toxins and physical trauma but also by chronic dysfunctional emotional-energy patterns and unhealthy ways of relating that drain energies and weaken the body. Emotional and mental energies can somatize into the body and express/manifest as "physical "problems as depicted in Figure 8.1 below. The energy approach employs the use of different forms of energy along with electromagnetic and subtle life energy to bring about healing changes in the body, mind and spirit.[588]

Figure 8.1 Emotional and Mental Energies Become Embodied

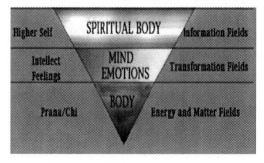

A wide range of soft and hard tissue healing occurs from magnetic pulses, whether from human hands or machines. A very low frequency of two hertz enhances nerve regeneration while seven hertz enhances bone growth, ten hertz stimulates ligament healing and 15 hertz stimulates capillary formation and limits skin necrosis.[589] Many companies now produce and market consumer devices for enhancing health and wholeness that range from light and sound machines, subtle energy builders and air ionizers.[590]

Conventional medicine is based primarily on a biochemical model while energy medicine is based on energy and informational systems as they influence downstream biochemistry. The energy model is based primarily on the principles of physics. All parts of the body are viewed as connecting together with a living tissue matrix that is the largest organ of our body. All living bodies depend on the use and transfer of electrical charges.The body is a liquid crystal that is capable of vibrating at a number of different frequencies, some in the range of visible light. The watery matrix of the human body interconnects fields that receive some 60 pulsations of electromagnetic energy from our hearts per minute. Our heart becomes a synchronizing electromagnetic master system influencing the entire living matrix.[591]

Conventional medicine is based primarily on a biochemical model while energy medicine is based on the principles of physics.

By focusing primarily on chemical reactions and chemistry, the important role of electromagnetic fields and physics is neglected. Some basic tenets of this energy model include:

- Energy joins and flows through all things.
- Living things are a local matrix that expresses as biological coherence.
- The living tissue matrix is body's largest organ.
- This living matrix connects all cells and organ systems together.
- The heart is an electromagnetic means for regulating the body.

The energy model of medicine uses therapies for the physical body (supplements and good nutrition) but it goes beyond to include emotional, mental and spiritual therapies in the form of stress-reduction and breathing/imagery techniques to connect to Source/Universal Intelligence.[592] Energy medicine uses less toxic, less expensive and gentler healing approaches that tap into the very energies of Mother Nature with simple acupuncture needles, tiny magnets, pocket lasers emitting beams of light which are all capable of quickly relieving pain and promoting rapid healing. *Energy medicine provides both ancient and modern healing tools that can relieve pain, balance body energies and alleviate physical symptoms while also healing emotional and spiritually related maladies.*[593]

People at the institute of Heart Math (www.heartmath.com), and elsewhere, are researching the effect of emotions on autonomic balance, cardiovascular function, hormonal and immune system health. Emotions like anger and frustration create less coherent electrical signals in the heart and bring imbalance in the autonomic nervous system and a suppression of the immune system. Greater coherence and health ensues when the electrical patterns of the brain are synchronized with the electrical patterns of the heart. Focusing on your heart with experiences of gratitude and love brings about increased coherence in the electromagnetic field of your heart, which entrains the brain and a greater hormonal balance in the body.

Heart health and emotions are connected. People can consciously alter their heart rhythms to enrich health. Coherence aligns the frequencies of the heart that increases the power of the heart and its efficiency. The heart generates the body's most powerful electric field and it pulls or entrains the other organ energy fields into alignment with it similar to how the sounds from the queen bee bring harmony to all worker bees in the beehive.

Traditional Chinese Medicine treats emotions as energy, believing they express and set into motion different energies as compressed in the conjunction 'e-motion.' The Yellow Emperor's Classic describes the connection between emotions and energy as follows: *Anger causes chi to rise up, joy causes chi to slow down, grief causes it to dissipate, fear causes it to descend and surprise scatters it.*[594]

The body stores energy in the electrolytes of its vital fluids similar to a battery. Electrolytes are non-metallic conductors of electricity and are carried by ions instead of electrons. Like battery fluid, the body's electrolytes accumulate and store electric charges as electric potential and release them upon demand as active energy currents.[595]

The body stores energy in the electrolytes of its vital fluids similar to a battery.

Individuals in good health show an electric charge of eight micro-amperes on average; tired people register one or two while very excited people measure up to 15 micro-amperes.[596] This life force that the Chinese call chi represents electrical potential. Daniel Reid contends that: *Vitality and health manifest by an abundant bioelectrical charge, by ion exchanges and by the harmony of all functions.*[597]

Research shows that 'healers' such as Reiki and Healing Touch channeled an average of 8.3 volts during a healing session (range of 4 to 221 volts) as compared to a control group of non-healers who channeled an average of one volt.[598] Studies in Japan found that 'healers' were able to emit strong pulsating magnetic fields from their hands that were 1,000 times stronger than normal human bio-magnetic fields.[599]

Energy medicine uses some of the most sophisticated diagnostic screening devices such as the Magnetic Resonance Imaging (MRI) and the Positron Emission Tomography (PET). Other machines measure the various magnetic frequencies emitted by the body in order to detect imbalance that may be causing illness or contributing to future disease.

An early device to measure the electrical conductivity of the skin was developed in Germany by Dr. Reinhold Voll, MD. Voll determined that the electrical conductivity of the skin increases dramatically at acupoints and each acupoint has a specific conductivity value for healthy people. A lower than normal conductivity indicated an inflammation or irritation in the organ corresponding to the acupoint being tested. A higher conductivity meant a fatigued or degenerating organ. Voll also created the Dermatron to diagnose diseases caused by bacteria or viruses along with food allergies and the presence of chemical toxins. He discovered that if a patient held vials containing homeopathic solutions of various disease-causing agents (such as bacteria and viruses), then the acupoint conductivity reading would return to normal when the patient held a vial containing the precipitating causal factor leading to that disease (homeopathic principle of like cures).

A network of energy pathways called meridians flow through the human body like rivers of energy. These rivers pass through each of the organs, supplying energy to the different parts of the body. For the body to function at an optimal level, the proper amount of energy must flow through the meridians. There are 20 pairs of meridians and each pair connects to a different organ in the body such as heart, lung, kidney and stomach. As a person moves away from health, their energy levels fall. A certain range of energy means the meridian is in balance. The energy can either move above or below an optimal range, indicating either a stressed or weakened and impaired organ.

> A network of energy pathways called meridians flow through the human body like rivers of energy.

Detecting energy level imbalances in the body provides an early warning system for disruptions that may lead to disease before chemical or structural disturbances occurs. Blocked or low energy will bring disease. Blocked energy can be cleared by stimulation with acupuncture or acupressure with finger pressure on acupoints located on the meridian. Disturbed energy flows can be returned to their normal healthy state through the input of electromagnetic signals that counteract the affected frequencies to restore a normal energy balance within the body.[600] Individuals can learn how to recognize their pains as signals of energy imbalance. People can reclaim their natural healing capacities by their own efforts claims Donna Eden, author of *Energy Medicine.*[601]

Dr. Valeria Hunt of UCLA built and tested the AuraMeter System to detect signature energy patterns of cancer, diabetes and heart disease before they manifest in the tissue/organ at the biochemical level.[602] The Acupuncture Department at the Vet General Hospital in Taipei also developed a technique to detect diseases in various organs and tissues long before they become acute by measuring changes in electric currents on a cellular level. The hospital achieved an 80 percent success rate in diagnosing the onset of a wide range of diseases before any physiological symptoms detectable by conventional Western methods such as blood tests, stethoscopes and X-rays appear.[603]

Medicine entered a third stage in the 1990s according to Larry Dossey.[604] In Chapter 3, this third stage called "transpersonal" or "non-local" medicine was reviewed. This state is characterized by research documenting the ability of the mind to affect the physical health of a distant living plant or person. Dossey cites prayer and transpersonal imagery as examples of the mind's ability to function at a distance. 'Conscious intentionality' affects things beyond what physical brains can do.

Elisabeth Targ, M.D., conducted a double blind study of forty advanced AIDS patients to determine if distant healers could promote healing at a distance. The healers worked from their homes from around the country on half of the patients having only the patient's picture, a first name and lab statistics. Neither the patients nor the doctors knew who was receiving the distant healing treatment. After six months the patients who had received the distant healing had significantly fewer new illnesses (2 vs. 12), fewer visits to doctors (185 vs. 260) and fewer days in the hospital (10 vs. 68) than the control group. They also experienced a markedly improved mood scores on standardized tests.

A number of programs train and certify "energy healing" work. One of the older organizations is the National Federation of Spiritual Healers. Their purpose is to train, license and coordinate spiritual healing, including distant healing. They publish the magazine *Healing Today* and have an active website at www.nfsh.org.uk. Other groups for energy work and training include Healing Touch, Therapeutic Touch and Reiki.

Rituals for rejuvenating and in-filling of energies for these types of healers include breathing (Qigong and Pranayama[605]), praying and imagining (Reiki and Healing Touch). Such rituals also facilitate the removal of one's self as an ego so as to channel outside pure energies for the patient to incorporate them if they are receptive.

Psychologist Lawrence LeShan studied energy healers and discovered that the most prevalent type of healer entered a prayerful altered state of consciousness in which the healers viewed him or herself and the patient as a single entity. No physical contact need occur nor is anything done outwardly, only the desire to become one with the patient and God/Universal Mind. Connecting to one's source is conducive to healing as it brings calm and coherence. Anything that dissolves boundaries and alleviates separation brings calm and wholeness, thereby stimulating the person's immune system.

How One Reiki Master Views Healing

Before doing Reiki on a client, I ask them to declare their intention for the session outwardly or silently. I then facilitate a centering exercise to focus inward, quieting my mind, and being receptive to receiving healing energy; I ask for healing on all levels for the other person; I ask for our guides and angels to work in concert for the highest good of all concerned.

During Reiki, I ask as a vessel, filling from Source, bringing loving energy through my energetic system. Working in the same space, our energy fields closely approximate, therefore, the energy I channel is offered to the client but is not directed consciously by me. During the session I hold the space for a large capacity of loving energy to be available. The person I work on then draws it from my energy field. It can be viewed in terms of diffusion: loving energy moves from an area of high concentration to an area of less concentration if no barriers exist for the movement. (The person seeking to be healed must be willing and receptive.) When equilibrium is achieved, the flow stops. When I feel the flow slowing I know that I can move to another area or that I am done with the session. In absentee or distant healing the same thing happens; I connect to the person's energy filed and the same process occurs! Barbara Rose, RN and Reiki Master of Knoxville, Tennessee

---

The following account of distant healing occurred in May 2005 with Kathy, a retired nurse. She continues to use her training in Reiki and Healing Touch to help people. Ahweh, an ancient entity came into Kathy's life in response to seeking guidance for her 'life purpose' in 2000. Kathy became a channel to this loving energy.

Kathy now uses (ahwehonearth@yahoo.com) to receive requests for guidance from Ahweh.

Kathy shared a copy of e-mails between herself and a man who was healed overnight as he was awaiting prostate surgery in the hospital. This healing occurred before the e-mails or any contact in the "ordinary world" as this man lives in a distant state. This story starts with the man's e-mail.

> *I want to tell you a story before I ask my question of Ahweh. I was in the hospital with my doctor who was reading x-rays on my prostate when this nurse appears behind him and starts telling me that I have other options beside surgery. I thought the nurse was part of the program until the doctor looked at me like I was talking to the wall. I am scheduled for surgery the next day. That night the same nurse comes walking into my room and puts her hand over my prostate. I had a feeling this was one of my other options. The next morning, I insisted on more x-rays [before surgery]. The doctor was "miffed." He finds my prostate is no longer enlarged and he seems upset that I no longer need treatments! I wanted to thank the nurse but no one [here] knows who she is.*

The man returned home and went online with his computer to e-mail relatives when Ahweh's website mysteriously 'popped up' as the man explained:

> *I read some of the content. This was a miracle in itself, because I don't have any tolerance for pop ups, but I guess I was just in the mood. I am putting two and two together and I have a suspicion [about that mysterious nurse and your website]. My question is: ARE YOU A NURSE AND DO YOU DO THIS KIND OF DISTANT HEALING? Does any of this make sense? I am really shooting in the dark here. Could you ask Ahweh about this nurse?*

Ahwey's reply:

Dear one, What you experienced is becoming more common now that we are in the shift of energies on Earth leading to the "Healing of all Life." Your story will give hope to many who are caught in despair because of the belief system they have been taught. "Reality" is changing. As people believe it CAN change, it WILL change. We chose you for many reasons. One reason is your clear ability to recognize Truth when you see it, and then speak your Truth with matter-of-fact clarity. WE LOVE YOU.

Kathy was not aware of the type of healing work she was doing until she received this e-mail from the man. In response to his e-mail, Kathy sent a photo of herself to the man and he replied:

You are the nurse! My God, you are the Mother Teresa of nurses to me. I love you. Thank you, thank you, thank you.

Kathy replied to him in another e-mail and wrote:

It's like the dream world and the 'real world' is merging. I have been having many dreams of being in the hospital recently and have been wondering why.

We are connected to each other by fields of energy that extend throughout and beyond our physical bodies. Use of these energy fields enables us to experience spiritual healing via distant prayer and other non-physical means.

> There is an endless net of threads throughout the universe. The horizontal threads are in space. The vertical threads are in time. At every crossing of the threads, there is an individual. And every individual is a crystal bead. And every crystal bead reflects not only the light from every other crystal in the net, but also every other reflection throughout the entire universe. THE RIG VEDA

We live in a most interesting and exciting time. With greater understanding of our self and our world, consciousness is expanding as we take more responsibility for our life and open ourselves to guidance from within. The power to create a healthier environment resides within each of us as individuals. As we each learn to appreciate our power in the greater scheme of things and respect our connectedness to all living things, we will experience the path to peace, harmony and health enrichment.

APPENDIX A
GLOSSARY OF TERMS

Acupressure—A technique whereby finger massage is applied to acupuncture sites to improve the balance and flow of qi energy in the body, thus preventing and treating disease and disability.

Acupuncture—A technique for preventing and treating disease that has been used in China for the last five thousand years. Thin, metallic needles are inserted into precise points on the body surface along meridian systems to improve the balance and flow of qi energy to promote health and to treat disease and relieve pain. Acupuncture has been scientifically studied extensively.

Applied Kinesiology—A diagnostic and therapeutic system that employs the practice of muscle-testing to identify nutritional deficiencies and health problems with the belief that weakness in certain muscles relates to respective imbalances and diseases in organs and the body.

Aromatherapy—This therapy uses concentrated essential oils from plants, often in association with massage to relieve symptoms and aid well-being. Each plant oil contains its own properties and is particularly effective for different conditions.

Allopathtic Medicine—The mainstream school of medicine whose therapeutic modalities are generally confined to surgery, radiation, and synthetic drug therapies. Allopathic medicine utilizes the principle of opposites and is characterized by specialization according to diagnoses or anatomy.

Ayurvedic Medicine—Based on the Hindu Vedic texts, Ayurveda is one of the oldest known systems of healing. It is the aggregate of diagnostic and therapeutic practices that approach health as the balance of body, mind, emotion, and spirit. It uses an understanding of qualities of energy and the application of preventive and corrective treatments such as yoga, purification regimens, dietary changes, and herbal remedies.

Bach Flower Remedies—Developed by homeopath E. Bach, these extracts of flowers diluted according to homeopathic principles are applied to cure subtle emotional roots of disease.

Bioenergetics—A therapeutic system that uses breath and body movement to release and transform blocked energy, body tensions, and inhibitions, and to restore health.

Biofeedback—A method for learning control of physiological responses of the body. It uses electronic equipment to amplify the electrochemical energy produced by body responses. This helps individuals to gain voluntary control. Biofeedback is the use of equipment to self-monitor physiological signals from the mind or body and thus to bring involuntary processes under voluntary control.

Biofield Therapy—The use of intention and energy to alter the biofield of another living being. All living things have an energy field permeating and surrounding them that can be manipulated therapeutically to treat illness and restore health. The three most prominent therapies using the hands are Healing Touch, Therapeutic Touch and Reiki.

Chelation Therapy—A process describing how certain molecules surround and bind to metal ions and the resulting variety of biochemical alterations that occur. Conventional medicine uses it as a standard treatment for poisoning with lead, iron, copper, zinc, aluminum, manganese, and other metals. Chelation is used for treating atherosclerosis and other chronic degenerative diseases, consisting of a series of intravenous infusions, accompanied by vitamins, minerals, and other supplements.

Chiropractic—Focuses on the spine as integrally involved in maintaining health, providing primacy to the nervous system as the primary coordinator for function, and thus health, in the body. Maintenance of optimal neuro-physiological balance in the body is accomplished in chiropractic by correcting abnormalities in the movement and function of the muscular and skeletal systems by means of massage and chiropractic adjustments.

Christian Science—This is a system of healing that believes that disease is a form of "mis-creation" by the individual who must be treated and healed in their mind by prayer and aligning with Divine Mind.

Craniosacral Therapy—A therapeutic technique developed by W. G. Sutherland, <u>DO</u>, (Ditto to query #1.) that uses very gentle manual pressure applied to the skull, spine, and membranes to restore proper rhythmic flow to the craniosacral system and relieve pain and certain disorders closely related to the skull and spine, such as headache, TMJ, and vertigo.

Dietary Therapy—A product taken in addition to the diet that supplies nutrients and other substances to promote health or to treat disease.

Electromagnetic Fields—EMFs, also called electric and magnetic fields are invisible lines of force that surround all electrical devices. The Earth also produces EMFs; electric fields are produced when there is thunderstorm activity, and magnetic fields are believed to be produced by electric currents flowing at the Earth's core.

Electrical Therapies—Use of electromagnetic energy directly for therapeutic purposes.

Electrical Stimulation—Use of electrical currents applied to the body to bring about healing. Some devices used to reduce pain are called transelectrical nerve stimulation, or TENS, instruments. Some physicians utilize computerized TENS type devices that deliver minute electrical impulses through the skin in response to electrical currents received from injured cells of the body. These instruments are used to treat all kinds of musculoskeletal injuries.

Fasting—A common component of naturopathy in which little or no food and/or drink is taken for a specific period to cleanse the body and to rest the digestive system.

Feldenkrais—This therapeutic method uses awareness of movements and teaches proper body movement through gentle massage, stretching and exercise.

Guided Imagery—Based on the principle that the imagination has the capacity to relieve pain and promote healing when it is optimistic and confident. The techniques of guided imagery are designed to teach individuals how to use their own powers of imagination to steer away from negative thoughts toward well-being. Guided imagery seeks to make beneficial physical changes in the body—e.g., a heart beating normally or a tumor shrinking—by repeatedly focusing on them.

Healing Touch—An energy-based technique that focuses attention on the hands with the intention to direct energy toward another for purposes of balancing their energy field for healing.

Herbalism—Therapeutic systems based exclusively on the curative power of herbal and mineral remedies prepared from a wide variety of plant materials—frequently the leaves, stems, roots, and bark, but also the flowers, fruits, twigs, seeds, and exudates (material that oozes out, such as sap). They generally contain several biologically active ingredients and are used primarily for treating chronic or mild conditions.

Holistic Medicine—An approach to healing that considers the whole person's body, mind and spirit in the process of treating disease and promoting health. This approach combines the use of conventional and complementary therapies by medical and non-medical practitioners in collaboration with the patient to both treat disease and promote health.

Homeopathy—A therapeutic system developed by S. Hahnemann, that uses extremely dilute medicines to trigger a person's innate capacity to heal, based on the law of similars that medicines can produce in healthy people the same symptoms they cure in the sick.

Hypnotherapy—Hypnosis is a state of attentive and focused concentration during which people are highly responsive to suggestion during such trance states. It is used to address a wide range of problems, including anxiety, phobias, and emotional problems and to help break habits like smoking. By inducing altered states of consciousness, hypnotherapists help clients use the resources of the unconscious mind to bring about psychological and physical benefits.

Iridology—Diagnosis by observation of the marks, patterns, and colors of the iris, which are reflections of body diseases and psychological makeup. Iridology helps identify inherited emotional patterns which can create or maintain physical symptoms, as well as identify lessons or challenges and gifts or talents.

Macrobiotics—Diets according to the principles established in Zen monasteries in which the grain-, vegetable-, animal-, salt-, heat- or cold-producing and yin or yang qualities of food are balanced appropriately.

Massage—Any technique (e.g., rubbing, stroking, tapping, or kneading) in which pressure and touch are applied to the body for the purpose of treating physical and emotional disorders, increasing blood flow, reducing pain, and promoting relaxation, muscle tension release, and general health and well-being.

Meditation—A general term for a wide range of practices that involve relaxing the body and stilling the mind. A discipline that uses intention to direct one's focus on a word or the breath as a means to increase awareness of the present, reduce stress, promote relaxation, and attain personal and spiritual growth.

Meridian—In traditional Chinese medicine, a circuit that loops throughout the body and carries the vital qi (Ditto to query #1.) along one of 12 main channels connecting, regulating, and balancing the functioning of the principle organs and body structures. In acupuncture and acupressure, specific points along the meridians are used to correct the flow of qi and to restore proper function. Through the meridians, the qi reveals the condition of the internal functions of the body.

Mind-Body Therapies—This approach recognizes the connection between the physical and mental/emotional aspects of disease and treats both. These therapies include art, biofeedback, dance, hypnosis, imagery, meditation, yoga and others.

Naturopathy—Emphasizes the body's ability to heal itself by living within the laws of nature and by the use of natural foods and medicines that support the self-healing mechanisms such as nutritional therapy. Only natural treatments are used including diet manipulation, vitamin, mineral and herbal supplements, exercise, massage, homeopathy and hypnotherapy. Therapies are noninvasive and have low incidence of side effects.

Orthomolecular Medicine—The adjustment of concentrations of molecules (e.g., vitamins, minerals, amino acids, hormones, and metabolic intermediates) that are normally present in the body for the prevention and treatment of disease. This approach takes the idea of dietary supplementation a step further, the belief that larger than usual doses of certain nutrients can actually prevent or cure disease.

Osteopathy—A system of medical practice, developed in 1874 by Andrew Still, who believed that diseases were due chiefly to loss of structural integrity and adequate nerve and blood supply to organs of the body. Manipulation is used to restore health supplemented by other therapeutic measures.

Placebo—An innocuous substance or treatment that is given for its suggestive effect. A substance or treatment given to the control group in a randomized controlled trial (RCT) in order to distinguish between effects of the substance or treatment being tested and the effects of suggestion.

Polarity Therapy—A therapeutic method based on the theory that positive and negative energies flow throughout the body along five predictable pathways and that the flow can be balanced by the placement of the polarity therapist's hands at specific points along the channel to correct certain disorders.

Psychosomatic Medicine—A field of medical research and practice that examines the influence of the mind and emotions on the development of bodily disorders and disease and uses physical and psychological means to treat them.

Psychotherapy—A form of treatment that uses "talk therapy" to gain an awareness, understanding, and resolution of emotional, behavioral, and psychiatric disorders and related physical disorders. The many types of psychotherapy include individual, group, or family psychotherapy that may be utilized by psychiatrists, psychologists and social workers.

Qigong—An ancient Chinese discipline that uses breathing exercises, movement and meditation to balance and strengthen the body's vital energy.

Reiki—Reiki is based on the belief that when subtle or universal energy is channeled through a Reiki practitioner, healing is promoted on a physical, mental, emotional, and spiritual level.

Spiritual Healing—The systematic, purposeful intervention that aims to help another by means of focused intention, by touch, or by holding the hands near the other being, without application of physical, chemical, or conventional energetic means of intervention.

Subluxation—The partial dislocation of the bones within a joint, interfering with proper neurophysiological function. Realignment of the bones is known as a chiropractic adjustment.

Supplements—A supplement is a product taken by mouth that contains a "dietary ingredient" intended to supplement the diet. Supplements include vitamins, minerals, herbs or other botanicals, amino acids, and substances such as enzymes, organ tissues, and metabolites. Dietary supplements come in many forms, including extracts, concentrates, tablets, capsules, gel caps, liquids, and powders. Under US law, dietary supplements are considered foods, not drugs.

Therapeutic Touch—A modern variation of the "laying on of hands," which claims to heal by correcting imbalances in the energy field that emanates from the body. Despite its name, therapeutic touch rarely involves physical contact; instead, the therapist moves his or her hands just above the patient's body. Healing is promoted when the body's energies are in balance; and, by passing their hands over the patient, healers can identify energy imbalances.

Traditional Chinese medicine (TCM)—TCM is an ancient system of health care from China that is based on a concept of balanced qi (pronounced "chee"), or vital energy, that is believed to flow throughout the body. Qi regulates a person's spiritual, emotional, mental, and physical balance and is influenced by the opposing forces of yin (negative energy) and yang (positive energy). Disease is proposed to result from the flow of qi being disrupted and yin and yang becoming imbalanced. The therapeutic components of TCM are herbal medicine, acupuncture, moxibustion, massage and qigong.

Transcutaneous Electrical Nerve Stimulation (TENS)—A therapeutic method in which a low-voltage electrical current is delivered to the nerves by attaching electrodes to the skin in order to relieve pain by stimulating endorphin production.

Vibrational Medicine—A system of healing that posits that disease originates from an imbalance or blockade of energy and that certain therapeutic methods such as homeopathy, sound and biofield therapies can be used to unblock and balance the energies and restore health and well-being.

Yoga—An ancient Indian philosophy that uses gentle stretching exercises, breath control, and meditation to gain self-mastery and self-realization. Yoga helps yoke or connect body and mind together to balance bodily energy.

APPENDIX B
CENTERS FOR CAM RESEARCH

1. Aging and Women's Health
   - Center for CAM Research in Aging and Women's Health, Columbia University, New York, New York
2. Arthritis
   - Center for Alternative Medicine Research on Arthritis, University of Maryland School of Medicine, Baltimore, Maryland
3. Cancer
   - Center for Cancer Complementary Medicine, Johns Hopkins University, Baltimore, Maryland
   - Specialized Center of Research in Hyperbaric Oxygen Therapy, University of Pennsylvania, Philadelphia, Pennsylvania
4. Cardiovascular Diseases
   - CAM Research Center for Cardiovascular Disease, University of Michigan Taubman Health Care Center, Ann Arbor, Michigan
5. Cardiovascular Disease and Aging in African Americans
   - Center for Natural Medicine and Prevention, Maharishi University of Management, Fairfield, Iowa

6. Chiropractic
   - Consortial Center for Chiropractic Research, Palmer Center for Chiropractic Research, Davenport, Iowa
7. Craniofacial Disorders
   - Oregon Center for Complementary and Alternative Medicine, Kaiser Foundation Hospitals, Portland, Oregon
8. Neurodegenerative Diseases
   - Center for CAM in Neurodegenerative Diseases, Emory University School of Medicine, Atlanta, Georgia
9. Neurological Disorders
   - Oregon Center for Complementary and Alternative Medicine in Neurological Disorders, Oregon Health Sciences University, Portland, Oregon
10. Pediatrics
   - Pediatric Center for Complementary and Alternative Medicine, University of Arizona Health Sciences Center, Tucson, Arizona

CENTERS FOR DIETARY SUPPLEMENTS RESEARCH: BOTANICALS

1. Botanical Center for Age-Related Diseases, Purdue University, West Lafayette, Indiana
2. Botanical Dietary Supplements for Women's Health, University of Illinois, Chicago, Illinois
3. Center for Dietary Supplements Research: Botanicals, University of California, Los Angeles, California
4. Center for Phyto-medicine Research, University of Arizona College of Pharmacy, Tucson, Arizona
5. Center for Phyto-nutrient and Phyto-chemical Studies, University of Missouri, Columbia, Missouri

CENTERS OF EXCELLENCE FOR RESEARCH ON CAM

1. Acupuncture
   - Neuro-imaging Acupuncture Effects on Human Brain Activity, Massachusetts General Hospital, Boston, Massachusetts

2. Antioxidants
   - Center of Excellence for Research on CAM Antioxidant Therapies, Oregon State University, Corvallis, Oregon
   - Translational Research Center for CAM Therapy of Asthma, University of North Carolina, Chapel Hill, North Carolina
3. Mindfulness-Based Stress Reduction
   - Center on Mindfulness-Based Stress Reduction, Stress Arousal, and Immune Response in Early HIV, University of California, San Francisco, California
4. Traditional Chinese Medicine
   - Alternative Therapies for Alcohol and Drug Abuse, McLean Hospital/ Harvard Medical School, Boston, Massachusetts

APPENDIX C
MIND/BODY THERAPIES

MD BETZ WITH RON FELIX: Therapies for enhancing coherence of body, mind and spirit.

Mind/body tools help focus attention, shift consciousness and reduce stress. Reducing stress is important because stress undermines health and leads to illness. "Stress related problems account for 60 to 90 percent of all U.S. doctor visits and mind/body approaches often are more effective and less costly than drugs or surgery" claims Herbert Benson,MD and author of *The Relaxation Response* and *Timeless Healing.*

Five mind-body tools that help link conscious intention to internal physiological processes are examined here. These tools include hypnosis, imagery, biofeedback, meditation and yoga. All five tools help restore balance and enhance healing, health and well-being. All can enrich health. These five tools are a small sample from a larger set of mind/body tools that are being used.

Mind/body tools expanded within the last 25 years. Increasingly mind tools are deployed in business, sports, problem solving and promoting health. We are empowering and creating new futures with an increasing number of tools as shown below.

Tools for enhancing body-mind coherence include:

Art therapy	Biofeedback
Dance/movement therapy	Dream work
Gestalt therapy	Hypnotherapy and regression
Holographic breath work	Imagery/visualization
Jungian analysis	Meditation
Music therapy	Neurolinguistic programming
Prayer/spiritual healing	Psychoanalysis
Psychodrama	Qi Gong
Relaxation response	Tai chi chuan and chi gong
Thought Field Therapy	Transcendental Meditation
Transactional analysis	Yoga

Therapies dealing with mind/body medicine can be found at www.cmbm.org and www.holistic-online.com.

The five tools discussed here all enhance coherence and unify separate dimensions of the self (body, mind, and spirit). They help dissolve boundaries and shift consciousness via slowing brain waves into the alpha and theta frequencies (4-12hz). Absorption, focusing and relaxation techniques help achieve this outcome. Absorption is the ability to shift attention from external stimuli via the five senses to internal processes so as to attain calm, focused attention and insight.

The dictionary defines mind as an abstract term for all forms of intelligence- the organized conscious and unconscious adaptive activity of an organism. Synonyms of mind include consciousness, reason, soul and spirit. John Dewey in *Experience and Nature* (1925 pp. 247-8) defined mind as "an organized field of meaning."

HYPNOSIS

Hypnosis is a way of relaxing the conscious mind to make use of heightened suggestibility for changing perception, memory, and behavior.

In the 1955 the British Medical Association approved its use and the American Medical Association in 1958 officially approved it as a valuable and safe treatment tool. The most common problems treated with hypnosis include smoking, overweight, stress, phobias, anxiety or panic attacks, sports improvement, test taking, public speaking and pain management. While effective and safe, controversy persists over what it is, how it works and why it works.

Willingness to be hypnotized is a necessary prerequisite but does not insure positive results. Research shows the best candidates for hypnosis are those able to imagine and three factors determine the level of success in hypnosis:

- The patient's level of motivation to change.
- The use of believable/credible suggestions.
- Repetition or reinforcement of the suggestion.

Hypnotic induction is a way to focus attention so as to access that natural hypnotic state. Once in this state, the "mental gate" opens and helpful suggestions can be given. Positive healing suggestions sink deeply into the mind much more quickly and strongly than when you are in a normal, awake state. Hypnosis is nothing more than fixating attention so that new frames of reference can be planted and nurtured. There are two steps: the relaxation stage which creates a receptive, open mind; and planting suggestions which creates a new frame of reference that fits the facts equally well. The new frame is used for reinterpreting reality for enhancing well being. [See page 148 in Joan Borysenko's book *Minding the Body, Mending the Mind*]

Fresh frames of reference are planted and nurtured by affirmations which neutralize a mind trap and reinforce a new viewpoint. New affirmations challenge and counter beliefs from the past or the unconscious. Affirmations are also called neuro-linguistic-programs (NLP) for creating new ways of "seeing" and reacting. Each of us have access to our own unconscious at the edge of waking and sleeping (called the hypnogogic state) which is the best time for planting affirmations. Those who work in this area contend that one positive affirmation (verbally or mentally repeated) can cancel out ten negative thoughts of "stinking thinking". Replace "I want" with "I intend"; replace "try" with "promise"; "should" with "I choose"; and "hope" with "I make a commitment". Establish your goal and align your intention and words to achieve what you envision!

Brain researchers refer to states of consciousness and brain wave frequencies in cycles per second. The four brave wave patterns are:

- Beta–fully awake (<12hz) peak concentration and cognition=16 hz)
- Alpha–alertness but calm relaxation   (8-12hz) visualization and hypnosis
- Theta–for meditation, learning and memory; early stages of sleep (4-7hz)
- Delta–for sleep and healing (>4hz).

Most individuals who choose alternatives therapies such as hypnosis seek more personal involvement in their health. Auto hypnosis fits their orientation nicely since all hypnosis is self-hypnosis. People can learn to self-induce relaxation and plant suggestions in their mind. Self-hypnosis is one of the easiest and fastest ways to relax. Often hypnosis is taught as a stress management technique.

IMAGERY

Imaging is a process of forming something within the mind that is not actually present to the senses; this internal creation arises from thinking less so as to experience more as mind and memory are activated. Greater coherence between left and right brain functioning occurs when one aligns conscious and unconscious states of mind. Activating the imagination draws upon the wealth of stored experiences and feelings from both the conscious and unconscious. From this well springs all new inventions and creations. Often referred to as seeing with the mind's eye or the third eye, it is the way we plan, dream and create but it is also the way we feed fear, phobia, anger and resentment. Becoming more conscious of how we deploy mind holds great health benefits!

Images are not just visual but can involve sound, taste, touch and smell. Surveys show that most rely on visual and auditory cues as sensory input in their "learning styles." All sensory memories can enhance imagination but people exhibit their "in-put" learning styles by the forms of their output of imagination.

The power of imagining in health and healing is not new but scientific research and proof was lacking until the late 1920s. We can thank technology itself for helping us rediscover imagery as a healing tool. Experiments done by Edmund Jacobsen in 1929 proved "that when people imagined themselves doing an action such as running, the muscles in their body associated with that action contracted in small but definite amounts." This linking of imagined thoughts to muscular action paved the way to more complex brain research and a new field of investigation including biofeedback.

Psychoneuroimmunology links the once separate disciplines of the mind (psychology), the brain (neurology), and the immune system. The National Institute of Health contains a unit devoted to mind/body research. Brain research shows a molecular code links emotions, mind and health. Imagery can enhance the immune system, skin resistance, affect vascular tone, change blood glucose, lower blood pressure and respiration and open the airways. Candice Pert of the National Institute of Health shows that brain and body communicate using a flood of chemical messengers that hook up to receptors on the surface membranes of cells; every thought, mood and attitude effect the body via chemical messengers. These opiate receptors translate every thought, reaction, and emotion into physiological changes. The brain, the immune system, endocrine system, heart, lungs, intestines are linked together into an integrated set of communicating circuits. Pert claims: *We are not a mind in a machine but a single integrated entity; these peptides constitute a 'psychosomatic communication network' in which the mind is literally spread throughout the body.* (See her book *Molecules and Emotion.*) Repressed emotions can be stored in a body part, thereafter affecting the ability to feel that part or even move it. Memories are stored in a psychosomatic network extending into the body, particularly in the receptors between nerves and bundles of cell bodies called ganglia. Massaging those parts can activate memories and their release.

Beliefs and attitudes effect the immune system positively or negatively. The creative mechanism within is impersonal. The body's task is to carry out thoughts, not judge whether they are positive or negative. Thoughts and beliefs affect biology. As in hypnosis, focusing attention in combination with nurturing or enriching an intention produces results. All thoughts and images effect the quality of our lives and health. For more, see the center for mind/body medicine web site www.cmbm.org.

The Imagination Institute seeks to understand the effects of imagery on mental and physiological outcomes. The majority of our thoughts are a product of creative imagination. Why? Because of the time spent imaging both 'positive" futures (in planning, hoping, dreaming, perceiving) and 'negative' pasts (by resenting, plotting, judging, and fearing). The images and feelings stored in memory and body tissues from the past can outweigh the present input of direct sensory data, thereby imprisoning one in a historical cubicle. Becoming more conscious of what and how images are used uncovers new choices and ways of enhancing health. (www.imagination-institute. com).

What we imagine expands what we can "see" and achieve, reversing the adage that what we see limits what we imagine and achieve. If you fill a person with knowledge, you have a person full of knowledge, but spark their imagination and their world expands! What you conceive and believe determines what you achieve. Support for this comes from sports, healing and problem solving.

What you conceive and believe determines what you achieve or C + B = A.

BIOFEEBACK.

Biofeedback is the use of instruments to monitor and provide information that facilitates the person learning how to regulate autonomic bodily functions. The autonomic system regulates heart rate, blood pressure skin temperature, breathing, etc. The term biofeedback arose in 1969 at the first conference of feedback researchers.

The idea behind biofeedback is not new, even though the name, its development and use of high tech equipment is. As early as the 18th century, stories of amazing feats by Indian gurus led to testing of their feats/abilities and an eventual change in understanding how the mind/body interacts. Their ability to slow their heart rate and maintain an animated state or their ability to withstand severe cold by controlling blood flow challenged old views of what was controlled by conscious vs. unconscious mind.

A typical biofeedback system contains a sensing device, an amplifier and a monitor. The sensing device, usually an electrode, is attached to a part of the body system to be measured. It is then amplified and the response is fed back in the form of tones, lights charts or gauges. The central purpose is to connect the cue with an internal physiological state.

As technology increased, biofeedback equipment could use blood pressure, activity of the bladder, esophageal motility, stomach acidity and the rectal sphincter. A person might use all or some of the above instruments depending on the disorder being treated. Some equipment is expensive and not designed for home usage but there are simpler and less expensive instruments for home use.

The therapy involves using this instrumentation for purposes of reducing symptoms and/or medication, enhanced quality of life and prevention. The equipment provides readings of internal bodily processes. It's like looking inside the body. The instruments enhance the capability of directing attention to internal states of muscular tension, heart rate, respiration and brain wave frequency. You gauge your success by noting any changes in the intensity, volume or speed of the signals from the machine. Gradually, you learn to associate "successful thoughts" and actions with the desired change in involuntary responses. Once the effective pattern is learned, controlling the "problem" becomes learned and the feedback device is no longer needed.

Biofeedback is being used to treat over 150 conditons including: asthma, epilepsy, ADD, chronic pain, hot flashes, irritable bowel syndrome, incontinence, headaches, cardiac arrhythmias, hypertension, substance abuse, Raynaud's syndrome and nausea and vomiting associated with chemotherapy. There are specific biofeedback therapists but in many instances biofeedback is now being incorporated into clinical practices like neurology, psychotherapy and dentistry.

The self-regulating aspect of biofeedback appeals to many people in the alternative health movement because it gives them a sense of mastery and self-reliance over their illness and health. Change requires effort and involvement because skills must be acquired and practiced. This requires willpower and determination. Patients become partners with the therapist.

MEDITATION

Meditation uses the focus on a word or the breath so as to increase present awareness; one deliberately suspends the stream of consciousness that usually occupies the mind so as to induce mental tranquillity and physical relaxation.

Meditation is a mind tool for dissolving usual boundaries between the physical and non physical worlds. Used throughout the ages as a religious and spiritual practice, it facilitates the experience of unity and peace. People experience something greater than themselves and a relationship to it. Among scientists who meditate and were asked why, most claimed: "It's like coming home."

Many different approaches to meditation are taught, each with its own specialized techniques. However, all require:

- A quiet environment where you won't be disturbed (limit light and noise)
- A comfortable position on the floor or in a chair, do not lie down
- A point of focus for your mind

Approaches to meditation fall into three major categories:

1. *Transcendental Meditation (TM)* is the most common form of meditation in the West. It involves mental repetition of a

mantra, usually a Sanskrit sound provided by the instructor. TM practitioners sit upright in a straight-backed chair with their eyes closed, and meditate for 15 to 20 minutes twice a day, morning and evening. A less spiritual off-shoot of TM, developed by Dr. Herbert Benson of Harvard University, achieves the same with his regimen called the "relaxation response."

2. *Mindfulness Meditation.* An outgrowth of a Buddhist tradition called vipassana, this approach focuses on the present moment and the feelng of every movement, muscle, and sensation that resides therein.

3. *Breath Medication* calls for concentrating on the process of inhalng and exhaling.

In the late 60's, Harvard cardiologist Dr. Herbert Benson developed a generic relaxation method. The relaxation response occurs with all techniques involving "repetition of a word, sound, prayer, or muscular activity and passive disregard of all other thoughts that come to mind." The purpose is to learn to let go within your own body and relax. Meditation does not involve getting somewhere but, rather, emphasizes being where you already are. As J. Krishnamurti once said, "meditation is not a means to an end, it is both the means and the end." And as the title of one book suggests, it is a journey without distance: *Wherever You Go, There You Are.*

A larger body of research exists on meditation than on all other mind-body tools. And we have the TM movement to thank for this. There is a compilation of over 500 research, review and theory papers by the Maharishi International University and under the direction of Dr. David Orne-Johnson. It is the work of over 360 researchers and 200 universities.

Physiologically, meditation slows the metabolic rate so the body uses less oxygen and produces less carbon dioxide. The respiratory rate, heart rate and blood pressure also decrease. Skin resistance increases, blood-lactate levels decrease and brain wave patterns change.All are measuring a decrease in stress. The body neutralizes the damaging effects of stress and revitalizes itself. People suffering from headaches, high blood pressure, insomnia, asthma, pain, and other stress related illnesses all benefit from meditation.

Research shows meditation slows the aging process. Robert Wallace studied a group of adult meditators over time to discover they were significantly younger biologically than their chronological age. The female subject who scored highest was twenty years younger than her chronological age.Years of continuous meditation practice correlated with how much benefit a person derived... the longer the better. A later study in England calculated that each year of regular meditation removes one year of aging. A 1986 Blue Cross–Blue Shield study of 2,000 meditators found them to be much healthier than the larger population in seventeen areas of serious mental and physical disease. Other studies since then confirm that meditators expend 30-87 percent fewer dollars on medial care. For more on meditation, see www.holistic-online.com/meditation.

YOGA

Yoga is a complete system of health that uses gentle stretching exercises, breath control and meditation; it originated some 5,000 years ago in India.The purpose is to gain self- mastery and self realization. Although the ultimate goal is to reach "oneness" or "enlightenment," yoga is not a religion. The word "yoga" means to yoke or join. Originally an oral tradition, yoga passed from teacher to student through time. Then about 2,000 years ago the Indian sage, Patanjali, systematized yoga philosophy in a single treatise called the Yoga Sutras. The Yoga Sutras consist of 195 aphorisms or statements of truth giving guidance on how to live a meaningful and productive life. The Yoga Sutras is the authoritative text on which all yoga is now based.

The physical or hatha yoga is predominant in the West. In Sanskrit, Ha means sun and Tha means moon which when combined implies balance.The balance that practitioners seek is union with the body, mind and spirit—different aspects of the self.

The three key elements to exercise and control are the breath, muscle, and the mind. During the deep relaxation pose, one systematically relaxes every part of the body, even suggesting that the brain itself is "relaxed." During conscious relaxation, thoughts are experienced more as an energy associated with the brain than as the sum of who we are. We have thoughts, but those thoughts no longer activate our bodies and minds by triggering tension, anxiety or other responses.

Yoga is a multi-purpose tool for physical conditioning, for cultivating mental or emotional calm and for clarity and spiritual awakening. Practicing yoga cultivates physical health which in turn allows one to cultivate good mental and emotional health which can lead to spiritual awakening. Good physical health creates the foundation on which the other conditions are built. Yoga increases the efficiency of the heart, slows respiration rate, improves fitness, lowers blood pressure, promotes relaxation, and reduces stress and anxiety. It also increases one's coordination, flexibility, range of motion, concentration, sleep and digestion. Research shows the practice of yoga increases brain endorphins, enkaphalins, and serotonin; yoga increases lymph circulation, nutrient supply to the tissues, and augments mental relaxation into alpha and theta brain wave patterns.

Exercises now called "yoga" are actually *hatha yoga*, a discipline intended to prepare the body for the pursuit of union. A typical session includes three disciplines: breathing exercises, body postures, and meditation.

Breathing. Cultivating control of breathing is an important part of hatha yoga.The life force is believed to enter the body through the breath. Shallow, hurried breathing inhibits the life force or "prana" and affects mind and body adversely. Deep, slow, diaphramatic breathing relaxes and enhances the life force.

Postures. Some yoga postures are intended to stretch and strengthen muscles, others to improve posture and work the skeletal system, while others aim to compress and relax the organs and nerves.The underlying purpose is to perfect the body, making it a worthy host for the soul.

Postures involve a series of poses that typically must be held for periods of a few seconds to several minutes. The goal is to mildly stretch all the muscle groups in the body, while gently squeezing the internal organs. Postures follow a specific order to balance the muscle groups. Breathing techniques remain important, facilitating gentle moves without jerking or bouncing as various postures are taken. Focus on exhaling during certain movements while inhaling during others.At the conclusion of the exercises, usually a period of rest or meditation follows.

Meditation. Meditation supplements and reinforces the disciplines of hatha yoga by focusing the mind and relaxing the body. Closely linked with focused breathing, meditation produces a quiet, calm mind. Many find that it reduces stress and increases energy. The interplay of these three facets of breathing, postures and meditation helps achieve yoga's benefits.Through controlled breathing, prescribed postures (called *asanas)* and meditation, hatha yoga enhances the life force in the body and helps achieve a balance and harmony between body and mind.

Half the health clubs in the US offer yoga classes replacing aerobics.Time Magazine contends that 17 million incorporate at least some aspects of yoga in 2001; 12 million were enrolled in yoga classes, double the numbers in 1996. We now have classes specializing in yoga for kids, partner yoga, yoga for round bodies, yoga for stiff bodies, yoga for pregnant women, corporate yoga, yoga for athletes, yoga for people with long term illnesses and more. For more information, visit www.holistic-online.com/yoga.

NOTES

[1] Disclaimer: Although I cancelled my medical health insurance that was my choice. What you choose to do in assuming more personal responsibility in promoting your health and life is just that—your choice and your responsibility.

[2] Cited by Daniel Reid, *The Tao of Health, Sex and Longevity*, NY: Simon & Schuster, 1989, page 233.

[3] Dysbiosis is commonly caused by repeated or long-term use of antibiotics or cortisone drugs. These drugs destroy both the good and bad bacteria, thereby allowing the gut to be colonized by unfriendly bacteria and parasites such as yeast-like fungi called *Candida Albicans*. Dysbiosis causes inflammation of the intestinal livings and activation of the immune cells. These cells release inflammatory cytokines which stimulate the adrenal to release the stress hormone, cortisol. Increased levels of cortisol cause the intestinal lings to thin and become more porous, allowing chemicals to get into the blood stream. These chemical proteins create an immune response, i.e., allergy. They also tax the liver's detoxification pathways disturbing the natural metabolism of hormones, cholesterol and toxins. This further causes the release of more cortisol and further thinning of the gut lining, thus creating a vicious cycle. Dysbiosis can give rise to irritable bowel, acne, food allergies, Chronic Fatigue and depression. See William Crook, *The Yeast Connection.*

[4] See Roger Battistella et al., "Crisis in American Medicine" Lancet 1: 581-86. March 16, 1968.

[5] Quoted in J. McKinlay and L. Marcean "The Impact of Managed Care on Patients' Trust in Medial Care and Their Physicians." Paper presented at the American Public Health Association, Washington DC, Nov. (cited in W Cockerham (ed) 2001, The *Blackwell Companion to Medical Sociology*, Oxford: Blackwell, p. 196).

[6] See www.practicalhealthreform.org . The entire issue of *Science* in May 26, 1978 is devoted to health maintenance and contains good articles on the need for a new way of looking at medical care.

[7] See *Death by Medicine* by Gary Null et al., October 2003, at www.garynull. com/documents/iatrogenic/deathbymedicine/deathbymedicine.

[8] The Foundation for Accountability in health care conducted a study in 2001 and found that two out of three patients were not advised by their doctor to make healthy behavior changes, one in three did not get enough information to manage their own health and half did not get recommended condition-

specific tests. *See Chronic Care in America*, a chart book for the Robert Wood Johnson Foundation, January 2002.

[9] The names of people I interviewed have been changed to protect their privacy.

[10] Quoted in *Integrative Medicine*, by David Rakel, Saunders, 2003, page 7.

[11] See Paul Starr's classic book *The Social Transformation of American Medicine* NY: Basic Books, 1984 for a discussion of the campaign to monopolize control of medical care.

[12] Both homeopathy and the Thompsonian herbalist were strong contenders in the practice of medicine at the turn of the 20th century.

[13] A December 2002 article in the *Annals of Int Med* by Druss et al shows non physician providers are specializing in more preventive care and less acute care over the 1986-97 period.

[14] Use of CAM-therapies increased from 60 million people in 1990 to 83 million in 1997. The total number of visits to alternative therapy practitioners increased 47% from 1990 (427 million) to 1997 (629 million). This number exceeds the total visits to all US primary care physicians. Expenditures for alternative professional services increased 45% between 1990 and 1997; this expenditure exceeds the 1997 out-of-pocket expenditures for all US hospitalizations. Total 1997 out-of-pocket expenditures relating to alternative therapies were conservatively estimated at $27.0 billion, which is comparable to out-of-pocket expenditures for all physician services. See David Eisenberg, et al. "Trends in Alternative Medicine in the US" *JAMA,* 1998, Vol. 280:1560-1575.

[15] See US government report, NIH 2004 at www.nccam.hih.gov/news/2004/052704.

[16] In a recent study in Washington State, patients who have used both conventional medicine and CAM for the same chronic illness reported higher levels of satisfaction with CAM (89% satisfied) than with conventional medicine (46% satisfied).

[17] See Kelner, M. and Wellman, B., 1997. Who seeks alternative health care? *The Journal of Alternative and Complementary Medicine* vol. 3 (2): 127-140.

[18] See F.M. Sirois, M.L. Gick, "An investigation of the health beliefs and motivations of complementary medicine clients," *Social Science and Behavior*, vol. 55 (6): 1025-1037 Sept 2002.

[19] See Kessler et al., "Long-term trends in the use of CAM," *Annals of Internal Medicine*, 2001, vol. 135: 262-68.

[20] From a 1987 report of the American Board of Family Practice.

[21] A 1999 article in *Am J of Health Promotion* asked: "Is it time for health promotion? The White House Commission on CAM Policy in 2002 declared that it was time.

[22] *Preventing Chronic Disease* is a peer-reviewed electronic journal, published by the National Center for Chronic Disease Prevention and Health Promotion.

[23] See Michael O'Donnell, *Health Promotion in the Workplace*, 3rd edition, NY: Thompson Delmar Learning, 2001: 35. Two books summarize data on cost-effectiveness published by the Association of Workplace Health Promotion:

Economic Impact of Worksite Health Promotion and *Worksite Health Promotion Economics*. (For more on best-of-practice methods, see www. awhp.org).

[24] See Annie Murphy Paul, "Self-Help" *Psychology Today*, March, 2001.

[25] See "An Overly Rosy View" in *USA TODAY*, Jan. 13, 2005.

[26] See *Learned Optimism* by E Martin and M Seligman, Free Press, 1998.

[27] A quote from *Quantum Change* by William Miller and Janet DeBaca, 2002.

[27*] See page 182-84 in his book, *A Whole New Life*, Plume/Penguin 1995.

[28] See Reynolds Price's book, *A Whole New Life*, Plume/Penguin 1995.

[29] See Esther Dunn, dept of Public Health and Preventive Medicine at Oregon Health Sciences University and her webpage at www.ohsu.edu .

[30] Self-help as behavioral modification tools can be effective 80-90% of the time. A meta-analysis of 40 well-designed outcome studies of self-help treatments concluded that self-help is just as effective in most cases of behavioral change as treatment administered by a therapist. See Scogin, F., Bynum, J., Stevens, G., and Calhoon, S. (1990). Efficacy of self-administered treatment programs: Meta-analytic review. *Professional Psychology: Research and Practice*, 21, 42-47.

[31] See www.cfah.org.

[32] Only 10% of research monies in NIH went to the behavioral sciences in 1998.

[33] See Eva Lindbladh and C.H. Lytkens "Habit versus choice" in *Social Science and Medicine*, vol. 5(3): 451-65 and "How to get healthier," *Time*, Feb 5, 2002.

[34] See Engel, "The need for a new medical model" in *Science* Vol. 196:129, April 8, 1977.

[35] See paradigm shift in Michael O'Donnell's book *Ibid* 2001: p 74-6).

[36] In 1997, "medical freedom of choice" legislation was introduced in the US Congress but it failed passage even after periodic reintroductions. Medical freedom of choice allows consumers to be treated by any health practitioner who is legally authorized to provide professional services in their state. (See Access to Medical Treatment Act HR 1964/S 1378.) Washington state passed their legislation in the early 1990s. (Read more at www.healthfreedom.org and www.holisticmed.com/www/medfree)

[37] See Jeffrey Levin "New Age Healing in the US," *Soc Sci &Med*, vol. 23 (9): 889.

[38] See www.templeton.org/courses98/highlights.

[39] See *Death by Medicine* by Gary Null PhD, Carolyn Dean MD ND, Martin Feldman MD Debora Rasio MD, Dorothy Smith PhD, October 2003. The Nutrition Institute of America, Inc., a New York not-for-profit corporation, founded in 1975, promotes better public health and nutrition through research and education.

[40] From being fingered for 180,000 deaths in 1994 by a Harvard study, to 225,000 deaths in 2000 by a Johns Hopkins study to over 780,000 deaths in 2003. See Leape, Lucian, "Error in medicine" in *JAMA*. 1994; 272(23):1851-7 and Starfield, Barbara, "Is US health really the best in the world?" in *JAMA*, 2000; 284(4):483-5.

[41] Consumer Reports issued a special issue on health entitled "Avoiding Hospital Blunders" in June 2000, vol. 12, number 6. Here are suggestions for avoiding being one of these medical errors:

- Be an active member of your health-care team. Take part in every decision about your care.
- Make sure all your doctors know every prescription medicine and over-the-counter product you're taking. That includes vitamins and herbal remedies. At least once a year, bring all your medicines and supplements to your doctor and discuss them to learn if there are any problems. This also helps your doctor keep your records up to date.
- Confirm your doctor knows about any allergies and adverse reactions you have to medicines.
- When your doctor writes a prescription, make sure you can read it. If you have trouble reading it, that means it may also be difficult for your pharmacist to read the prescription.
- Ask for easy to understand information about your medicines. What is the medicine for? How am I supposed to take it? For how long? What side effects are likely? What do I do if they occur? Can I take this medicine with other medicines or dietary supplements that I'm taking? What food, drink or activities should I avoid while taking the medicine?
- When you pick up the medicine from the pharmacy, ask if it's the medicine your doctor prescribed.
- If you have any questions about the directions on the medicine labels, ask your pharmacist about them.
- Ask about the best way to measure liquid medicines.
- Get written information about any possible medicine side effects.
- If you're having surgery and have your choice of hospital, pick the one where your type of surgery is most common. Research shows patients have better results when they're treated in hospitals with the most experience dealing with their condition.
- When you're in hospital, consider asking all health-care workers whether they've washed their hands.
- When being discharged from hospital, ask your doctor to clearly explain your home treatment plan.
- If you're having surgery, ensure that you, your doctor and surgeon all agree and are clear on exactly what will be done during surgery.
- Speak up if you have questions or concerns.
- Make sure that someone is in charge of your care.
- Make sure that your health information is known by all health-care workers involved in your care.
- Ask a family member or friend to be there with you and act as your advocate.
- Find out why a test or treatment is needed and how it may help you. More isn't always better.

- If you have a test, don't assume that no news is good news. Ask for the results.

[42] The entire March/April 2003 issue of Health Affairs is devoted to quality and patient safety issues.

[43] Nationwide poll on patient safety: 100 million Americans see medical mistakes directly touching them [press release]. McLean , VA : National Patient Safety Foundation; October 9, 1997.

[44] See the CDC website at www.cdc.org

[45] Accessed at www.cdc.gov/nccdphp/announce on Aug 8, 03. Arthritis is the number one cause of disability.

[46] See "Gut Reaction: treating a disease called GERD" by Mark Teich in *Newsweek*, Fall 2002.

[47] See "The Costly Case of the Purple Pill" Neil Swidey, *The Boston Globe Magazine*, 11/17/02.

[48] See "Fire Down Below" 12/23/02 at www.hsibaltimore.com

[49] See "Fire Down Below" with Allan Spreen, MD. Health Sciences Institute e-Alert, 12/23/2002 at www.hsibaltimore.com.

[50] See "putting out fires" at Health Sciences Institute e-Alert. January 30, 2003 at www.hsibaltimore.com

[51] See the *Physicians Desk Reference* book for drugs.

[52] See "Risk of community-acquired pheumonia and use of gastric acid-suppressive drugs" *Journal of the American Medical Association*, vol. 292 (16), Oct. 27, 04.

[53] David Eddy journeyed from conventional medical practitioner to learned critic. Trained as a cardio-thorasic surgeon, Eddy began his career at Stanford University. Like many, he assumed that most treatments were supported by rigorous research (i.e., research that followed the accepted scientific methodology of clinical trials with randomized assignment of patients to treatment and control groups.) Random assignment is the only way to know with any degree of certainty that the treatment produces the intended effect, since the group that gets the treatment in question and the group that does not (the control group) are similar in all other respects.

After several years in practice, Eddy became increasingly concerned with the frequent failures of his recommended treatments. He turned to the research literature in the mid-1980s, beginning his systematic studies with an examination of the supportive evidence for the various treatments for glaucoma. He searched the medical reports back to 1906, but could not find one randomized controlled trial of the standard treatments for glaucoma. The confident statements in textbooks and medical journals on treating glaucoma had simply been passed down as "conventional wisdom." He then extended his inquiry to other treatments and found the same absence of scientific research support.

[54] See Nelda Wray et al, (July 11, 2002) *New England Journal of Medicine*.

[55] Accessed from the CDC website, Jan. 2000.

[56] Perhaps the rising chorus of criticism will shift the paradigm. The research on the impact of genes on cancer points to such a shift. The July 2000 issue of the New England Journal of Medicine found that in 44,000 pairs of twins, genetics provided an explanation for only one quarter of the cancers, while lifestyle and environment explained two-thirds and access to medical care one tenth.

[57] Also see John Robbins 1996 book *Reclaiming Our Health* (Tiburon, Calif., HJ Kramer Press.

[58] Accessed at www.cdc.gov/nccdphp/announce on Aug 8, 03. A 1996 estimate of the cost of chronic conditions was published in the *Journal of the American Medical Association*. The total loss to the economy amounted to $161.3 billion.

[59] See August 21, 2003 issue of *New England Journal of Medicine*.

[60] The cost per patient with chronic conditions is more than three times higher than the cost for those with acute conditions. More telling still, the cost for those with two or more chronic conditions is over two and one half times greater than for those with only one chronic condition. If nothing is done to prevent or delay the onset of chronic conditions, the nation's spending on medical care will continue skyrocketing. In 1990, the lost productivity associated with chronic conditions was estimated to be $73 billion.

[61] See Eileen Crimmins and Y Saito "Trends in Healthy Life Expectancy" in *Soc Sci and Med* 52 (11):1629-41.

[62] See Jeffrey Johnson and Lyle Bookman "Drug Related Morbidity and Mortality" *Arch Internal Medicine* Oct 9, 1995: 155: 1949-56.

[63] Frank Ernst and Amy Grizzle J Am Pharm, vol. 41 (2):192-97 "Drug-Related Morbidity and Mortality" 2001.

[64] See Frank Ernst and Amy Grizzle, "Drug-Related Morbidity and Mortality", in *J Am Pharm Assoc* vol. 41 (2):192-97 2001.

[65] See *CMAJ* 1993 Nov 15; 149 (10):1401-7, "Interactions between physicians and the pharmaceutical industry" by J. Lexchin.

[66] See "Direct-to-Consumer Prescription Drug Advertising 1989-1998" by Robert A. Bell in *J Fam Pract* 2000; 49:329-335.

[67] See "Prescription Drug Trends" by Kaiser Family Foundation at http://www.kff.org/.

[68] See Wazana Ashley, MD. "Physicians and the Pharmaceutical Industry" *JAMA* 2000;283:373-380.

[69] See Wazana Ashley, MD. "Physicians and the Pharmaceutical Industry" *JAMA* 2000;283:373-380). Also see Michael Fisher et al, *JAMA*, April 20, 04 at www.JAMA.ama_assn.org.

[70] See Friedberg, M et al., *JAMA* vol. 282 (15):1453-57.

[71] See Horton, R., "Sponsorship, authorship, and a tale of two media" in *The Lancet* 1997; 349: 1411; Lexchin, Joel, "Pharmaceutical industry sponsorship and research outcome and quality", *British Journal of Med.*, 2003; 326: 116;7-70; Chan, A. et al, "Association of funding and conclusions in randomized drug trails" in *JAMA* 2003; 2909: 921-28.

[72] See "Cholesterol panel highlights medical conflicts of interest" by Marilynn Marchione. Accessed at www.InsideVC.com on 10/17/2004.

[73] See *On the Take*, NY: Oxford University Press, 04.

[74] The drug industry spent $2 billion in 2001 on events for doctors—double what it spent five years earlier.

[75] Other related books on the drug industry include: *Powerful Medicines* by Jerry Avorn; *Overdosed America* by John Abramson; *The Big Lie* by Katharine Greider; *Your money or Your Life* by David M. Cutler; *Internal Bleeding: the truth behind America's terrifying epidemic of medical mistakes* by Robert Wachter, Kaveh Shojania, *The Brave New World of Health Care* by Richard D. Lamm.

[76] See the National Institute for Health Care Management, "Prescription Drugs and Intellectual Property Protection," August 2000.

[77] See "States to sue Drug Makers" *New York Times* Feb 14 2003 by Reed Abelson and Jonathan Glater.

[78] See "Documents Detail Big Payments by Drug Makers to Sway Sales" By Milt Freudenheim, *NYTimes* March 13, '03.

[79] The FDA has a bias for prescription medications and against natural herbal products. It studiously examines the interactions between prescription drugs and herbal products. If an interaction occurs, the FDA recommend "cease taking the herbal product as it is dangerous". The FDA is already warning that we must not take some herbs in combination with the much stronger patented drugs! The assumed state of normalcy is that we are already popping the FDA-approved pills.

[80] Overuse of drugs is not simply an American problem. A similar study conducted in France found that 3% of hospital admissions, between 5 and 9% of hospital costs, and 7.6% of all hospital days resulted from ADRs. See Moore N; Lecointre D; Noblet C; Mabille M in *Br J Clin Pharmacol*, 45(3):301-8 1998 Mar} Also see a Canadian study Adverse drug reactions in hospital patients by JS Buechner in *Med Health R I*, 279(15):60-1, 1998 Feb.

[81] Serious ADRs were defined as those that required hospitalization, or were permanently disabling, or resulted in death.To calculate the overall incidence of ADRs in hospitalized patients, they combined the incidence of ADRs occurring while in the hospital with the incidence of ADRs causing admission to the hospital.

[82] See " Incidence of adverse drug reactions in hospitalized patients: a meta-analysis of prospective studies" by Lazarou J; Pomeranz BH; Corey PN in *JAMA*, 279(15):1200-5 1998 Apr 15

[83] See Bates, *JAMA* vol 279 (16): 1216-1217); and "Time to Act on Drug Safety" in *Journal of the American Medical Association* 279 (19): 1571-73.

[84] See William Campbell Douglass II, "The Depressing Truth", *Daily Dose,* March 26, 2004.

[85] See http://healthy.net/scr/news.asp accessed July 8, 04.

[86] See "Time to Act on Drug Safety" in *Journal of the American Medical Association* 279 (19): 1571-73.

[87] See Barbara Starfield "Is US health really the best in the world?" in *JAMA,* 2000; 284(4):483-5.

[88] See "Treatment of Antidepressant-Associated Sexual Dysfunction With Sildenafil" *JAMA* 2003, Jan 1:289(1):56-64. "Viagra May Fight Antidepressants' Sex Side Effects" Reuters Health, 1/1/03 "The Shameless Factor - Antidepressants Become Friendly With Viagra" Nicholas Regush, *Red Flags Daily*, 1/2/03 "Study Urges Use of Drugs to Treat Antidepressant-Related Impotence" Dr. Joseph Mercola, www.mercola.com; "Urologist Recommends Daily Viagra To Prevent Impotence" Ray Moynihan, *British Medical Journal*, 1/4/03.

[89] See RA Levy, *Medical Interface*, 1989. Also see Sullivan SD et al. *J Res Pharmaceutical Econ.* 1990.

[90] See Dunbar-Jacob "Adherence in chronic disease. *Annu Rev Nurs Res* 2000:18; 48-49; Bernard Bloom, "Daily regimen and compliance with treatment" *British Medical Journal*, 325: 647 (Sept 2001).

[91] Ibid, Bernard Bloom, *British Medical Journal*, 325: 647 (Sept 2001).

[92] See Heidi Nelson et al, August 20, 2002, Annals of Internal Medicine and the August 21 *Journal of the American Medical Association.*

[93] See Daniel Reid, *Guarding The Three Treasures*, NY: Simpon & Schuster, 1993.

[94] Angell Marcia. Is academic medicine for sale? *N Engl J Med .* 2000 May 18;342(20):1516-8. Also see her book, *The Truth About the Drug Companies*, N Y: Random House, 2004.

[95] After the FDA approves a drug (phase IV), there is no mandatory post approval research to ensure safety or to report side effects or adverse reactions. In regard to drugs, the nation has a voluntary monitoring system with only 52 full-time FDA employees to monitor the safety record of over 5,000 brand-name drugs. (In a 1993 article, Med Watch notes that there is a budget of only $140,000 to watch over $90 billion in sales of prescription drugs. In 2000, there were over $110 billion in sales of some 10,000 prescription drugs on the market.

[96] This is a hot debate with many involved such as Hrobjartsson, A., "Is the placebo powerless?" in *N. E.J. of Med.*, 344 (21): 1594-1602, and Golomb, B, "Paradox of placebo effect, *Nature*, 375: 530, and Golomb, B "Are placebos bearing false witness? In *Chemistry and Industry*, 21: 900, 1995.

[97] See O.P. Corrigan "A risky business: the detection of adverse drug reactions in clinical trials and post-marketing exercises" in Social Science and Medicine, Aug 2002, 55 (3): 497-507.

[98] See Golomb, B., "Using placebos", in *Nature*, 379: 765; Golomb, B., "Are placebos bearing false witness? In *Chemistry and Industry*, 21: 900, 1995 and larger debate on "About Follies and Fallacies, but mostly about placebo" at www.thincs.org/discuss.placebo.htm.

[99] Ibid.

[100] See Beatrice Golomb, "Are placebos bearing false witness? In *Chemistry and Industry*, 21: 900, 1995.

238

[101] See Diedtra Henderson "FDA Reviewer says Vioxx is not only risky drug," AP 11/19/2004 accessed at www.healthynet.com.

[102] See "Adverse Drug Evens in Ambulatory Care" by Tejal K. Gandhi et al, in *New England Journal of Medicine* vol. 348 (16): 1556-1564.

[103] See Elmer Green's article "Mind over Matter" in *ISSSEM*, 1996.

[104] See "Glaxo sees red over changes" *Dailey Mail*, Dec. 9, 2003.

[105] See Drug-Induced Nutrient Depletion Handbook, Pelton, Lavale, Hawkins, and Krinsky, American Pharmaceutical Association, 1999-2000.

[106] See *The Kellogg Report* - The Impact of Nutrition, Environment & Lifestyle on the Health of Americans, Joseph Beasley, MD & Jerry Swift, MA, 1989). In addition to drugs, poor diet, carbonated drinks, coffee, alcohol, stress and emotional upsets play a part in wiping out the bacteria we need for metabolizing our food for health!

[107] See *JAMA* 2002; 287:598-605.

[108] These results from the 1998 National Ambulatory Medical Care Survey. See "Sociological influences on antidepressant prescribing" *Social Science & Medicine* vol. 56 (6): 1335-1344 March 2003 by Betsy Sleath and Ya-Chen Tina Shiha.

[109] From Jenny Thompson Health Sciences Institute, Newsletter Oct 25 2001.

[110] Leape LL. Error in medicine. *JAMA*, 1994 Dec 21;272(23):1851-7.

[111] The Advisory Commission on Consumer Protection and Quality was appointed in 1997 and reported in 1998 that 180,000 die every year of medical errors—52 percent of which were preventable. Such errors are responsible for injury in 1 out of every 25 patients (4%)and one in seven of those injured die each year. See "Reducing Errors in Medical Care. Research in Action Fact Sheet." AHCPR Publication No. 98-P018, September 1998. Agency for Health Care Policy and Research, Rockville, MD.)

In November 1999, the Institute of Medicine (IOM) downsized the Advisory Commission's estimate of 180,000 deaths to focus only on the preventable deaths, which they estimated to be up to 98,000 in their report *To Err Is Human: Building A Safer Health System.*

[112] HealthGrades, a medical-care-rating organization, found 195,000 deaths resulting from preventable medical errors on average per year in 2000, 2001, and 2002. See "New study puts hospital error death rate at twice IOM's total" by Don Long, Medical Device Daily at www.bioworld.com accessed July 28, 04.

[113] See Death by Medicine October 2003, Gary Null et al, found at www. garynull.com/documents/iatrogenic/deathbymedicine/deathbymedicine 1

[114] Ibid. 2003. Sources for this data include: Lazarou J, Pomeranz BH, Corey PN. Incidence of adverse drug reactions in hospitalized patients: a meta-analysis of prospective studies. *JAMA,* 1998 Apr 15;279(15):1200-5; Drug giant accused of false claims. MSNBC News. July 11, 2003. Available at: http://msnbc.com/news/937302.asp?0sl=-42&cp1=1. Accessed December 17,2003; The Institute of Medicine, To Err is Human, 1999, Publication No. AHRQ 00-PO37.; Xakellis GC, Frantz R, Lewis A. Cost of pressure ulcer

prevention in long-term care. Am Geriatr Soc. 1995 May;43(5):496-501; Barczak CA, Barnett RI, Childs EJ, Bosley LM. Fourth national pressure ulcer prevalence survey. Adv Wound Care. 1997 Jul-Aug;10(4):18-26; Weinstein RA. Nosocomial Infection Update. Emerg Infect Dis . 1998 Jul-Sep;4(3):416-20; Weinstein RA. Nosocomial Infection Update. Emerg Infect Dis . 1998 Jul-Sep;4(3):416-20; Fourth Decennial International Conference on Nosocomial and Healthcare-Associated Infections. Morbidity and Mortality Weekly Report. February 25, 2000 , vol. 49, No. 7, p.138; Burger SG, Kayser-Jones J, Bell JP. Malnutrition and dehydration in nursing homes: key issues in prevention and treatment. National Citizens' Coalition for Nursing Home Reform. June 2000. Available at: www.cmwf.org/programs/elders/burger_mal_386asp Accessed December 13, 2003; See Starfield B. Is US health really the best in the world? *JAMA* . 2000 Jul 26;284(4):483-5. Starfield B. Deficiencies in US medical care. JAMA . 2000 Nov 1;284(17):2184-5; Injuryboard.com. General Accounting Office study sheds light on nursing home abuse. July 17, 2003 . Available at: www.injuryboard.com/view. cfm/Article=3005 Accessed December 17, 2003; See Frank Ernst and Amy Grizzle, "Drug-Related Morbidity and Mortality", in J Am Pharm Ass vol. 41 (2):192-97 2001; For calculation details see "Unnecessary Surgery." Sources: HCUPnet, Healthcare Cost and Utilization Project. Agency for Healthcare Research and Quality, Rockville , MD. Available at: http://www.ahrq.gov/ data/hcup/hcupnet.htm . Accessed December 18, 2003 . US Congressional House Subcommittee Oversight Investigation. *Cost and Quality of Health Care: Unnecessary Surgery.* Washington , DC : Government Printing Office;1976. Cited in: McClelland GB, Foundation for Chiropractic Education and Research. Testimony to the Department of Veterans Affairs' Chiropractic Advisory Committee. March 25, 2003; and HCUPnet, Healthcare Cost and Utilization Project. Agency for Healthcare Research and Quality, Rockville , MD. Available at: http://www.ahrq.gov/data/hcup/hcupnet.htm . Accessed December 18, 2003; Zhan C, Miller M. Excess length of stay, charges, and mortality attributable to medical injuries during hospitalization. *JAMA.* 2003;290:1868-1874.

[115] See Robert Blendon, Cathy Schoen, Catherine DesRoches, Robin Osborn, and Kinga Zapert "Common concerns amid diverse system: health care experiences in five countries" in *Health Affairs* vol.22 (3): 106-121.

[116] These numbers are significantly higher than the other four countries. As the number of doctors seen and the number of prescription drugs taken increase, the probability of an adverse event increases dramatically.

[117] The US ranked poorly on care coordination, medical errors, overall rating of doctors, and getting questions answered relative to the other four countries.

[118] Edgar Cayce gave over 15,000 readings until his death in 1945; two-thirds of these readings were for health and disease-related problems, many with intractable diseases. Cayce conducted readings by lying down and going into a deep trance.

[119] See John Astin, "Why Patients Use Alternative Medicine" *JAMA*, volume 279 (19): 1548-53.

[120] See Larry Dossey M.D. and James Sawyers, in their introduction to the 1995 NIH report *Expanding Horizons on Alternative Therapies*, US Government Printing Office 1995.

[121] See Dossey and Swyers, introduction to *Expanding Horizons*, 1995

[122] See her book, *Dr. Judith Orloff's Guide to Intuitive Healing*, Three Rivers Press, 2001 and *Second Sight*

[123] See *Simply Well* by John Travis and Sara Ryan Berkeley, CA. Ten Speed Press, 2001. In *Simply Well* authors John W. Travis, MD and Regina Sara Ryan condense a comprehensive wellness program into a series of simple actions that people can use in cultivating a more vibrant and healthy life. From breathing exercises, meditation and massage, to nutrition and the cultivation of inner silence, they offer 32 ways to use on the path to high-level wellness.

[124] See Lynn Robinson's *Compass of the Soul*, Andrews McNeel Publishing 2003 and *Divine Intuition*, 1997.

[125] Eisenberg et. al., Trends in Alternative Medicine Use in the US" *JAMA*, vol. 280 (18): 1569-1575, found that 58% of all alternative usage was for prevention or maintenance while Ramsey et al 1999 found 81% was for prevention.

[126] See Thomas, W. H. (1996). *Life worth living: How someone you love can still enjoy life in a nursing home: The Eden alternative in action*. Acton, MA: Vander Wyk & Burnham.

[127] See James Oschman *Energy Medicine*, NY: Churchill Livingstone, 2000).

[128] Miriam Wilson of Memphis, Tennessee wrote this.

[129] See Ted Kaptchuk and David Eisenberg "The Persuasive Appeal of Alternative Medicine" in Annals of Internal Medicine vol. 129 (12): 1061-64.

[130] See Gina Kolata, "Vitamins" in *New York Times*, April 29, 2003 and Waring and Tseng 1998.

[131] See Reuters/Zogby America, May 2000).

[132] The term CAM applies to a wide range of therapies. Some like chiropractic are well known to the public, but others like energy healing are just entering the public's consciousness. Unlike mainstream medicine, many CAM therapies are rooted in ancient practice.

[133] See Vegetarian Times, July 2001.

[134] See Deepak Chopra's *Ageless Body, Timeless Mind*, Harmony, 1994 and Andrew Weil's Eight Weeks to Optimum Health.

[135] Adapted from Eisenberg et al, "Trends in Alternative Medicine Use in the US" *JAMA*, vol. 280 (18): 1569-1575

[136] See Ron Kessler et al., "Long-term trends in the use of CAM", *Annals of Internal Med*, 2001, vol. 135: 262-68.)

[137] Adapted from David Eisenberg et al, "Trends in Alternative Medicine Use in the US" *JAMA*, vol. 280 (18): 1573.

[138] For more, see David Eisenberg, et al, "Trends in Alternative Medicine Use in the US, 1990-97" *JAMA* vol. 280(18):1569-75).

[139] See Nancy Melville at Health Scout Reporter, Yahoo News assessed InterSurvey 2000, July 24, 2000.

[140] See National Institutes of Health, 2002 *White House Commission on Complementary and Alternative Medicine Policy*, Washington, DC: US Government Printing Office.

[141] See John Astin, "Why patients use alternative medicine" in *JAMA*, 279 (19):1548-53.

[142] See Robbie Davis-Floyd and Gloria St. John, *From Doctor to Healer: the transformative journey*, Rutgers University Press, 1998

[143] Quoted in "Cross-cultural primary care" in *Annals of Internal Medicine* 1999, vol. 130: 829.

[144] IBID, see page 155.

[145] See the chapter on "Conversion" by David Snow and Richard Machalek in *Annual Review of Sociology* 1984 vol. 10: 167-90.

[146] See www.nccam.nih.gove/news/2004/052704.htm accessed 5/28/2004

[147] A short list of CAM professional organization can be found at www.healthynet.com

[148] See HSC's 2000-01 Community Tracking Household Survey at the Center for Studying Health System Change at www.businessandhealth.com accessed 4/25/03.

[149] See US Government Accounting Office report AIMD-96-86, 1996).

[150] See *Cultural Creatives*, Harmony Books, 1999, by Paul Ray and Sherry Anderson

[151] See p 47-8 of *Cultural Creatives*, Harmony Books, 1999, by Paul Ray and Sherry Anderson.

[152] See Paul Ray and Sherry Anderson, *Cultural Creatives*, 1999.

[153] See June Lowenberg, in *Caring and Responsibility* University of Pennsylvania Press 1989 pp. 79-91.

[154] Eisenberg et al's (1998) profile of CAM users illustrates the effects of education and affluence. CAM use is more common among those with post-secondary education (50.6%) than among those with no post-secondary education (36.4%) and more common among those with incomes greater than $50,000. (18) In another large national survey, users of CAM therapies supported these same demographic correlates and were more likely than non users to view alternative care as being compatible with their values and granted more personal control over their health care decisions. (19)

[155] See Michel Goldstein, "The culture of fitness and CAM" in M Kelner, *Complementary and Alternative Medicine*, 2000.

[156] Central to this separation was the 16th Century mathematician, Rene Descartes, who brokered a compromise with the Catholic Church, permitting science to proceed without Church interference. Henceforth, science could study the physical body, leaving the mind (psyche or soul) under the care of the Church.

[157] See www.ahha.org

[158] See Larry Dossey, *Reinventing Medicine* Harper San Francisco, *2000.*

[159] See Harold Koenig, "Use of religion by patients" in *Mind/Body Medicine* 1997; and Harold Koenig in the *Journal of Gerontology*, 1999

[160] See Levin, Jeffrey, *God, Faith and Health*, John Wiley & Sons, 2001.

[161] See Jeffrey Levin, *God Faith and Health*, John Wiley & Sons, 2001.

[162] See WWW.templeton.org/courses98/highlights

[163] See David Larson and Susan Larson "Spirituality in Clinical care" p 101 in *The Role of CAM,* Daniel Callahan (ed) Georgetown University Press, Washington DC 2002).

[164] Op cit, Larson and Larson, 2002.

[165] See Eva Lindbladh, C.H. Lytkens "Habit versus choice" in *Social Science and Medicine*, vol.55(3): 451-65 and "How to get healthier, Time, Feb 5, 2002.

[166] Over six million adults a year have contact with addiction self-help groups and such groups are the most frequently accessed resource for alcohol and other drug problems. They also have the highest success rates at 83% according to Hester and Miller, *Handbook of Alcoholism Treatment Approaches*, Allyn & Bacon, 2003.

[167] See Stanton Peele, *The Diseasing of America*, 1999. Peele contends that support systems are central to helping motivate individuals to want change, feel they can change and that they should change.

[168] See Robert Wuthnow, *Sharing the Journey*, Free Press 1994.

[169] See The Futurists October 2000, and Ron Kessler et al, "Differences in the use of psychiatric outpatient services" in *New England J of Medicine*, 336, 551-57.

[170] See "Self-help Comes of Age" in *Social Policy* vol. 30(4):47-8).

[171] Adapted from Frank Riessman and David Carroll, *Redefining Self-Help*, San Francisco: Jossey-Bass, 1995.

[172] See Lyn Freeman, Mosby's *Complementary and Alternative Medicine: A research-based approach*, Second edition, St Louis, Missouri: Mosby, 2004.

[173] Dean Ornish, Love and Survival, 1999.

[174] Edward Hollowell, *Connect: 12 Vital Ties That Open Your Heart, Lengthen Your Life, and Deepen your Soul,* Pantheon, 1999.

[175] See Meta-analysis of medical self-help groups" by Barlow SH, Burlingame GM, Nebeker RS, Anderson E *Int J Group Psychotherapy* 2000 Jan;50(1):53-69; and Berkman, LF, and Syme, SL, "Social networks, host resistance and mortality" *Am J of Epidemiology* 109(2): 186 1979.

[176] See H. Roth, "Relationship between attendance at a Parents Anonymous Adult Program and children's behavior" in *Children & Youth Services Review*, 7(1): 39-43.

[177] See Spiegel et al "Complementary Medicine" in *West J of Med* 1998; and Dean Ornish "Support groups and metastic breast cancer" in *Advances in Mind-Body Medicine* 2001 vol. 17: 19-21); Isolating social conditions contributed to more than 700 deaths during a week-long wave of heat and humidity in Chicago in 1995 according to *Heat Wave: A Social Autopsy*

of Disaster. The author examines key social factors relating to the elderly: "aging in place" while the surrounding environment changes; the idealization of personal independence among seniors; and lacking friendships and connectedness with others. Lacking social connections were risk factors, causing the isolated, the poor and the elderly to die disproportionately. More discovered. of the elderly died by the heat wave because they were socially isolated and poor. And when they died alone in their rooms, time also expired before they were see Eric Klinenberg, *Heat Wave: A Social Autopsy of Disaster,* University of Chicago Press. 2002.

[178] Kathryn Davison et al, "Who Talks," *American Psychologist* Feb 2000 vol. 22 (2):205).

[179] See *Newsweek,* March 16, 1998 issue which featured the story of Dean Ornish, MD

[180] Two scientific journals are primarily devoted to the publishing literature on self-help groups: *Social Policy* and *International Journal of Self Help and Self Care.*

[181] See Gartner and Riessman, *Social Policy,* 28(3): 83-6).

[182] See Jerome Groopman "Hurting All Over" pp. *New Yorker* Nov 13, 2000.

[183] See Lee et al *J of Nat Cancer Institute,* 2000, p 42-47; and Boon, et al "Use of CAM by breast cancer survivors" in *J of Clin Oncol* vol. 18(13):2515-21, 2000.

[184] See "Self-Help Groups: Tool or Symbol?" Kurt Bock and Rebecca Taylor *in Journal of Applied Behavioral Science,* 1976, 12, 3, July, 295-309.

[185] See Audrey Gartner and Frank Riessman, "Self Help" in *Social Policy* vol. 28(3): 83-6

[186] See Simmons, D. 1992 "Diabetes Self Help Facilitated by Local Diabetes Research" *Diabetic Medicine* 9: 866-869.

[187] See Gilden, J. L., Hendry, M. S., et al. (1992). Diabetes Support Groups Improve Health Care of Older Diabetic Patients. *Journal of the American Geriatrics Society* 40: 147-150.

[188] See David Spiegel et al, "Effect of psychosocial treatment on survival of patients with breast cancer", *Lancet,* 1989: 888-911 and Dean Ornish "Support groups and breast cancer", *Advances in Mind-Body Medicine,* vol. 17: 19-21.

[189] See Fawzy, I. et al, "Structured psychiatric intervention for cancer patients" *Archives of General Psychiatry* vol. 47(8): 729-35 1990.

[190] See Classen, C et al, "Supportive-expressive group therapy and distress in patients with metastatic breast cancer" in *Archives of Gen Psychiatry,* 58(5): 494-501 2001.

[191] See Hinrichsen, Revenson, and Shinn, 1985).

[192] See Parkes, 1972.

[193] See Riessman and Carroll, 1995: 131.

[194] See Riessman and Carroll, 1995: 131.

[195] See Jason et al. 1987.

[196] See Emrick et al. 1993.

[197] See "Can substance abuse patients in self-help groups reduce demand for health care? by Humphreys, K and Moos, R in *Alcohol Clin Exp Res*, 25(5): 711-6.

[198] see James Spira in *Group Therapy for Medically Ill Patients* NY: Guilford 1997:3).

[199] See Scott Wituk et al. in *Social Work* vol. 40(2): 157-65).

[200] See Wuthnow, *Sharing the Journey*, Free Press 1994: 259.

[201] "The use of patients' stories by self-help groups" Yaphe, J Rigge,M Hexheimer, A, MvPherson A, MillerR, Shepperd S, Ziebland S in *Health Expert*, 3(3): 176-181   2000)

[202] See Frank Riessman "The Peer Principle" in *Social Policy ,* Winter vol. 29 (2): 10-12, 1998.

[203] *The Public Perspective*, published by the Roper Center for Public Opinion, found the numbers engaging in charitable or social service activities has increased from 46 to 54% from 1991 to 1995; 48% of the population volunteers about four hours a week to organizations and causes; per capita charitable giving in constant dollars has increased from $280 in 1960 to $522 in 1995.

[204] See Allan Luks and Peggy Payne, *The Healing Power of Doing Good.* NY: Fawcett Columbine, 1992: 17 and 83.

[205] Stephanie Brown et al., *Psychological Science* Nov 2002. The study was a random community-based sample of 423 older couples who were first interviewed in 1987 and studied for five years to see how they coped with the inevitable changes of life. During the first set of interviews, the husbands and wives were asked a series of questions about whether they provided any practical support to friends, neighbors or relatives, including help with housework, childcare, errands or transportation. They were also asked how much they could count on help from friends or family members if they needed it. Finally, they were asked about giving and receiving emotional support to or from their spouse.

[206] They sought to rule out the linked possibilities that older people give less and are more likely to die, that females give more and are less likely to die, and that people who are depressed or in poor health are both less able to help others and more likely to die.

[207] 75 percent of men and 72 percent of women reported providing some help without pay to friends, relatives or neighbors.

[208] From Sally Thorne, *Negotiating Health Care*, 1993: 200.

[209] See Robert Wuthnow in *Sharing the Journey*, Free Press 1994: 86 and 171.

[210] Nearly half of adult Americans with chronic illness sought additional information beyond their MD in the previous year according to a national survey by Health System Change entitled "Majority of Americans Don't seek health information" March 16, 2003 at www.hschange.com.

[211] See Ron Kessler et al. *Social Policy* 1997.

212 See Ross Gray and Margaret Fitch "Cancer Self-help Groups are Here to Stay" in *J of Palliative Care* 2000 vol. 17 (1):53-8) (see Wolfgang Sollner in *Cancer*, Aug 15, 2000 vol. 89(4): 873.

213 See Robert Wuthnow *Sharing the Journey*, Free Press 1994

214 See Morton Lieberman and Lonnie Snowden "Problems in Assessing Prevalence and Membership Characteristics of Self-Help Group Participants", Journal of Applied Behavioral Science vol. 29(2): 166-80 1993.

215 See Kathryn Davison et al, "Who Talks," *American Psychologist* Feb 2000 vol. 22 (2):205).

216 .See Wituk, S et al A Topography of self help groups" in *Social Work*, 2000 vol. 40(2): 157-65.

217 If we use marriage as the unit of study rather than couples, this percent rises to 75%.

218 The Clearinghouse can be accessed at www.mentalhelp.net/selfhelp.

219 Herbert Benson, *Timeless Healing*,

220 Rhea White "Exceptional Human Experience," Institute of Noetic Sciences, 1994

221 See her story "MS as a Spiritual Guide" and others at www.selfgrowth.com/article/olsen

222 Duff, *The Alchemy of Illness*, pp.45-6)

223 For more case histories of healing and transformation, see www.wholisticmed.com/cases .

224 See Raima Larter, "Life lessons from the newest science" in *IONS,* August 2002 #59: 65.

225 The 12 steps can be found in *The Big Book of Alcoholics Anonymous.* Page 59-60.

226 See Lee et al J of Nat Cancer Institute, 2000, p 42-47; and Boon, et al "Use of CAM by breast cancer survivors" in *J of Clin Oncol* vol. 18(13):2515-21, 2000).

227 See Ross Gray et al 1999 in *Cancer Prev Control* vol. 3 (1):80).

228 See Kathryn Davison et al, "Who Talks," *American Psychologist* Feb 2000 vol. 22 (2):205.

229 See Pew Internet and American Life Project- www.pewinternet.org.

230 See www.grohol.com.

231 See Tom Ferguson *Health Online* Addison Wesley Publishing Company 1996.

232 Madara and White "On-Line Mutual Support" in *Information and Referral* vol. 19, 1997:92.

233 See Mandara and White "On-Line Mutual Support" in *Information and Referral* vol. 19, 1997:92.

234 See Alem, F et al "Electronic self-help and support" in *Med Care* vol. 34(10) suppl: os32-44. Oct 1996.

235 Cited by Tom Ferguson in *Health Online* Addison Wesley Publishing Company 1996: 278.

[236] See Edward Madara "The Mutual-Aid Self-Help On-Line Revolution" in *Social Policy*: Spring 1997: 23.

[237] See Tom Fergurson "Running a Self-help Group by Computer" at www.healthynet.com.

[238] See "Who Talks" by Kathryn Davison, James Pennebaker and Sally Dickerson *American Psychologist* Feb 2000 vol. 55(2): 205-17.

[239] See Keith Humphreys, "Individual and Social Benefits of Mutual Aid Self-Help Groups" *Social Policy*, 1997: 16).

[240] Wuthnow, *Sharing the Journey*, 1994: 195

[241] Quoted in *Integrative Medicine*, by David Rakel, Saunders, 2003, page 7.

[242] See John DeGraaf et al, *Affluenza*, Berrett-Koehler Publishers 2001.

[243] See *American Mania: When More Is Not Enough* by Peter Whybrow, W. W. Norton & Company, 2005.

[244] In the next chapter, several reforms in our institutions and practices are recommended with an eye toward transforming a system that fosters pathology to one that nurtures health and wellness. Here we diagnose some root causes of the ailment.

[245] See Daniel Reidpath, "An ecological study of the relationship between SES and environmental determinants of obesity" in *Health and Place* vol. 8 (2): June 2002, pages 141-45.

[246] See national Restaurant Association, 1999 p. 3.

[247] See *The Nation's Health* 12/01/03, "Legislative effort calls for nutritional listing at restaurants" by Kim Kriesberg found at www.healthy.net.

[248] See National Restaurant Association 1999 and Charlene Price, "Fast food chains penetrate new markets. USDA *Food Review*, Jan 1993, US Dept of Commerce.

[249] See p. 6 in Fast Food Nation.

[250] See *Fast Food Nation,* 1st edition 2001 by Eric Schlosser p, 130; and Laurent Belsie, "World wants 'fries with that'" in *Christian Science Monitor*, Jan 2, 2002).

[251] See David Theno "Raising the bar to ensure safer burgers" *San Diego Union Tribune* Aug 27, 1997.

[252] Cited in Max Boas and Steven Chain, *Big Mac*, 1976, p. 218.

[253] See historian Harvey Levenstein discussed in *Fast Food Nation* p.113.

[254] See p. 114 of *Fast Food Nation*, 2000.

[255] Annemarie Colbin in *Food and Healing* 1988 contends it may even be up to seven thousand additives. p. 48.

[256] Overall, nutritionists recommend consuming a diet that consists of 20 percent of total caloric intake from protein, 50 percent of caloric intake from carbohydrates (mostly from complex ones), and 30 percent of calories from fat. Fat has nine calories per gram, compared to protein and carbohydrates which each contain four calories per gram. Fat is almost two-and-a half times more fattening per gram.

[257] See April 1999 issue of *Journal of Am Dietetic Assoc.*

258 See "Obesity," in the *Journal of American Dietetics Association*, vol. 104 (3): 335-36, March 2004.

259 See USDA survey in 1994-95.

260 See "Hospital Cafeteria Food Is a Recipe for Illness" September 15, 2005 by Healthy News Service.

261 See *Historical Statistics of US and US Yearbook.*

262 See Joseph Pizzorno, *Total Wellness*, Prima Lifestyles, 1997.

263 See Francine Kaufman *Diabesity,* Bantam, 2005.

264 See "Many Americans have undiagnosed diabetes" in *Diabetes Care*, vol. 24:2065, 2001.

265 See "Diabetes, Cholesterol, and Blood Pressure" *The Barron Report*, vol. 11, Issue 5, June 2002.

266 See "Many Americans have undiagnosed diabetes" *Diabetes Care* vol. 24:2065-2070. Nov 26, 2001.

267 See "For Strong Bones East more Vegetables, less Candy" *Canadian Press*, 9/9/02).

268 See "Consumption of high-fructose corn syrup in beverages may plan a role in the epidemic of obesity" *American Journal of Clinical Nutrition*, vol. 79, (4), April 2004 at www.ajcn.org. Also see "Fructose, Weight gain and the insulin resistance syndrome? *Amer J of Clincial Nutrion*, Nov 2002, vol. 76 (5): 911-922.

269 See Judy Putnam "US food supply providing more food and calories USDA Food Review, Oct 1, 1999.

270 See "Liquid Candy" at www.cspinet.org.

271 Ibid.

272 Ibid.

273 See Marion Nestle, *Food Politics*, University of California Press, 2002.

274 See Annemarie Colbin in *Food and Healing,* Ballantine Books, 1988 contends it may even be up to seven thousand additives. p.48. See Michael Jackson at the Center for Science in the Public Interest for a short list of chemical additives in the food supply at www.cspinet.org.

275 See Ruth Sombrook "Do you smell what I smell?" *Institute of Food Research* 1999.

276 See Schlosser, *Fast Food Nation* pp.124-5.

277 See Allan Spreen, *Nutritionally Incorrect*, Woodland Publishing, 1999.

278 See Annemarie Colbin in *Food and Healing, 1988* p.49.

279 See "Diet and Behavior in Children" by David Schardt, March 2000 issue of *Nutrition Action Newsletter* at www.cspinet.org.

280 Divide your weight in pounds by the square of your height in inches, multiply by 703 for your body mass index or BMI. If the resulting number is below 25 you are not overweight. If it is 25 to 29, you, like 61 percent of Americans age 20 to 74, are overweight. If your BMI number is 30 or higher you, like 27 percent of adults, are super-sized or obese.

281 See Jacobson "Liquid Candy" reported in 2001.

[282] See David Allison et al in Journal of American Medical Association, June 4, 2004.

[283] See research published in the Sept 2001 issue of *Public Health*.

[284] See A. Bergstrom, et al. "Obesity ups kidney cancer risk in men and women" British Journal of Cancer 2001;85 :984-990.

[285] See "National Medical Spending Attributable To Overweight And Obesity" by Eric Finkelstein et al, in *Health Affairs*, May 14, 2003.

[286] See Greg Critsler, *Fat Land,* 2003.

[287] See Francine Kaufman *Diabesity,* 2005.

[288] See www.betterhealthcampaign.org, "Healthy kids, Healthy Families accessed June 2004.

[289] Many Americans know the value of nutrition. A large survey of consumers in year 2000 found 74% ranked nutrition ahead of exercise and family health history as central to achieving good health; 61% claim they have a great amount of control over their own health and thirty-three percent of Americans are adding particular foods or ingredients to their diet in an effort to improve or maintain their health. In regard to specific changes in diet, 13% are adding more fruit, 22% are eating more vegetables and 24% are reducing their fat intake. See International Food Info Council report, December 2000.

[290] See "The Dish on Comfort Food" at www.napsnet.com/food/52686.

[291] Reuters Health, New York, Sept 13, 2001 "High-fat diets trigger changes in brain chemistry."

[292] See Anne Underwood, "Health" in *Newsweek*, February 3, 2003.

[293] American families have more disposable income to spend on food prepared outside the home since food costs as a percentage of household expenditures fell from 13.4% in 1980 to 10.7% in 2000.

[294] Marion Nestle, a nutrition and food sciences professor at NY University discusses the role of marketers in her book, *Food Politics*, U. of California Press, 2002.

[295] See "Legislative effort calls for nutritional listing at restaurants" by Kim Kriesberg, *The National's Health* at www.healthy.net on 2/11/04.

[296] From "Promoting Healthy Eating," 1999: 2; also White House Commission on CAM Policy statement March 2002.

[297] See David Bassett, Patrick Schneider and Gerturude Huntington, "Physical activity in an old order Amish Community," *Medicine & Science in Sports & Exercise*, vol. 36 (1): 79-85, 2004.

[298] See "Do Suburbs Make You Fat?" Associated Press, CBSNews8/28/03 at www.cbsnews.com.

[299] See Nataliya Schetchikova, "Children with ADHD Medical vs. Chiropractic Perspective and Theory," Part 2, in the *Journal of the American Chiropractic Association*, August 2002.

[300] See "Excessive TV viewing Sets Up Kids for Attention Disorders" by Derrick Jackson 4/8/04 at www.healthy.net

[301] See Hurst WA. "Sense Modality Coordination" *Global Contacto.* vol. 35, No.1. 1991.

[302] Stress-related illnesses cost the US 10 percent of GNP each year.

[303] See http://www.cdc.gov/niosh and the annual "Attitudes In The American Workplace" Gallup Poll.

[304] See http://www.cdc.gov/niosh.

[305] Accessed and adopted from http://www.cdc.gov/noish.

[306] See Economic Policy Institute and *Time Magazine*, May 26, 2003, p. 47.

[307] See Heilbroner and Thurow 1994.

[308] See Holly Sklar and her associates.

[309] See Rousseau 1997.

[310] See Useem and Cappelli 1997.

[311] SeeUseem and Cappelli 1997.

[312] Griffin (1993).

[313] See Useem and Cappelli p. 62.

[314] See NPR and Kaiser Foundation survey on Health care June 5, 2002 at www.npr.org/morningedition.

[315] Stress is destructive but fortunately there are things individuals can do to reduce its harmfulness. Three key habits help: eating nutritiously, sleeping the right amount for your body, and keeping a regular exercise program. Stress management may be one of the most feasible things individuals can implement to maintain health. Recognize the things that trigger stress. Make a list of the stress factors in your life. Talk about your stress with someone you trust. Diffuse stress. See "Practical Stress Management Program Found to Improve Health of People" American Psychological Association, 8/24/02. "Management Program Found to Improve Health of People" American Psychological Association, 8/24/02.

[316] Over eight hundred healthy employees were followed for an average of 25 years. See Mika Kivimaki et al "Work stress and risk of cardiovascular mortality: prospective cohort study of industrial employees" *British Medical Journal*, 2002;325:857-860).

[317] See Benjamin Amick et al in 2001 May/June issue of *Psychosomatic Medicine.*

[318] See Robert Karasek and Tores Theorell, *Healthy Work*, Basic Books, 1992.

[319] See Elizabeth Warren, *All Your Worth*, Free Press, 2005.

[320] Every year Americans spend more than $4 billion on non-prescription headache drugs alone. See Linda Strowbridge, *HIS Newsletter*, Oct 2002, vol. 7 (4).

[321] Pills are not only big business—they are, since the 1980s, the most profitable industry in America The pharmaceutical industry since 1980 experienced a return on investment greater than that of any other industry. In 2000, Fortune Magazine again rated pharmaceuticals the most profitable industry, with pharmaceutical profit margins being nearly four times the average of all Fortune 500 companies.

[322] See Jeff Donn "Americans Buy Much More Medicine" 4/16/05 at www.healthy.net accessed 4/19/05.

[323] See "Attention Deficit Drugs May have Long-Term Effects," December 8, 2003 Reuters News and William Carlezon in *Journal of Biological Psychiatry*, Dec. 15, 2003 and www.ritalindeath.com/board.

[324] See *Drug Topics* May 7, 2001 p. 58.

[325] See Jarry Weber "Americans Still Don't Get It When It Comes To Health" 02/25/04, found at www.healthy.net, assessed 03/05/04.

[326] See *Cured to Death* by Arbella Melville, published by Stein & Day, 1983.

[327] See Barrie Cassileth, "After Laetrile, What?" *The New England J of Medicine*, 1982, p. 1482

[328] See "Promotion of Prescription Drugs to Consumers," Meridith Rosenthal et al, *New England Journal of Medicine*, 346 (7): 500-501; also see Kaiser Family Foundation and data from IMS Health, Inc. at www.IMShealth.com.

[329] See "Prescription Drug Trends" by Kaiser Family Foundation. The consumer watchdog group, *Families USA*, uncovered the fact that pharmaceutical firms spend over three times more on marketing (34% of drug cost) than they devote to research and development (11% of cost), even though they tout R&D as the justification for high prices and wide profit margins.

[330] Table Dollar value of drug purchased by aging baby boomers in the US 1996-2006 ($ millions)

Year	1996 ($M)	1997 ($M)	2002 ($M)	2006 ($M)	1996-2006 % Growth
Menopause	1,202	1,370	2,808	5,037	15.4
Impotence	65	74	152	302	16.6
Skin Care	450	520	943	1,459	12.5
Sunscreen	220	246	490	828	14.2
Hair Growth	150	180	270	344	8.7
Total	$2,087	$2,390	$4,663	$7,970	14.3

Source: Business Communications Company, Inc. ($ millions at manufacturers' level)

[331] See *Pharmacy Times* April 2001 p.15.

[332] See "I Want It Now" by the *Natural Marketing Institute*, July 2005 at www.npicenter.com.

[333] See Jerry Avorn, "Advertising and prescription drugs" Health Affairs, Feb 26, 2003.

[334] See Richard Kravitz et al, "Influence of Patients' Requests for Direct-to-consumer Advertised Antidepressants" *Journal of the American Medical Association*, vol. 293 (16), 4/27/05 at jama.ama.assn.org.

[335] See "Two advertisements for TV Drug Ads" by Thomas Bodenheimer in *Health Affairs*, Feb 26, 2003.

[336] See WHO, "Model List of Essential Drugs" in *The Use of Essential Drugs*, Ninth Report, Technical report series, no. 895 (Geneva: WHO, 2000).

[337] See Tony Pugh **"Doctors are sick of drug salesmen"** *Mercury News Bureau*. Sept 2, 2002 at www.bayarea.com.

[338] See *Rx News*, Dec 2001.

[339] These "prescriber profiles" allow drug reps to tailor their presentation to individual physicians. The cost of these computerized prescriber profiles account for $16 billion out of the $19 billion pharmaceutical companies spent on marketing in 2001 according to IMS Health, a Connecticut-based company that collects prescriber data. See more in Liz Kowalczyk "Drug companies' secret reports outrage doctors" in *Boston Globe* on page A1 on 5/25/2003.

[340] Op. Cit. *National Institute of Health Care Management*, "Prescription Drugs."

[341] See: *Drug-Induced Nutrient Depletion Handbook*, Pelton, Lavale, Hawkins, and Krinsky, American Pharmaceutical Association, 1999-2000); also see C. Tschanz 1996 "Interactions between drugs and nutrients" in *Advances in Pharmacology* 35:6-10.

[342] See The Kellogg Report - The Impact of Nutrition, Environment & Lifestyle on the Health of Americans, Joseph Beasley, MD, & Jerry Swift, MA, 1989). In addition to drugs, poor diet, carbonated drinks, coffee, alcohol, stress and emotional upsets play a part in wiping out the bacteria we need for metabolizing our food for health!

[343] An early book on the negative effects of prescription drugs was *Cured to Death* by Arbella Melville Stein and Day, 1983 that examined the bedroom relationship between drug manufacturers and the government.

[344] Frank Ernst and Amy Grizzle *J Am Pharm Ass* vol. 41 (2):192-97 "Drug-Related Morbidity and Mortality" 2001.

[345] See "Adverse Drug Evens in Ambulatory Care" by Tejal K. Gandhi, et al, in *New England Journal of Medicine* Vol. 348 (16): 1556-1564.

[346] See David Bates, a researcher at Boston's Brigham and Women's Hospital, the foremost authority on this subject.

[347] See *Advance Data* No. 346. 44. pp. (PHS) 2004-1250 from US office of HHS. US government, and "Heath Behaviors of Adults: United States, 1999-2001. Series Report 10, Number 219. 89. pp. (PHS) 2004-1547.

[348] See October 15, 2002 issue of *American Family Physician*.

[349] See "Adverse Drug Evens in Ambulatory Care" *New England Journal of Medicine,* vol. 348 (16):1556-1564.

[350] This story was told by Surgeon General David Satcher and reported in "Population Based Medicine" by Penny Tselikis in The 2002 edition of *The State of Health in American* by Business and Health.

[351] See www.practicalhealthreform.org.

[352] See *American Journal of Health Promotion*, vol. 17(2): 5, Dec. 2002

[353] The CDC contends that 89% are preventable.

[354] Medical costs for seniors who died at younger ages (65-74) were considerably higher near the end of life than the costs for those who died at age 85 and older because more heroic medical interventions were used on those in the younger age cohort. By living longer, many baby boomers will pass the ages at which the most expensive efforts are likely to be made to prolong their lives. The research came from 25,954 elderly people enrolled in Medicare

from 1982 to 1998 and is published *Journal of Gerontology,* Jan 2002. In the month before death, the cost for people aged 65 to 74 averaged about $7,580, while the cost for those 85 and older was $5,254. See "Health costs for oldest not as high as feared" *Scripps Howard News Service/Nando Times,* Jan 2002.

[355] The quality crisis in medicine remains hidden and not focused on promoting health. Donald Berwick, MD, founder of the Institute for Healthcare Improvement (IHI) based in Boston, has estimated the net savings from systematically managing quality would amount to 30 percent of current national expenditures. In addition, virtually every disease-by-disease examination in the scientific literature of "quality waste" finds numerous opportunities for both clinical and economic improvement.

[356] Estimates of the annual cost range from 6 to 14 percent of total expenditures.

[357] See Surgeon General report, *Health Effects of Smoking* at www.CDC.gov/tabacco.

[358] Blue Cross and Blue Shield of Minnesota is reducing tobacco use with the "5-C" guidelines:

1. Cover effective treatment—Provide benefit coverage for cessation medications and medical care provider counseling. (Over-the-counter items such as the nicotine patch or gum, prescription drugs like Zyban, reimburse providers for time spent counseling and offer financial incentives for pushing smoking cessation.)
2. Counsel members who smoke—Offer no- or low-cost access to behavioral counseling and a personalized smoking-cessation program with phone counseling.
3. Capitalize with significant financial resources and dedicated staff to reducing tobacco use.
4. Collaborate with the medical plan policy and community personnel.
5. Count—Conduct research to monitor progress, measure return on investment and improve quality. See Health and Business Institute website June 24, 03, News and trends.

[359] See www.thecommunityguide.org.

[360] See Kim Kriesberg, "The National's Health," Dept of HHS, Dec. 2003. The journal *Health Affairs* estimated this cost at $93 billion for the previous year of 2002.

[361] See Business and Health June 1, 2003.

[362] See "Preventive care highlighted as key to improving health" by Markian Hawryluk in *Health & Medicine Week,* June 24, 2002 p7.

[363] See "Employers plan campaign to fight obesity" in New York Times June 19, 03.

[364] See Aldana, Steve "Financial impact of health promotion programs" Am J of Health Promotion 2001 May/June, vol. 15(5): 296-320).

[365] See www.cdc.com.

[366] See www.mylifepath.com .

[367] See Eve Raskin and Lynora Williams "Lowering the business cost of alcohol problems" in *Business and Health*, June 1, 2003.

[368] See Health and Human Services *Report on the Impact of Poor Health on Business*, HHS, US gov. 2003.

[369] See www.ccam.org and results of study funded by the Office of Alternative Medicine.

[370] See Robert Fletcher and Kathleen Fairchild, "Vitamins for chronic disease prevention" Journal of the American Medical Association, 2002, volume 287(23):3127.

[371] DNA does not determine disease for over 99 percent of us.

[372] The results of the Task Force deliberations were first published in 1989 and again in 96.

[373] The first international conference on health promotion was held in 1986 (the Ottawa Charter). The momentum toward health promotion began building in the US since then.

[374] The Department of Veterans Affairs (VA) established the VA "Preventive Health Care Pilot Program" in June 1979. The Veterans Health Care Amendments in November 1983, authorized the provision of preventive health services to any veteran under care at VA facilities. To implement the law, the VA established The Preventive Medicine Field Advisory Group and The Preventive Health Care Task Force. Further expansion of the Disease Prevention Program followed passage of Pub. L 102-585 in November 1992, which called for the creation of a VA National Center for Health Promotion and Disease Prevention.

[375] See "Few Americans Follow Health Advice, Report Says" Reuters, 4/26/05, reuters.com.

[376] See website www.cdc.gov/nccdphp/bb_brfss.

[377] Congress allocated $17.5 million in 2002 and $28 million in 2003. This will identify at-risk populations and replace fear with facts and to strengthen the public health forces. See more at www.healthyamericans.org.

[378] Publications appear in journals such as AM J of Health Promotion, J of Occupational Medicine, and others.

[379] See www.alternativelink.com.

[380] The first major conference concentrating exclusively on health and productivity arose in 2001- the HERO International Health and Productivity Conference

[381] See Goetzel, R et al, "Cost savings through work site health promotion" pages 490 in Integrating Complementary Medicine into Health Care, edited by Nancy Faass, 2001.

[382] For more about the Vitamin Relief USA program, see, www.vitaminrelief. org. Accessed 8/5/04.

[383] The Quality Interagency Coordination Task Force (QuIC) was created in 1998 within the Department of Health and Human Services. The goal of the QuIC is to ensure that all 12 Federal agencies that purchase, provide, study, or regulate medical care services are working in a coordinated way toward

the common goal of improving quality. The QuIC provides information for making choices, thereby developing the infrastructure needed to improve the care purchased and delivered by the Government.

The National Quality Forum (NQF) is a not-for-profit membership organization created to develop and implement a national strategy for medical care quality measurement and reporting. The NQF arose in 1999 out of the government's QuIC Task Force to precipitate change in medical care. Today the NQF has broad in-put from consumers, public and private purchasers, employers, medical care professionals, provider organizations, medical plans, and labor unions. They developed a consensual set of standardized hospital-performance measures for use by the Center for Medicaid and Medicare Systems.

Minnesota became the first state to adopt all the error-reporting standards set by the National Quality Forum in Spring 2003. The Minnesota Dept of Health will collect information from hospitals on 27 different types of medical errors and adverse events. These data will be shared with the state legislature and the public. See Modern Healthcare's *Dailey Dose*, June 10, 2003.

[384] See The Dean Ornish's Program for Reversing Health Disease by Dean Ornish, Ivey books, 1996.

[385] Millions of patients receive treatments each year that are unneeded, leading to complications, reduced productivity, and significantly higher costs of medical care. Experts estimate that approximately 20 to 30 percent of medical care treatments are unnecessary. Overuse has been well documented for numerous types of invasive surgery and tests; an estimated 16 percent of hysterectomies and 17 percent of coronary angiograms performed each year are unnecessary. Further, antibiotics are routinely over prescribed or mis-prescribed for virus infections for which they are ineffective. Half of all patients diagnosed with a common cold are unnecessarily prescribed antibiotics. This overuse of antibiotics has led to bacterial strains resistant to antibiotics, resulting in added costs of up to $7.5 billion a year.

[386] See "How good is the quality of health care in the US?" by Mark Schuster, Elizabeth McGlynn, and Robert Brook in *The Milbank Quarterly*, vol. 76(4): 517-63, 1998).

[387] Elizabeth McGlynn et al, "The quality of health care delivered to adults in the US," New England Journal of Medicine, vol. 348 (26): 2635-45.

[388] See Elizabeth McGlynn et al, "The quality of health care delivered to adults in the US," New England Journal of Medicine, vol. 348 (26): 2635-45.

[389] See FACCT, "The Foundation for Accountability Summary report to RWJF, Sept 2000.

[390] See the Agency for Healthcare Research and Quality report of year 2001.

[391] See Chronic Care in America by FACCT, 2002, a chartbook for the Robert Wood Johnson Foundation, 2002, See www.facct.org.

[392] See www.nqf.org.

[393] See Research!American, 2001, Survey of Congress conducted by Harris Interactive, Inc.

[394] See Research!America 2000, Survey of the Public conducted by Charlton Research Company.

[395] See *A Study of the Cost Effects of Multi vitamins in the Elderly Population* by J. DaVarzo et al, Oct Lewin Group, Inc. 2003.

[396] See "Preventive care highlighted as key to improving health" by Markian Hawryluk *American Medical News*, May 20, 2002 v45 i19 p.12(1).

[397] See article in the Chicago Tribune; *American Medical News* May 20, 2002, vol. 45: 2; and Health and Medical Week, June 24, 2002, p. 2.

[398] See John O'Donnell, *Health Promotion in the Workplace* 2001, p. 8.

[399] See Oct 2001 issue of *The Physician and Sports Medicine*.

[400] See the Partnership for Prevention and the Centers for Disease Control and Prevention.

[401] Nearly three in five Americans feel smokers should pay more for insurance than non-smokers, says a new survey by Harris Interactive in 2003. On the other hand, only 27 percent favored different levels of health premiums based on people who are overweight and people who do not exercise regularly.

[402] The cost of voluntary turnover is estimated to range from $6.9 million for a smaller plan (143,000 members) to $55.9 million for a larger plan (995,000 members). The cost, for each member lost, is $240-$300. It's much cheaper for HMOs to retain their members than to attract new ones.

[403] The average duration of enrollment was only 3.8 years.

[404] The average employee switches insurance carrier every two years according to a recent survey.

[405] The Insurance Portability and Accountability Act of 1996 is being phased during 2003. This act protects enrollees who move by allowing them to buy into their previous employers' plans if they so choose. The reduced paperwork and improved efficiency of this plan is expected to save $1.5 billion during the first five years. How many people will benefit from it, however, is an open question.

[406] See Jeff Tieman Sept 9, 04 in *Modern HealthCare Alert* and the 2002 edition of *The State of Health Care in America*, produced by Business and Health.

[407] See "The Underused Method of Controlling Health Care Costs" by Bradford Myers Jan 20, 2003, *Business and Health*.

[408] There is still much overuse of services. For example, a) defensive medicine where doctors order more test to avoid future law suits; b) over use of the emergence room by Medicaid enrollees and other; c) doctors schedule appointments to fill their calendar; d) over use of surgery as opposed to therapy.

[409] Employers attempted to cut medical insurance costs in the 1980s by turning to heath maintenance organizations (HMOs) in what looked like a mass conversion. Their motives were transparent—managed care could save millions of dollars with such devices as tightly controlled utilization review, case management, pre-authorization and capitation. Employers pushed their

cost concerns onto their insurance carriers to implement cost containment. (HMO enrollment climbed steadily from 1990 through 1999, when it peaked at 80.5 million. Nationwide HMO enrollment dropped to 74.2 million in 2003, according to InterStudy Publications, St. Paul, Minn. See Modern Healthcare's *Dailey Dose* May 03) Limiting access to care and capitation of costs was successful and transformed the delivery of medical care. Mainstreaming managed care came in a short time period. By year 2000, 89 percent of employees at companies with 10 or more workers were enrolled in some form of managed care.

[410] See *Talking Straight* by Lee Iacocca, NY: Bantam Books, 1989.

[411] See "*I gotta tell you*" speeches of Lee Iacocca, Detroit: Wayne State University Press 1994, page 85.

[412] See "Now can we talk about health care?" by Hillary Rodham Clinton in the New York Times, April 18, 2004, accessed at www.nytimes.com.

[413] In 2002, more chief financial officers were treating benefits as an investment in employee-health, driving productivity and profit. See "CFOs Take a Fresh Look at Health and Productivity" by Thomas Perry and William Molmen, in *Business and Health*, Mar. 18, 2003. While productive companies provide basic coverage, they are creating a financial tension designed for capturing employee attention, encouraging more proactive behavior in worker health planning and lifestyle choices. But employers face a significant challenge in educating their workforce and building long-term behavioral change among employees. Company leadership provides information and decision support tools that allow good choices. More companies are moving toward a new defined-contribution medical system, whereby individuals design and create their own medical-care reimbursement account. See Maureen Cotter "Why are some employers surviving the health care crunch?" in Business and Health, May 15, 2003.

[414] See Paul Greenberg of the Analysis Group and Ron Goetzel of the MEDSTAT Group respectively.

[415] See www.hhs.gov and the www.cdc.gov. Chronic diseases consume more than 70% of the national $2.1 trillion cost for medical care.

[416] Medical care is no longer confined to the human resource or benefits department, but a CEO-level concern. Employees are encouraged to take more responsibility for their medical care needs and costs. Employers are increasingly informing and empowering workers to make their own choices. See "New Rules for Managing Health Costs" at www.watsonwyatt.com/research.

[417] See "Discover the power of wellness" by David Hunnicutt, in *Business and Health*, March 2001

[418] See J. Lee Hargraves, Sally Trude, "Obstacles to Employers' Pursuit of Health Care Quality" Sept. 4, 2002 *Health Affairs*, Vol. 21, No. 5. Also see Towers Perrin, *The changing Face of Health Care*, October 2002, a TPTrack research programs.

[419] See Katherine Capps and Sandy Mau, "Yet another silver bullet for health care" in *Business and Health*, June 1, 2003.

[420] See Hewitt survey, "Health Promotion/Managed Health Provided by Major US Employers" at www.was4.hewitt.com/resource/newsroom/pressrel/2003/08-26-03.htm.

[421] See Healthcare Intelligence Network, an advisory service on the business of healthcare. See their website at www.hin.com.

[422] The *Quality Dividend Calculator*, based on HEDIS data, is a sophisticated on-line tool for choosing medical-care plans. This information tool that arose in early 2003can help an employer reduce employee sick days and disability wages associated with various illnesses. It also shows employers how many of their employees are likely to have one or more of eight key medical conditions, such as asthma, diabetes or heart disease. Users have the option of comparing different categories of plans: those in the top 10 percent, the average NCQA-Accredited plan, and a non-accredited plan. Getting higher quality in medical care means getting better value, and giving the right care at the right time for a specific patient and their condition. The Quality Dividend Calculator is available at www.ncqa.org, the NCQA Website.

[423] See Eve Raskin and Lynora Williams "Lowering the business cost of alcohol problems" in *Business and Health*, June 1, 2003.

[424] See Employee Benefit News/Forrester Research 2005 Benefits Strategy and Technology Study.

[425] See "Are Health Savings Accounts an answer to higher costs?" by Bob Sanders New Hampshire Business Review on 5/5/2004. Cigna, Aetna, Humana, Definity Health and Destiny Health off HAS's.

[426] See Tony Fong, "HSAs" from *Modern Healthcare Alert*, March 23, 2005.

[427] The Washington Business Group on Health established an Institute on Health Care Costs and Solutions in November 2001, reflecting their concern with keeping their cost of production "internationally competitive." This Institute focuses on three issues: identifying safety measures; employee cost sharing strategies; and a more consumer-driven system such as medical reimbursement accounts. Companies like Definity Health, Health Market, and Humana are expected to experience their consumer-directed medical plan enrollment grow more than 200% in 2004. But the bulk of enrollment gains will occur later this decade as total CDHP enrollment breaks through the 20 million level by 2008. Forrester expects 40% of current PPO member to eventually choose a CDHP, but only 20% of HMO members to jump ship.

[428] More employers are requiring workers to share the premium-cost and to pay higher co-payments and with higher deductibles (43% in 2002).

[429] See Helen Darling, "Containing Costs" in *Health Affairs*, April, 2003 page 91. A growing number of employers are asking workers to choose the level of coverage that best suits their individual/family needs. The more frequent user of medical services may select a lower deductible plan with a higher premium and a broader network of providers; a less frequent user may choose a higher deductible with a lower premium with a narrower choice of providers. But the

biggest obstacle to the growth of these medical reimbursement accounts is the lack of readily accessible cost and quality information that is comprehensible to people at all levels of education and income. See Katherine Capps and Sandy Mau, "Yet another silver bullet for health care" in *Business and Health*, June 1, 2003; and Jon Christianson et al, "Defined-contribution health insurance products" in *Health Affairs*, Jan/Feb, 2002.

[430] The concept of health risk assessment has been around for over three decades, but modern assessment tools date from the early 1990s. Risk assessment is the first step in helping individuals identify behaviors that erode health and cause disease and hopefully change them.

[431] The best example is the Dean Ornish "by-pass" plan for patients with heart disease to reverse their artery problems with diet-changes, exercise, stress management and group support.

[432] Worksite health promotion is a growing business because they are cost effective. Companies such as the Wellness Councils of America are dedicated to helping organizations build and sustain results-oriented wellness programs. See Wellness Councils of America website at www.welcoa.org.

[433] See Robert McCarthy's article "Who's in charge of health?" in *Business and Health's* 2002 edition of The State of Health Care in American.

[434] See Health and Human Services *Report on The Impact of Poor Health on Businesses*, US Gov. 2003.

[435] See Robert McCarthy "Who's In charge of health?" in Business and Health's 2002 edition of The State of Health Care in American.

[436] Other tools to limit demand in the short term include patient education and sharing more of the cost of premiums, higher deductibles and higher co-payments. These tactics and the other two discussed all encourage greater awareness and personal responsibility for health, rather than dependency on doctors and entitlements of insurance for disease care services.

[437] See "New paths to a healthier workforce" by Michael Kriner in *Business and Health*, July 15, 2003.

[438] The top two percent of enrollees cost a typical commercial plan $39,000 annually, according to the Forrester Report at www.forrester.com. The "Pareto principle" suggests an 80/20 rule; 80% of the resources would be consumed by 20% of the enrollees.

[439] See "Target your health dollars to the root causes" by Robert McCarthy in *Business and Health*, Dec. 1, 1999, page 23.

[440] Ibid, page 23.

[441] Case management emerged in the late 1980's to prevent the patient and doctors from over using services and inappropriate settings.

[442] See *New England Journal of Medicine*, Aug 2002.

[443] See Penny Tseliki "Population based medicine" 2002 edition of *The State of Health in American* by Business and Health.

[444] See "Is the Informed Consumer any healthier?" by Mary Kouri in *Business and Health*, Sept 2002, p.3.

445 See page 134 of "Spending and service use among people with the 15 most costly medical conditions" by Joel Cohen and Nancy Krauss, in *Health Affairs* vol 22(2). Also see "Physical activity key to preventing disease," 2002, NIH.

446 See Feb 28 2003 issue of Modern Healthcare's *Dailey Dose*. Average expenditures ran about $13,243 compared with $2,650 per person without diabetes.

447 Se Aldana, S "Financial Impact of Health promotion programs" *Am J of Health Promotion* vol.15(5): 296-310.

448 Se Aldana, S "Financial Impact of Health promotion programs" *Am J of Health Promotion* vol.15(5): 296-310.

449 See "The business case for quality" by Sheila Leatherman, Don Berwick, Debra Iles and Lawrence Lewin, *Health Affairs*, April 2003.vol 22(2): 17-21.

450 See "New report shows health care system's ills" NCQA News, Sept 18, 02, page 1 at www.ncqa.org.

451 See Kate Lorig et al, "Chronic Disease Self-management Program" in *Medical Care*, vol.39 (11):1217-23.

452 See www.bradholmes@forrester.com.

453 See "Reconsidering Community-Based Health Promotion by Cheryl Merzel and j. D'Afflitti, in *American Journal of Public Health,* vol. 93 (4): 635, April 2003.

454 Ibid.

455 See August 04 issue of Journal of Clinical Psychiatry, vol. 65: 948-58.

456 See Business and Health Website, news, July 11, 2003

457 It was 44 percent in 2002. See CMS *Report on Managed Care* March 24, 2003, Executive summary, p. 10.

458 See Hewitt's recent study Health Promotion/Managed Health Provided by Major U.S. Employers in 2001 in "Is the Informed Consumer any Healthier?" in Business and Health Aug 29, 2002 (#10) By Mary Kouri.

459 The cost of these is estimated as follows: diabetes costs $132m, obesity costs $100m, inactivity $76m.

460 Patient management programs might invest $2,000 to $4,000 to motivate behavioral changes in a person who would otherwise use $40,000 or more medical expenditures within the next three to six months. The dollar return on investment is from 10:1 up to a 20:1 ratio according to Penny Tseliki "Population based medicine" 2002 edition of *The State of Health in American* by Business and Health.

461 From *Modern Healthcare* Feb. 28, 2003.

462 The Healthy Lifestyle and Prevention Act of 2004 reimburses prevention services for the first time.

463 See www.thecommunityguide.org.

464 See "Lessons from a health promotion victory" by Christine Guico-Pabia and Debbie Endsley in *Business and Health* Sept 2000, pp. 43-44.

465 Only 27 percent participated in the 1999 screening but the most common risk factors were high body fat and physical inactivity; 21 percent of the participants had three or more major risk factors for cardiovascular disease.

[466] See Schauffler and Chapman 1998.

[467] See "Obstacles to Employers' Pursuit of Health Care Quality" by J. Lee Hargraves, Sally Trude Sept. 4, 2002 September/October 2002 *Health Affairs,* vol. 21, No. 5.

[468] The Center for Practical Health Reform (CPHR) was formed at the turn of the millenium to precipitate reform of the medical care system. CPHR is a multi-constituency, non-partisan, not-for-profit organization espousing ten realistic and sustainable principles for reform.

[469] A group of business and health care professionals agreed on ten principles for reform of the system:

1. Essential care for all Americans- universal coverage.
2. Opportunities for choice through supplemental care.
3. Maintain an accountable private sector system, with incentives for performance.
4. Promote compatible information technologies, permitting secure, private information sharing.
5. Adopt, publish, update and promote evidence-based practice improvement processes.
6. Promote Continuity and Coordination of Care.
7. Publicly Disclose Quality Information on Professionals, Institutions and Procedures.
8. Publicly Disclose Risk-Adjusted Pricing Information for Patients.
9. Promote Individual Awareness Of and Responsibility For Choices Affecting Health Care.
10. Create Practice Standards and Greater Accountability to Reduce Medical-Legal Liability. Their website is www.practicalhealthreform.org.

Basic medical coverage could be made available to the nation's uninsured if total U.S. medical care spending were increased by $69.9 billion, an additional 5%, according to a study by the Kaiser Commission. See Modern Healthcare's Dailey Dose June 11, 03 by Laura Benko.

[470] See *Wilk vs. American Medical Association* 719 F. 2nd 207 (7th cir. 1983).

[471] See Terri Winnick, "From Quackery to Complementary Medicine" in Social Problems Feb 05, vol. 52 (1): 38-61

[472] See White House Commission on CAM Policy, March 2002 chapter 1.

[473] Don Powell of the American Institute of Preventive Medicine in Michigan.

[474] In its final report, the White House Commission on CAM called for the government to substantially broaden its support of complementary therapies. The core suggestions were:

1. Increase funding for basic, clinical and health services research related to CAM.
2. Create an office within the Dept. of Health and Human Services to coordinate CAM research and other government activities.
3. Increase CAM educational opportunities for conventional health professionals, including medical school curricula development.

4. Make accurate information about CAM available to the public and ensure that modalities and products are safe such as establishing good manufacturing practices and improved product information for nutritional supplements.

5. Improve access and ensure accountability with regulatory frameworks.

6. Broaden insurance coverage for those practices shown to be safe and effective.

In its report (http://www.whccamp.hhs.gov) the commission repeatedly acknowledges that many CAM therapies have not yet been scientifically studied and found to be safe and effective. "The fact that many Americans are using CAM modalities should not be confused with the fact that most of these modalities remain unproven by high-quality clinical studies", the report says. Alternative medicine should be evidence-based and research into CAM practices should be held to the same rigorous standards of good science as are required for research in conventional medicine, the report says.

"Substantially more funding for research is needed to determine the possible benefits and limitations of a variety of CAM modalities, especially those that are already in widespread use," the report says. The report also calls for tighter regulation of dietary supplements and advertising of CAM-related products and services.

The key emphasis of the report is to encourage the generation and rapid distribution of better information about CAM therapies to practitioners, conventional medical providers, and the public—including information about which alternative therapies work and which do not. (See Michael McCarthy's "US panel calls for more support of alternative medicine" in *Lancet* June, 2002.)

[475] CAM practices may be the most efficient means of achieving 54% of the 26 major objectives of Healthy People 2010 objectives

Promoting healthy habits and attitudes could help prevent many of the negative behaviors and lifestyle choices that begin in childhood or adolescence. Poor dietary habits, lack of exercise, smoking, suicide, substance abuse, homicide, and depression are epidemic among young people.

[476] See page 13 of Executive Summary of *White House Commission Report* on *CAM Policy, 2002.*

[477] Complementary therapies can have more than a simple additive effect, as it can be more effective than relying on any one approach by itself as noted by William Collinge (See his "Integrative Medicine Wheel" article at www.ahha.org/articles.)

[478] See page 13 of Executive Summary of *White House Commission on CAM Policy,* 2002.

[479] See the CDC website at www.cdc.org.

[480] Portland Oregon-based Complementary Healthcare Plans surveyed their credentialed chiropractors, naturopathic physicians And acupuncturists to see if they were asking about smoking, drinking, exercising etc and found that

they were much more active in promoting healthy habits than "big Medicine."
See John Weeks in *Towsend letter* 2001.

[481] The recent Institute of Medicine suggested that the federal government needs to become a leader in quality improvement and implement it in its many programs in HHS.

[482] HealthyPeople now has established goals over three decades, from 1990 to 2010.

[483] Critics say the commission should have been more forthright identifying which CAM modalities were worth researching and which were not.
The report set no research priorities. Instead, it calls for NCCAM to work with the Institute of Medicine (IOM) to "develop guidelines for establishing research priorities," which is what happened 2 months later when it was announced that IOM would do this.

Gordon did suggest research on CAM approaches that can't be patented, such as herbs and areas of energy therapies that do not have the prospects of financial support to do the expensive research for gaining acceptance. Failing to sponsor promising unpatentable therapies insures higher prices because unpatentable therapies can never undergo study to gain the expensive legitimation process.

NCCAM's 15 specialty research centers, they noted, already are exploring much of the research recommended by the panel. (See *Science & Government Report,* April 1, 2002 v32 (i6): 4.)

[484] See Alliance for Health Reform, *America's Most Ignored Health Problem: Caring for the Chronically Ill.* Washington, DC: Alliance for Health Reform, 2001.

[485] Failing to sponsor promising unpatentable therapies insures higher prices because such unpatentable therapies can never undergo the expensive study to gain acceptance. Herbs and many of the energy therapies are examples.

[486] People use CAM therapies primarily to maintain or promote health—as high as 60% according to Eisenberg in his 1998 article. CAM interventions focus on the physical, mental, spiritual, and emotional aspects of one's life, presenting many new opportunities for enhancing health.

[487] See "Managing stress is most Effective Action to Prevent a Heart Attack" American Journal of Cardiology 2002;89:164-168

[488] See Blumenthal JA, et al: Stress Management and Exercise Training in Cardiac Patients with Myocardial Ischemia: Effects on Prognosis and Evaluation of Mechanisms. *Archives of Internal Medicine* 1997;157: 2213-2223).

[489] Millions of Americans now regularly consume herbs and dietary supplements. The U.S. dietary supplement market is estimated to be about $19 billion a year. Since 1993, the FDA has received about 7,000 reports of people experiencing adverse reactions as a result of using supplements. (See "The FDA to regulate dietary supplements," Washington Post March 10, 2003.)

[490] See John Diamond, The Clinical Practice, NY: CRC Press 2001, page 5.

[491] See David Rakel, *Integrative Medicine*, Saunders, 2003, page 7.

[492] See www.onemedicine.com which is a Boston-based company seeking to combine the best of CAM with conventional medicine for optimal healthcare. Founded in 1998, it is based in Newton, Mass.

[493] See John Weeks, "Major Trends in the Integration of CAM" p 8 in Nancy Faass, *Integration of CAM into Health Care*, Aspen, 2001.

[494] A survey by the American Assoc. of Health Plans-Health Insurance Assn. of America found 94% offered Chiropractic care, 70% offered massage/relaxation therapy, 70% Acupuncture, 58% herbal medicine and 58% Biofeedback. See AAHP-HIAA, 2002.

[495] CHEF has over 125 members representing medical and health care purchasers, payers and providers such as hospitals and health systems, national professional associations of CAM, employers and medical care purchasers and payers, managed care organization, integrative medical clinics, academic medical institutions, educators, and researchers.

[496] See chapter 2 of Final Report of White House Commission on CAM Policy, 2002, page 12.

[497] See "Hospital get alternative" by Jodi Schneider in U.S. News & World Report, July 22, 2002.

[498] See "About the ABC code development process" at www.alternativelink.com/ie3/code-dev.

[499] Dr. Andrew Weil, director of the University of Arizona's integrative medicine department hosted representatives from 12 other prominent medical schools in the country.

[500] See The Integrator newsletter, Jan 2003 and Feb 2004.

[501] See AHA/Health Forum 2003 in the Nov 25, 2003 issue of The CHRF News File #59; and "Hospitals get alternative" by Jodi Schneider in *U.S. News & World Report*, July 22, 2002.

[502] They share ideas about how to introduce integrative medicine into medical education and practice. They hope to be a significant voice in the way future physicians are trained. The prestigious medical schools founders included Harvard, Duke, Stanford, Arizona, Columbia, San Francisco and others.

[503] See chapter 2, page 12 of the White House Commission on CAM, March, 2002.

[504] The report shows significant decreases in inpatient admissions and emergency department admissions among those patients in the Ornish program compared to controls. This type of disease management program, which "shifts the focus from a person's disease to his or her entire lifestyle," distinguishes it from more limited disease management strategies that make it "difficult to quantify clinical results and cost savings." The report concludes that the more comprehensive approach "can yield dramatic results that compensate for extra personnel and time such an approach takes."

[505] See Helen Lippman, "Can complementary and conventional medicine learn to get along?" Business and Health, vol. 19 (9): 15-9, Oct 2001.

[506] See Elizabeth Thompson, "The alternative model" in *Modern Healthcare*, May 15, 2000, page 28.

507 Cited by John Weeks in Nancy Faass (ed) *Integrating CAM into Health Care Systems,* Aspen, 2001: 8.

508 Sixty percent of physicians referred patients to CAM practitioners in 1998 according to Wayne Jonas; supra).

509 See "The Alternative Model" by Elizabeth Thompson in *Modern Healthcare* Magazine, May 15, 2000.

510 See "Hospitals get alternative, Acupuncture, massage, and even herbs pop up in mainstream medical settings" By Jodi Schneider in *US News and World Report* July 22, 2002 p 68,70.

511 See "Integrative Clinics" from Integrative Medical Leadership Summit Conference, April 2002.

512 See Quackery No more" by Rebecca Gardyn in *American Demographics* Jan 2001, page 11.

513 Over 60 percent of those who used CAM therapies did so on the advice of a friend or relative and less than 25 percent on the advice of a physician . See "Alternative Medicine Merging With Mainstream" by Nancy A. Melville at *HealthScout Reporter,* Yahoo News 24th July 2000.

514 Jane Guiltianan co-founded the King County Natural Medicine Clinic, the first publicly funded integrated health clinic in the nation. She is also dean of clinical affairs at the Bastyr University. See this story in "The Alternative Model" by Elizabeth Thompson in Modern Healthcare Magazine, May 15, 2000.

515 Integrative medicine at the Group Health Cooperative of Puget Sound collected data from 492 members who used acupuncture, naturopathic or massage benefits offered by the HMO; 76% of these patients had their condition for longer than 1 year.

Care for this condition provided by:	Conventional M.D.	CAM provider
Was helpful:	46%	89%
Perceived a decrease in their use of conventional medical physician		49%
Perceived a decreased use of prescription medications		56%
Would return to the same CAM provider with the same condition again		85%

See "The Role of the Consumer in Coverage Decisions," Washington Health Policy Forum, Seattle, WA, December 4, 1997.

516 Only 5% of the total expenditures for "healthcare" go to public health and on average, the conventional doctor devotes at most 10% of his time with health promotion and/or prevention. The remaining 90% is devoted to detection and/or management of disease. With an eight to ten minute office visit, the average physician has little or no time to teach patients or promote health skills.

517 See Integrator newsletter Dec 2003 Integrative Medicine at Evanston Northwestern Healthcare: A Success Story.

518 See "The Alternative Model" by Elizabeth Thompson in *Modern Healthcare Magazine*, May 15, 2000, page 33.

519 See "Trends in care by non physician clinicians" by Druss BG, et al, *N Engl J Med* 2003;348:130-137.

520 See David Eiesenberg, et al, *JAMA* 1998 vol. 280 (18): 1569.

522 Ibid.

523 See "Trends in care by non physician clinicians" by Druss BG, et al, *N Engl J Med* 2003;348:130-137.

524 Ibid.

525 See "So much to do, so little time: physician capacity constraints" by Sally Trude, *Health System Change*, May, 2003 at www.hschange.com.

526 From "Envisioning the Future" by Clement Bezold in Nancy Faass (ed) *Op. cit.* p 708-18.

527 See John Weeks, "Major Trends in the Integration of CAM" p 4-11 in Nancy Faass, *Integration of CAM into Health Care*, Aspen, 2001.

528 There were 684,000 practicing medical doctors, and 2,559,000 registered nurses in 2000. See David Eisenberg, et al. "Credentialing CAM Providers" A*nn Inter Med.* Vol137:968, 2002. Also see Cooper RA, et al. "Economic and demographic trends signal an impending physician shortage" *Health Affairs* (Millwood) 2002;21:140-154.

529 The number of accredited schools for acupuncture is 37, for homeopathy is 4, chriprators is 16 and naturopaths is 4.

530 The states vary greatly in their policies from Washington state which certifies all CAM providers from an accredited educational program while Minnesota certifies all CAM providers unless a problem or question arises.

531 See K. Hirschkorn and I. Gourgeault "Conceptualizing mainstream health care providers' behaviors in relation to CAM" in *Social Science & Medicine*, vol. 61(1): 157-70, July 2005.

532 See Eisenberg et al "Credentialing CAM providers" in Ann Intern Med. vol. 137: 965-73 2002.

533 See the February 9, 04 issue of American Medical News, "Empowered by insurers and states, nonphysicians push practice limits" by Myrle Croasdale. For the full article: http://www.ama-assn.org/amednews/2004/02/09/prl10209.htm.

534 Eight states have passed practice protection bills for physicians to refer patients to CAM providers or use CAM therapies on their patients.

535 Six secondary subjects include: botanical medicine, homeopathy, ethno-medicine, manual medicine, bio-molecular therapies, and health promotion.

536 In many states, conventional medical doctors can provide alternative treatments without demonstrating competency in them because of their broad license to practice. There are exceptions to this: New Mexico requires licensed medical doctors to obtain a separate license to practice acupuncture; Arizona requires MDs and DOs to take a separate exam to demonstrate competency in homeopathic medicine to practice homeopathy.

537 See their website at www.salugenecists.com accessed on 4/14/05.

[538] The NCQA provides an accrediting process of managed care and insurance providers, using 60 standards in five areas, including whether the insurance plan thoroughly check the credentials of all its providers. This by-passes the total emphasis on state practice acts.

[539] See John Weeks, "Insurance Coverage of Alternative Therapies" in *Current Review of Complementary Medicine* edited by Mark Micozzi, 1999.

[540] They target employers with 51 or more employees to offer complementary health benefits as a supplemental rider. Employers can choose among varying co-payment amounts and visit limits. (See www.ashnetworks.com accessed Feb., 2004-02-12.)

[541] A widespread belief among CAM practitioners is that they must dramatically alter or dilute their approach to practice in a physician-dominated system that often focuses on biological universalism where a given physical problem arises from the same cause. See chapter 2, p 12 of Final Report of WHCCAM policy.

[542] Some of the nation's top medical schools–including Harvard, Duke, and Stanford–are teaching complementary medicine to first- and second-year medical students, stressing therapies like acupuncture and herbal medicine which are used most by patients. (See "Hospitals get alternative" by Jodi Schneider in US News and World Report July 22, 2002 pp. 68-70.)

[543] See "Medical Schools Embrace the Healing Arts" The Associated Press, 6/5/05, ap.org.

[544] "Do Physicians Not Offer Useful Services Because Of Coverage Restrictions?" By Matthew Wynia, Jonathan VanGeest , Deborah Cummins , Ira Wilson in *Health Affairs*, vol. 22 (4) July 2003

[545] See "Quackery No More" by Rebecca Gardyn in *American Demographics*, January 2001, page 11.

[546] In 1997, "medical freedom of choice" legislation was introduced in the US Congress but it failed passage even after periodic reintroductions. Medical freedom of choice allows consumers to be treated by any health practitioner who is legally authorized to provide professional services in their state. (See Access to Medical Treatment Act HR 1964/S 1378.} Washington state passed their legislation in the early 1990s. (Read more at www.healthfreedom.org and www.holisticmed.com/www/medfree.)

[547] Offering members of a medical insurance plan access to CAM at a discount seems a winning strategy for all. The insurance plan gains a new, consumer-oriented feature without assuming much financial risk; the member gets a discount on CAM, as well as reassurance of a credentialed CAM provider; and the CAM provider gains recognition and perhaps more business by being included in the plan's network of providers.

[548] See Janet Thorpe "How to offer CAM without losing your shirt." Also employees represented by the Natural Health Union in 2003 gained access to medical insurance that covers CAM therapies, including chiropractic, acupuncture, massage, homeopathy, and herbal remedies. The union president predicts there will be 6,000 members by the end of 2004. This medical plan

funds a savings account for each participating employee (and dependents) to pay for routine medical expenses. When those funds are exhausted, an employee must meet an annual deductible of $500, $1,000, or $2,500. After the deductible has been met, the plan then reimburses for covered expenses at 90%, 80%, or 70% of the allowable charge. Alternative and natural therapies are covered with no deductible. Benefits are insured by American Travelers Assurance Company. The cost is generally comparable to Blue Cross medical plans. It does not rely on restrictions such as pre-certification because the people who are attracted to this program are health conscious, take good care of themselves, and are "smart shoppers." For more information: www. thenaturalunion@aol.com.

[549] See John Weeks, "Insurance coverage for Alternative Therapies" page 110, in *Current Review of Complementary Medicine*, 1999, edited by Marc Micozzi, Current Medicine, Inc.

[550] See www.ashplans.com accessed April 04.

[551] See Stanford University/American Specialty Health Plan, "Understanding consumer trends in CAM". Presented at a conference at Stanford University, September 18, 1998.

[552] See David Rakel, *Integrative Medicine*, Saunders, 2003, page 9.

[553] See Wonderling, D., Vickers, A. Grieve, R. and McCarney, R. (2004) "Cost effectiveness of a randomized trail of acupuncture for chronic headache in primary care." *British Medical Journal*. March 15, 2004. koi:1136/ bmj.38033.896505.EB.

[554] See "Acupuncture for Chronic Headache in Primary Care" British Medical Journal, vol. 328 (7442).

[555] See Claire Cassidy, (1998) "Chinese medicine users in the United States Part I: Utilization, satisfaction, medical plurality. *The Journal of Alternative and Complementary Medicine*, 4(1): 17-27.

[556] See Chapter 2 in IOM, *CAM Use by Americans*, at www.books.nap.edu/ catalog/11182.html.

[557] More than eighty-five percent of CAM users would return again if they had the same condition because they found the therapy helpful. See "Utilization, patient satisfaction, and cost implications of acupuncture, massage and naturopathic medicine offered as covered health benefits" by Stewart, D., Weeks, J. and Bent, S. in *Alternative Therapies in Health & Medicine*, Jul/ Aug 2001 vol. 17 (4):66-73 and John Weeks, "The Role of the Consumer in Coverage Decisions," Washington Health Policy Forum, Seattle, WA, December 4, 1997.

[558] See Meredith Rolley, "Business Model Allows Full CAM Integration" in *International J of Integrated* Med. vol. 18 (1) Jan 2000.

[559] See Dumoff, *Alternative Therapies*, July 2002 vol. 8(4): 32.

[560] See recent studies on the cost-effectiveness of different tools comparing drugs vs. support groups for addiction, heart, diabetes, hypertension, obesity, etc. See entire June issue of J of Consulting and Clinical Psychology, volume 70(3), but especially pages 482-93. Also see R Hester and W Miller (editors),

Handbook of Alcoholism Treatment Approaches, Allyn & Bacon 2003 chapter 2.

[561] See Meredith Rolley, "Business model allows full CAM integration" in *International J of Integrated Med.* vol. 18 (1) Jan 2000.

[562] To create these codes, Alternative Links management asked input from nine CAM organizations and schools and numerous experts. For example, the CPT has 4 codes for chiropractic services while the ABC system contains 28 codes. The codes are part of the American National Standards Institute, X-12N implementation guide for electronic commerce as an administrative classification system for filing electronic claims. The Alternative Link system of coding has been published by the National Institute of Health in the Unified Medical Language System and meets all requirements for update process controls. (See "About the ABC code development process" at www.alternativelink.com/ie3/code-dev).

[563] See Melinna Giannini, "Testing of ABC Codes Approved for Complementary and Alternative Medicine and Nursing" Alternative Link press release, Internetwire.com, 2/3/03.

[564] The 13 CAM practitioners include holistic medical doctors, chiropractors, midwives, massage therapists, homeopaths, naturopaths, acupuncturists and those prescribing herbs.

[565] The American Medical Association convened several meetings in late 2002 and early 2003 to expand the Current Procedural Terminology (CPT) to incorporate new CAM codes for the new Health Insurance Portability and Accountability Act (HIPAA). The AMA and Alternative Link met in January 2003 and split the cost to discuss incorporating more CAM therapies. Representatives of the AMA panel said they are not a proactive, idea-generating organization but they did encourage requests for CAM codes and a representative from the CAM community to sit on the advisory committee overseeing CPT codes. The Health Insurance Portability and Accountability Act is to become operational in April 2003.

[566] The White House CAM commission recommended: "The National Committee for Vital and Health Statistics and DHHS should authorize a national coding system that supports research on CAM usage in clinical settings.

[567] Ibid.

[568] ABC codes have the ability to convey the cost, legality or efficacy of the services performed, offering business parity to licensed practitioners.

[569] See their website at www.medimerge.com.

[570] See more on this integrative effort at www.hawaiihealthcare.info.

[571] See more on this integrative effort at www.hawaiihealthcare.info.

[572] See Laura Benko "Reduced investment earnings hurt Pa. Hospitals" From *Daily Dose* Feb 27, 2003. Growing expenses have forced hospitals to rely more on investments, but the report shows that the financial market's poor performance "has severely damaged this critical financial safety valve for hospitals," association officials said. Of the state's 185 hospitals, 41% lost

money in the fiscal year ended June 30, 2002, compared with 33% in 2001, according to the Pennsylvania Health Care Cost Containment Council, a state agency. See "Fewer premium dollars going to medical care" by Laura Benko *Daily Dose,* Modern Hospital Feb 24 '03. A study released February '03 by the Blue Cross and Blue Shield Association, Chicago, reveals a decline in the percentage of medical insurance premium revenue going toward payment of medical claims. The percent of premium revenue covering medical costs dropped to 84.7% in 2002 from 85.7% in 2001, and 85.4% in 1998 according to the study by the actuarial firm Milliman USA, Seattle. Meanwhile, pretax profits grew to 3.7% of premium revenue in 2002, up from 2.7% in 2001 and 1.7% in 1998. Administrative costs consumed 11.6% of health plans' premium revenue in both 2002 and 2001, down significantly from the industry's 12.9% administrative cost ratio in 1998. The report was based on data drawn from both for-profit and not-for-profit organizations. The average annual growth in pretax profits as a percentage of premium revenue was 21.8%, but off of a much smaller base. We're talking about less than 4 cents on every premium dollar.

[574] See J.Barnes, et al, "Articles on Complementary Medicine" in *Archives on Internal Medicine* vol. 159: 1721-25.

[575] See IOM, *CAM Use in America,* 2005 at www.books.nap.edu;/catalog/11182. html.

[576] ibid, 2005, chapter 5, page 135-136.

[577] ibid, 2005, chapter 5, page 135-136.

[578] See Janet S. Thorp -President, Alternative Healthcare Systems of Maine. "Making Alternative Medicine a Viable Part of the Health Insurance System" July 2000 National Association of Health Underwriters.

[579] They are working with members of the Congressional Caucus on CAM.

[580] See Kaiser Foundation study of 2001 on the physical and psychological impact of having no insurance at www.kaiser.com.

[581] See recent studies on the cost-effectiveness of different tools comparing drugs vs. support groups for addiction, heart, diabetes, hypertension, obesity, etc. See entire June issue of J of Consulting and Clinical Psychology, vol. 70(3), but especially pages 482-93. Also, see R Hester and W Miller (editors), *Handbook of Alcoholism Treatment Approaches,* Allyn & Bacon 2003 chapter 2.

[582] In December 1995, the AMA passed the following resolution: "Unconventional Medical Care in the US." The AMA encourages the Office of Alternative Medicine of the National Institutes of Health to determine by objective scientific evaluation the efficacy and safety of practices and procedures of unconventional medicine; and encourages its members to become better informed regarding the practices and techniques of alternative or unconventional medicine. (Policies of House of Delegates - I-95; H-480.973; BOT Rep. 15-A-94, Reaffirmed and Modified by Sub. Res. 514, I-95.) The Federation of State Medical Board's special committee on questionable and deceptive Healthcare Practices in Fall 2000 selected 3 outside consultants to assist them in reviewing their CAM policy. (David Eisenberg of Harvard,

Kenneth Pelletier of Stanford Univ. and Russell Greenberg of Univ. of AZ) This committee oversees licensing board activity for medical doctors and recommends positions to licensing boards relative to other CAM practices.

[583] See chapter 7 of IOM, *CAM Use in America*, NAP, 2005 at www.books.nap.edu/catalog/11182.html

[584] See Henri J. Roca III, MD "Toward an integrated wellness delivery system-2000" in Connections, Dec 2002 Holistic Wellness Network newsletter, page 13.

[585] See page 4 of Richard Gerber, *Practical Guide to Vibrational Medicine*, NY: Quill, 2001.

[586] See Leonard Wisneski and Lucy Anderson, *The Scientific Basis of Integrative Medicine*, NY: CRS Press, 2005.

[587] ibid, page 233.

[588] See James Oschman *Energy Medicine*, NY: Churchill Livingstone, 2000; and *Energy Medicine in Therapeutics and Human Performance*, NY: Butterworth Heinemann, 2003.

[589] See page 4 of Gerber, *Practical Guide to Vibrational Medicine*.

[590] See *Energy Medicine in Therapeutics and Human Performance*, NY: Butterworth Heinemann, 2003.

[591] See the website www.ToolsforWellness.com.

[592] See James Oshman, Energy Medicine and Therapeutics, NY: Butterworth Heinemann, 2003.

[593] See Richard Gerber, *Practical Guide to Vibrational Medicine*, NY: Quill, 2001, page 405.

[594] *Ibid*, 2001 page 406.

[595] Quoted by Daniel Reid in *The Tao of Health*, Sex and Longevity, NY Simon & Schuster, 1989, page 40.

[596] See Daniel Reid, *The Tao of Health*, NY: Simon & Schuster, 1989, page 40

[597] See Daniel Reid, *The Tao of Health*, page 39.

[598] ibid, page 39.

[599] See Elmer Green et al. "Anomalous Electrostatis Phenomena" in *Subtle Energies*, vol. 2 (3): 69-94 and Elmer Green et al "Gender Differences in a Magnetic field" in *Subtle Energies*, vol. 3 (2):65-100

[600] See page 107 in James Oschman, *Energy Medicine in Therapeutics*, NY: Butterworth Heinemann, 2003.

[601] An excellent 'how-to' book on acupoints is by Donna Eden, *Energy Medicine*, NY: Tarcher/Putnam, 1999.

[602] Her workshops can be found at www.innersource.net.

[603] See Valerie Hunt, *Infinite Mind : Science of Human Vibrations of Consciousness*, Malibu Publishing,2000.

[604] See Daniel Reid Op Cit, page 40.

[605] See Larry Dossey, *Reinventing Medicine* Harper San Francisco, 2000.

[606] See Andre van Tysebeth, *Pranayama*, London: Unwin paperbacks, 1979.